Remarkable Miracles

Remarkable Miracles

by G.C. Bevington

Bridge Publishing, Inc., South Plainfield, NJ 07080

REMARKABLE MIRACLES

Contents

Foreword

After much prayer, I have finally concluded I must make another effort to set forth certain incidents of my life which have been of great importance to me. I pray an equal sense of importance will be felt by those who are directly or indirectly touched by this record. Please read this foreword carefully for it contains a very useful key to the rest of the book.

As soon as I ventured out from the mission work in Cincinnati, where I spent several years, I began to realize I had definitely not entered into a feather bed vocation. God had called me to labor among the poorest of people, few of whom had ever entered a church. From the start, mine was destined to be a life depending entirely upon faith.

I never took an offering for myself, asked anyone else to do so or made my wants known except to God alone. I had no objections to those who did take up offerings, I just could not. Many times I thought I would, but upon reaching the platform I would invariably begin to inventory the expectant faces before me. My thoughts would go like this: There is dear Brother Jones with that large family. He's not any too well and his little place is not paid for, I can't expect him to give anything. Next to him is Brother Smith. He just lost a cow last week and he certainly can't spare anything. And there is Sister Bell who has those four hungry children to feed and care for, she won't be able to give at all. Brother Brown has seven mouths to feed and backs to clothe! He had to hire another horse last week after his was injured. He couldn't give anything, either.

And through the entire congregation I would go, excusing everyone. I believed my work was to be a work of trusting God and Him alone. I found myself in a unique position, however, of such concern for other's needs that I became aware of many situations that otherwise would have been ignored, overlooked or classified as impossible.

As I watched these many situations, I became increasingly impressed with their significance. I selected a large writing book and whenever I found time for a little rest, I would record these incidents as a stimulus to my faith. Many times after coming home from a long, hard pull with no money and few visible results for my labor, feeling none the best I would look into that book. Invariably I would be greatly encouraged. Time after time, whenever I was getting low in faith, those precious records would lift the clouds and give me great victory. Knowing that what God had done once, He would do again if conditions were met, I began keeping a close watch on conditions.

As others began to lay hold of these records, many insisted I should put them into book form. That was so far from my intentions and ability, I paid little attention to them at first. However, they persisted until I brought the matter before God. At first I felt such encouragement in the mentioning of this to my Father, I just had to say yes. Then as reality overtook me, I began to look at the obstacles to such a task. I had no money to live on while writing the book and I had no typewriter to satisfy a publisher's requirements for a manuscript. So I dropped the matter—but the Lord didn't. Soon the way was opened for a typewriter through Reverend John Fleming.

One obstacle was removed. But the next obstacle, equally as large if not larger, still loomed before me. I had no money to live on while writing the book. As I pondered this, an invitation came from Ashland, Kentucky, and I went to preach Saturday and Sunday meetings in the Ashland Heights Church.

A dear brother and sister in the Lord, Brother and Sister Simpson, invited me into their home and presented me with an intriguing proposal. As Brother Simpson's work required him to be away from home the better part of the day, Sister Simpson was overwhelmed with caring for the needs of a large house full of children. Sister Simpson put it quite simply, "We believe God wants you to stay in our home to live before these children." I prayed over the matter and it did, indeed, seem quite clear I should stay with them.

With the obstacle of living expenses so beautifully resolved, I finally began to write. When I was about half done, I began tiring of my confinement in such a lively household and went out for a few meetings. At this time, Reverend John Fleming's brother invited me to come to his home in Willard, Kentucky, and finish my book there. Thanking the Simpson's for their generosity, I went on to Willard to finish my book.

Before I had completed it, however, I found myself called out again for meetings. I continued to hold meetings, believing that somewhere along the way a favorable opportunity would present itself to finish my manuscript. I was content to wait for such a time, but I guess the Lord wasn't. My nearly completed work was destroyed by a fire, along with everything else I owned, while I was living in yet another city.

The object in writing this foreword is to set forth the reason for the absence of specific names and dates. This manuscript has been drawn from the book of actual records that was burned. I had long given up any idea of rewriting the lost records, yet through the past winter and this spring many have urged me to rewrite the story of my life. Others have written me with the same intentions, some knowing nothing of the former book.

Of late, dear Brother Heins of Kingswood, Kentucky, has also importuned me to write my story. I related all of the above to him, explaining the loss of names, dates and places. He stated quite simply that such details are of little importance in such a work as this. Again I went to my Father in prayer and concluded to rewrite the incidents. I pray you will read as impartially as you can for all that follows is true.

I hope these incidents will be as great a blessing to you and others as they have been to me. If they are, pass the book on. Keep it traveling to spread the deeper truths of the many hidden nuggets contained in God's great gold mine—the Bible. Read, pray, lay hold, take in and give out. Eat and get fat.

G.C. Bevington

Preface

For the past several years this amazing volume has been passed about in an almost clandestine fashion. The format of the original editions printed in the 1920's and the controversial contents have served to keep it under wraps. Few bookstores knew about it and fewer still would stock it.

Bridge Publishing is privileged to present this entirely new edition to the public. The publisher has updated the language for today's readers, reset the type and redesigned the format to produce this more readable volume.

Introduction

It gives us very great pleasure to commend this little volume which was conceived in prayer and brought forth from one of the most consecrated lives we have ever witnessed. We have known Brother Bevington for fifteen years and have always found him to be the same true, loyal, prayerful, holy and devout Christian with a burden for a lost and dying world.

Since the days of George Muller, we doubt if there has been another man who has prayed more, had more direct answers or witnessed more remarkable cases of Divine healing than has the author of this book. We believe it will reach many and heartily commend it to all lovers of deep spiritual things.

John and Bona Fleming

1
A Sketch of My Beginnings

Every story must have a starting point. My name is Bevington, which was my father's and mother's name as well. I suppose that is why I have carried that long name more than seventy-four years. My father was a Methodist preacher and they say he was a "rattler," too—making men's hair stand straight up on their heads. He was especially led to preach on hell. He preached to the Indians in Wyandotte County, Ohio, and several adjoining counties. He also built log churches and schoolhouses. This was all before I made my appearance.

By the time I came on the scene, my father was filling the place of a backslider while blacksmithing, wagon making and carpentering at Little Sandusky, Ohio. He had backslidden over a barrel of soap. Mother had held onto her God and prayed faithfully with us children. Her prayers had much to do with the after life and with our finding God and keeping Him. The most beautiful features of her life were never seen until she was gone.

Then they seemed to stand out on every corner or crossroad as sign boards pointing out the right direction.

Now, you may wonder how Father came to backslide over a barrel of soap. Satan can use almost anything to get a preacher to backslide. And "over" the barrel it was, not in it as one might surmise. If he had gotten into the barrel, especially headfirst, there might be some logical conclusion as to how he backslid. During the time Father was building churches and schoolhouses where the people were too poor to do so for themselves, he took pledges from them of meat, corn, wheat, potatoes and so forth as payment on the buildings. One man promised him a barrel of soap and, of course, Father expected that soap. But the man never delivered it.

Soon after this man broke his word, Father settled in Little Sandusky, Ohio. This same man came to live in the area where Father was preaching. After this matter had run as long as Father thought it ought to, he demanded that this man be put out of the church for being a liar (as Father called him). Father concluded that if the man was not fit for Heaven, he was not fit for the church Father pastored.

As this man was a good-paying member and a class leader, the congregation put the matter to a vote with quite a majority voting to let him remain. So, Father handed in his resignation and never went into the church again. Of course, he backslid after this.

Our home remained open to preachers as long as they did not disagree with Father. And into our home they came. I have always supposed every one of them said, "He is an old friend of mine. I will go and get him back into the church." I remember being in the blacksmith shop one time when the preacher who was conducting the quarterly meeting came up to draw Father over to the church.

2

He was using quite tempting bait or so it seemed to me. But Father grew tired of the preacher's discourse and said, "This whole thing reminds me of an incident that occurred when I was a boy. We had a neighbor, a farmer with three sons and two daughters. All were married except for one son, Jim, who was considered quite foolish as he never had attended school. After the father and mother were laid beneath the sod, these children concluded to divide the property and stock. Jim was so weak-minded, the others believed they could easily dupe him—especially on the stock line.

"They had a lot of sheep, quite a number of which were poor, bony, scrawny and old. They said, 'Now Jim has that pet sheep of his that he has raised and we know he would never part with it. So let us take all of the poor sheep, put them in a pen with his pet and tell Jim to go ahead and take his choice.' They supposed, of course, that he would take the pen his beloved sheep was in.

"So Jim went and looked at them all and the last pen held his pet. As he looked over the fence and saw his dear pet in there, he said, 'Mickey, we have been together for three years. We've eaten out of the same dish, drunk out of the same pond and slept in the same bed. We've had many good times together. But, Mickey, you've managed to get yourself in such bad company, we're going to have to part.' So Jim selected a pen of the choicest sheep."

Father then said, "That is the condition here—bad company—and we can't fellowship. We part as Jim and Mickey did." How Father laughed as he told that story. No one ever got him back in that church, nor in any other, although I hope he got back to the Lord. Satan indeed comes up with some pretty reasonable excuses as viewed from the backslider's angle. I know the only hope for me is

3

to keep in the middle of the road and never backslide. That way Satan can't get a hold on me.

I was born quite unhealthy and never went to school until I was ten years old. I had a disease that baffled all the physicians. Father, having a drug store in connection with his other work, had studied medicine some. He concluded to take me out to an uncle who had a tamarack swamp in Indiana. He believed chewing on tamarack gum would cure me.

So Mother fixed me up when I was thirteen years of age and I went out to my uncle's. I chewed and chewed that gum and, sure enough, it cured me in less than a year. I prospered in health, becoming strong and hearty. I got so strong, I decided I would fool my father, whose rules I considered quite unreasonable. Boys often think they know more than their parents and I decided he would never put his rules on me like the older boys. So, I foolishly ran off from my uncle's and went to Michigan.

The point I am coming to here focuses on the indelible impression my mother's life and her family prayers made on me. I could never get away from either one. Fifty-nine years ago on Christmas morning, I started down the pike in snow that was knee deep to trudge nearly twenty miles to Kindleville, Indiana. I had a pair of overalls and one shirt wrapped up in an old-fashioned, colored handkerchief which constituted both wardrobe and suitcase. My pockets contained one dollar and twenty-five cents saved from having washed sheep the previous spring for a neighbor. I had even managed to save this precious sum over the Fourth of July and all through the fall and winter for such a time as this.

I arrived at Kindleville near daylight and found a train about to embark for Elkhart. I purchased a ticket and then paused in an alley to count my remaining funds. I

4

had forty-five cents. Since I would still have sixteen miles to go to Edwardsburg, then twelve miles beyond to Cassopolis, I had to go a little slow with my money. But I was hungry. I went into a grocery and got some bologna and cheese. I must have presented quite a picture with a hunk of cheese in one hand, a piece of bologna in the other and my handkerchief "suitcase" tucked under my arm. There I was, stalking importantly down the main street of Elkhart, the largest town I had ever visited.

The sights in the windows and the busy folk running here and there were all so new to me, as I chewed on my cheese and bologna I fell to gaping in spite of trying to appear worldly. I must have been a laughable scene to any passerby. As I gawked, suddenly I heard someone call out, "Hello, Bub." That was the name some had called me at my uncle's. My name, Guy, seemed difficult to remember, so Bub was what I usually went by. Now I was terrified to hear it. I never stopped to see who had called, I just struck out up the street on the run. I supposed someone had picked my trail and followed me that far to take me back.

I ran like a trooper even though the man shouted, "Wait! I won't hurt you!" I ran as hard as I could, but he and several others managed to head me off and corner me with my cheese and bologna and suitcase. After persuading me that he had never seen or heard of me before, he finally convinced me to go with him. I was cold and still hungry and obviously a stranger to the sights in Elkhart, so I went when he invited me back to his house. Upon entering the home where his wife was eating breakfast, he said, "Mamma, here is our boy. I just found him." She came over and took off my cap for a better look. Then she brushed back my hair and gently kissed me.

It was the kiss that did it. I had not had such since I left

5

home over a year before. I broke all up, but I was so bashful and shy I could not show appreciation of her motherly affection. Although she relieved me of my cheese and bologna and bandana suitcase, they could not relieve me of the embarrassment I was suffering. I was miserable in their presence in that home, but she did get me to eat a good breakfast. Anxious to get out from under the terrible strain, I spied a nearly empty wood box and asked their permission to fill it. I rushed outside when the man pointed the direction of the wood house.

I sawed and split wood until they came out and asked me to join them for dinner. Immediately uncomfortable again, I felt unworthy to go back into that fine kitchen and sit at their nice table. I began to stammer out excuses like people did of old. They listened thoughtfully at first and then the man called out, "Oh, Mary! Come out here, will you?"

A rosy-cheeked, plump girl about my size and age came bounding out of the house towards us. She was laughing and smiling as she rushed up, took hold of me and began to hug and kiss me. "You will come in, won't you? We all love you." She got me started and I found my feet moving towards that house. I wondered what in the world had made them love me, as no one but Mother had ever used that expression toward me. I knew this lady was not my mother. But I stumbled inside and ducked into a corner.

Mary finally persuaded me to sit down at the table by saying, "Now I am your sister and you are my brother. Come sit down right here by me and Mamma will give us some fine buckwheat cakes and maple syrup." Well, the cakes and Mary were quite inviting, but oh, how I wished I could only have the cakes and syrup out in the wood house! But there I was and what could I do? Such fine linen was on that table and real forks

6

and knives—they were something I had never seen or heard of at home.

I managed to eat something after Mary kindly cut it up for me. She was very nice, but I was suffering untold agony. Boys these days are further advanced at the age of eight years than I was at fourteen. As soon as I dared, I got up and blundered out what my Mother had taught me, "Excuse me!"

Then I hurried outside to the wood house and brought up wood until I had piled it way up in the box. I saw the empty water bucket and filled it as well as the tea kettle from the big stove. These were things I knew to do, for Mother had drilled such tasks into me.

I have always found it to be helpful in the work of the Lord to be helpful. I have been able to hold meetings in homes that others could not get into just because I would chop up some wood, carry water and help out. They let me in for the work I would do and that gave me the chance to preach the Gospel to them. Many of these people had never heard the real message of the Gospel, for they had been brought up on "meetin' house crumbs," with never a square meal issued to them. It pays to be prepared for almost anything to win people to the kingdom of God.

But back to my dilemma at this home as I want you to see what a praying mother can do. As far as my mother knew at this time, I was still at my uncle's as any boy should have been. But her prayers were not confined to that tamarack swamp in Indiana, they were focused to me and that meant wherever I was. Glory to God! Those prayers leaped the bounds of my uncle's home as soon as I did and followed my every step thereafter, as you will see. God always hears a mother's prayers. Amen and amen! Oh, how I praise God for a praying mother!

I kept on sawing wood all day as I struggled with many

thoughts. I had not told these nice people who I was or where I had come from, although they had tried every conceivable scheme to find out. I just would not tell them as I was afraid it was some kind of scheme to get me back to my uncle's. When late afternoon came, I was pretty homesick and I decided to crawl behind the large stove and curl down for a nap. But Mary soon bounced in the door from school and the first thing she cried out was, "Where is my brother, my twin brother? Where is he?" Spying my shoes, she pulled me from behind the stove and out into the yard to play ball.

When supper was called, I mustered up the courage to go inside without so much persuasion as before. But as soon as supper was over, I was back behind the stove. When the dishes had been washed and put away, Mary grabbed me by the feet and pulled me out again. The next thing I knew, I was in the parlor singing along with some of the good old Sunday school songs my Mother had taught me. The more I sang, the bigger the lump grew in my throat and to my horror, I was soon crying.

Sensing my embarrassment, Mary changed tactics on me and got a picture book. The next thing I realized, Mary had pulled everything out of me, pumping me dry. She got my first and last name, where I had just come from and where my people lived. Mary's father had been listening and although he was not a Christian, he felt the proper thing for me to do was return to my uncle's. I refused to go. In the first place, I was afraid to go back. In the second place, I had no money to go back. The man said kindly, "I will give you money enough and you need never pay it back."

I persistently refused. I did want to go home, but I was too proud to do so. He then said he would give me a ticket

8

to Upper Sandusky which was no more than seven miles from my home. I still said no.

I stayed there that night and in the morning I made sure the wood box and water bucket were both filled again. When Mary's father came in, he said, "Mamma, we need just such a boy. Let us try to get him to stay here with us." So they began to make many propositions. Finally he said, "All you will need to do is sweep out my room, clean a few glasses each morning, build the fire, look after the wood and water, go to school and share equally with Mary."

Then he added, "We lost our only boy just a year ago, a twin to Mary. Mary says you are here to take his place as you are much like him. We have all fallen in love with you. Since Mary is our only child, when Mamma and I are gone, all our property would be yours and Mary's. We have a farm out in the country and just came into town to give our children a better education. When Mary graduates, we expect to return to the farm. But whatever we do, you shall share equally with Mary."

Well, that appealed to me wonderfully as it would help me get an education and stay out from under the galling yoke (as I looked at it through my carnal, young eyes) of my home's discipline. I went outside and started splitting wood again so I could think. As Mary came out on her way to school, she kissed me and said, "You will be my brother, won't you? I need a brother to go to school with me." Well, I tell you that kiss went further than my chin. But there was one thing that kept bothering me and that was the washing of those glasses. What could that mean?

By and by, the man came out and called me into dinner. I met Mary at the kitchen door as she came in from morning classes. She clasped my hand and cried, "Oh,

9

my brother, my brother!" She made me feel considerately like I really was her brother. After we had finished dinner and Mary had gone back to school, the whole thing was gone over again preparatory to clinching the deal.

I finally mustered the courage to speak out what was bothering me, "What you said about my washing some glasses and sweeping your room. What is this?"

The silence that fell could be felt even by an inexperienced boy. The man finally raised his head as if to speak, but no words came. He was struggling inwardly with something I could diagnose. So his wife spoke up, "Guy, he doesn't like to mention the business he is in. He has a saloon in front and we are all ashamed of it, even he is. But it seems he cannot get out of it without losing all he has put into it."

Then the man rallied and began to speak, "Yes, Guy, we wanted to give the children a better chance than they could get out on the farm. So we moved in here to town. Since times were hard, I could not get any work. After hunting work for about eight months, the only thing I could find was this saloon. The man wanted to sell out and offered me quite a bargain. Not fully realizing all that was involved in the business, I finally bought him out. We have been here three years and neither of my children has ever been in the saloon even though it is right there in front of us. Neither has my wife been in there."

Now comes what is involved in a mother who knows and does what is right. When I left home to go to my uncle, Mother called me to her and raised my chin as I knelt before her. Looking in my eyes, she said softly, "Guy, you are going away from home, away from my personal care. I want you to promise your mother one thing. Will you promise it?"

"What is it, Mother?" Tears were falling because of my near departure from her.

"Guy, do you believe your mother would ask you to do a thing that you could not do or that would hurt you?"

That was a stunner. I quickly answered, "No, of course not, but what is it?" Then as I looked again into her eyes, I quickly promised, "Whatever it is, I will do what you ask, Mother."

"I want you to promise never to go into a saloon."

"Oh," I sighed in relief, "that is nothing. I am glad it is no harder than that. I promise." I placed little emphasis on her request at that time, for I had never been in a saloon and supposed I never would be. I actually felt I was let off remarkably easy. But as time went on, I saw that Mother's vision had been much broader than mine.

Now I told these people what Mother had made me promise, unsure as to their response. Mary's father jumped to his feet, threw his arms around me and cried, "God bless that mother of yours. Give me her name and I will write to her and tell her that I have her boy. I will tell her of the proposition I made you and how you refused it as a result of her covenant with you. I will adopt you if your parents will give their consent and you will never go into the saloon as we will soon be leaving here anyway. You stay here, do the other chores, go to school with Mary and be my boy until we hear from your mother and father."

But I was afraid of that saloon. I saw there must be some evil attached to it or Mother would have never singled that out for me at that time. Suddenly I knew I had to leave, so I told them I must go to Michigan.

Sensing my resolve, the man said, "If you are determined to go, because it is so bitterly cold, I will have a friend of mine who is going to Edwardsburg in the morning take you in his bobsleigh. He's going anyway and I'm sure he won't mind."

After breakfast the following morning, the precious Mary kissed me good-bye as tears rolled down her cheeks and I never saw her again after that. As I got into the sleigh and covered all up, a package containing an overcoat, a pair of rubbers and some underclothing was handed to me. There was also a basket of provisions. "When you get to Edwardsburg, go in and eat at the hotel," they said.

The trip was fairly uneventful and we arrived in fine shape. We went into the office of the hotel where the man who had brought me asked if I might have the privilege to sit behind the wood stove to eat my dinner. With permission, I slipped out of sight and eagerly pulled the lid off the basket. To my utter amazement, I found a five dollar bill rested on top of the goodies. I was sure it had gotten in there by mistake.

When the sleigh driver came out from his dinner, I said, "Somebody put this five-dollar bill in here by mistake. Please take it back to them."

"No," he replied, "that is from Mary. I saw her put it there. She had intended to put it into a pair of furs this week, but she said she would and could do without those furs. So, it is yours."

In spite of myself, I began to feel tears welling up in my eyes. I brushed them away angrily. Seeing the tears, the driver said, "Would you like to go back? If you want to, I will take you and charge you nothing."

I realized then that he was not some friend of Mary's father who had been coincidentally coming this way. He was running a hack and Mary's father had paid my fare. I said, "No, I want to keep going."

Thus began the main incident of my whole life, the

reason for relating all of the former as this book is to be about the results of prayer. I began a twelve-mile walk with more to carry than before. As I trudged down the road, I was flooded with feelings. I had a longing to be with Mother. I thought about the kindness and the remarkable proposition made at that home, with the lovely Mary as a prospective sister. That made me think of my own sister just two years younger than me. These thoughts all combined to get me in a mixed-up state, weaving a web around my heart that threatened to engulf me.

Finally I raised my head and saw a large tree several rods from the road. I walked up to the tree and dropped down to the ground where I thought I should say the only prayer I had ever undertaken to say, "Now I lay me..." I thought that might lift me out of the despondency that seemed to settle down on me like a dark, heavy cloud. I began with the familiar words that, being fourteen years old, I supposed were quite enough. I believe I was about to offer the finest prayer I have ever offered up to God for I began to really pray and then got lost in prayer.

I was under that tree for nearly two hours. I don't even know what all I prayed, but I well remember that the clouds began to break and roll back and it seemed I was being lifted up onto a plane I had never visited before. I remember saying, "God, just lead me to a religious home where they read the Bible and pray as Mother did."

I became very happy and rose from under that tree most wonderfully blessed. I believe I was regenerated then, but not yet knowing what regeneration was and being so young, Satan kept me from realizing that this was conversion. I do not remember all that I asked or promised, but have ever since believed that all was included that was required for my regeneration.

I ran down the road and hollered and laughed and jumped and cried aloud! I had never experienced such inward rapture. I ran for hours under that mighty something that made me feel as I had never felt.

Not supposing it to be regeneration, I never testified to it. But this was such a marked experience in my life, it stuck to me for years. In fact, I never did get entirely away from under its influence. I look back to that tree with great reverence. I remember saying, "Lord, if You will take me to a religious home, I will serve You the best I know how." I supposed I had to be older to get salvation. I ought to have known better as I am sure Mother never gave me this impression. But Satan is always right on his job and knows just where to get in his diabolical work. He cheated me out of what God had just given me.

While I had been at my uncle's, a niece of his from Michigan had spent several months there. She was a friend of my uncle's old schoolmate whom he had not seen or heard of for years. They used to speak often about this Mr. N--- who was a wealthy farmer in Michigan. I was aiming to reach him and tell him of my uncle. I reached S--- in the early evening and asked the way to Mr. N---'s. As it was only four miles farther, I set out again until I was sure I had walked at least four miles. However, I had not seen the sign I was told would mark the way to go. About three hours later I met a man on his bobsleigh and asked how far it was to Brushridge Schoolhouse. He said, "My dear boy, you are twelve or fourteen miles from there."

"No, " I said, "they said it was only four miles from S---." He told me that was quite true, but somehow I had taken a wrong road at the lake and was now ten miles from the lake. If I was to go back to S--- now, it would be another fourteen miles.

Recognizing my plight, he asked me to go home with

14

him and spend the night as he lived only five miles from where I wanted to go. But some of that old fear arose in me that a trap was being set to take me back to my uncle's. That inner bell, as Brother Kulp calls it, in my innermost being kept ringing. I declined his offer. So the man said the farm I sought was only about seven miles away as the crow flies. The moon was shining brightly on the snow and the man told me he would show me how to sight a line by using certain trees to make a path straight to the place.

He worked with me for over an hour and when I began to finally understand the trick of keeping the line, I started off across the countryside. I was in for a fierce struggle. The snow was drifted over the fences and I went down three times, way over my head. I had a terrible time digging out. I would then get on my feet and go back along my track and get my line again. As the temperatures fell, a crust formed on the snow and I kept breaking through. Finally I sighted my goal, a great mansion larger than any building I had ever seen.

It stood three stories high and was all lit up from top to bottom. I wondered what could be going on at that time of morning. I ventured closer and saw no signs of anything to fear. Leaving my meager belongings at the gate, I cautiously walked up on the porch. I heard unusual noises for that time of night, noises I did not understand. I stood there, hungry as a bear, yet trembling from head to foot like a kitten. Oh, how I dreaded to knock on that door!

But I knew I just couldn't stand there as someone might come out and accuse me of being a sneak. So I stepped up to knock, but my courage failed me. I hurried off the porch and started back the way I had come. But then, I argued with myself, perhaps someone inside was sick which might explain the strange noises. With that argument in favor of knocking, I walked back up on the porch, plunged right to the door and rapped quickly before I lost my courage again.

Someone called out, "Come in," so I opened the door and peered inside. I saw a great big, fat man who looked so fatherly, I felt safe to step inside. He said, "Take a chair, Bub." Shivering from the long exposure to the cold and my as yet unsettled nerves, I sidled up to the big stove.

I swallowed and cleared my throat and then said, "I am from Uncle Dave Voorhees in Indiana." The man's face brightened immediately and he began to ask after the welfare of his old school chum.

His wife came in and the man said, "Mamma, bring this boy something to eat." Being too stingy to break the five-dollar bill Mary had slipped into my basket the morning before, I felt I hadn't eaten for days. I said nothing and just sat there trembling. I thought I would eat whatever she brought as long as the people making all the noise stayed elsewhere in the house. I was quite fearful of the sounds I could hear coming from many parts of the house.

Finally Mrs. N— placed a nice, steaming meal in front of me on a little stand with a white cloth. Oh, it looked so tempting—hot mashed potatoes, hot mince pie and a tempting piece of cake. It was all so inviting and appealing to my stomach, but I was torn between looking at it and still watching all the doors.

The man said, "Well, Bub," (there it was again—Bub) "come now, sit up and have something to eat." I buckled up the courage and was just about to take a bite when a large door swung open and out marched a lady and a gentleman in fine clothes. The lady's dress had a long silken train and the man wore long coattails and everyone had flowers. I ducked my head between my knees and huddled as close to the stove as I dared to get. They stared at me as they passed through until I felt like a whipped dog.

Trembling fearfully after they had left, I said, "I must be going."

"Going!" said Uncle N---. "Where are you going?"

I replied, "To C---."

He looked at me thoughtfully and then told me to sit down, eat something and go to bed. He said I looked tired and obviously needed a good night's rest. If I had to go to C---, the boys would take me in the morning. "Who do you know at C---?"

"No one," I answered truthfully.

"Well, then you will stay here," he announced.

By now I was so scared by the display and fixings all around me, I knew I could never stay. So I got up and just walked out and headed for C---, four miles away. I had never been so hungry and tired! Just before dawn, I arrived at C--- and the girl who had been at my uncle's lived yet another nine miles farther. I continued to trudge on, wondering what I was doing. But God was on my track. Although I had made what seemed terrible blunders, I believe everything that happened was in accordance with His will that He might answer the prayer I had prayed the day before under the tree.

As I walked down a snow-covered sidewalk, I heard sleigh bells, a most unusual sound at that early hour. I stopped and listened and soon the sleigh overtook me. The driver pulled up and said, "Good morning, Bub." There was that name again. "Where are you going?"

"Going to D---," I replied.

"What are you going to do there?"

"Get work."

"Well, you're a pretty small boy to be out hunting work

17

this time of year, let alone this time of morning. You come here and get in my bob and come home with me now. If you still want to go to D--- after you've warmed up a little, I will help you."

Somehow I felt my fear and timidity melting away under the entreaties of his soft, mellow voice. He drove up to the walk and I jumped in. We had only another mile to drive to his home. In his house was a brightly lit and wonderfully warm kitchen where a sweet-faced woman was waiting for him. He was returning from South Bend, Indiana, with a load of black walnut for the Singer Sewing Machine Company. This accounted for his traveling at such a strange hour.

He said, "Well, Em, here is our boy." She jumped up, took hold of my cold hands and rubbed them briskly and kissed me. Then she retrieved some hot water and washed my hands and face. Setting me down to the table, she began to pull out one dish after another from the warming oven and set them on the table. I will never forget her motherly actions toward me that morning and that fine table so deliciously spread before me.

The man asked a blessing as we sat down and thanked God for sparing his life and allowing no accident on the trip. He thanked God for so much money for his load and, last but not least, for picking up a little boy. He just talked to Jesus until he had me crying again. As he said amen, his wife took her clean apron and wiped away the tears and then kissed me again, saying, "There, there, now. Have some of this nice, fried chicken and warm mashed potatoes and gravy." I dove into the delicacies spread before me, all bashfulness washed away by my hunger pangs. I ate and ate and ate.

After breakfast, the man took down a well-worn Bible and read the fourteenth chapter of John. I was so wonderfully impressed, I investigated where it was and that chapter has been a great blessing to me. I have often preached holiness as a second work of grace from that notable chapter with many being brought into God's sanctifying grace through it.

You see, this was the answer to my prayer I had offered up under that tree. God had brought me into a religious home, the home of a staunch Methodist at that—the same as I had been brought up. I was to soon give God my heart in such a way, I would know beyond a shadow of a doubt that salvation was truly mine.

2
Beginning, and Some Work At Sixth Street and Freedman Avenue Cincinnati, Ohio

As this book is also to treat of the results of sanctification, the blessed second work, I want to focus on incidents that have occurred as a result of the sanctification I received thirty-two years ago at St. Louis. It came on the fourth floor of a six-story brick building after tarrying nine days in real soul agony—wrestling and dying out.

Every sanctified man and woman enters a school, not simply a holiness school, but a holy school. Thirty-two years ago I entered this holy school. My first training came during several years in Cincinnati. I was kept in that period of training for what has since developed. At that time, though, I had no idea what everything that was happening really meant.

One incident that stands out during this time occurred while I had been having cottage prayer meetings that resulted in much good. I would entreat those who were the most dependable to meet at the mission and have prayer before going on to the cottage meeting. One evening I felt strangely led to be somewhat more aggressive. I said, "Brethren, how many of you will clasp hands in a circle and enter into a covenant for at least one soul to be saved tonight? We have seen no one saved or sanctified for several meetings." I thought it time to be more aggressive.

Several agreed and when we finished praying, we set off for the meeting. We had a fine time during the meeting, which was held at the house of a sister who was a widow about my age. As the meeting progressed, one brother whispered to me, "Where is that soul?" Not one sinner was present in the house.

"He will be here soon," I assured him. The meeting continued under a heavy anointing of the fire of the Holy Ghost. We had a blessed time amidst much shouting of the praises of God.

Again the brother whispered, "Where is that sinner?"

I replied, "He will be here."

The leader finally closed the meeting about 10:00 p.m. and those who had prayed with me earlier began getting their wraps and prepared to leave. But I remained seated with my head bowed, praying for that sinner. Soon one who had not been in the circle earlier came to me and asked, "Aren't you going home?"

I felt silenced and when I did not reply, those speaking to me seemed to draw their own conclusions from knowing that the woman of the house was a single woman and I was a single man. Glances were exchanged and they finally all left leaving me sitting there alone with the woman. I felt embarrassment, but I was unable to open my mouth and explain why I was still sitting there when all else had gone except the widow, and her seven-year-old daughter.

I did not dare raise my head. All I could do was continue to pray and hold on, saying, "Lord, Thou didst impress me to make that vow and here I am." While I wanted to tell her why I was still waiting there, I could not get my mouth to do it. So there we both sat—she becoming increasingly disgusted and I perfectly dumb. The clock struck 11:00. I said to the Lord, "Only one more hour left to our covenant for one soul." The clock struck 11:30. "Lord, just thirty minutes more for that soul."

The house stood on the edge of the pavement and I had hardly spoken that last statement when there was a rattlely-bang and the front door burst open. The woman jumped up, screamed and ran into the kitchen. Through the door fell a drunken man, sprawling out onto the floor. As soon as I saw him tumble in, a voice said, "There is your man."

I jumped up and tried to haul him in, but he was so drunk he was about lifeless. The woman, seeing what had happened and being anxious about her carpet, came back and ordered, "Put that man out!"

"Sister, this is in answer to prayer," I said.

"I will not have him in here with his filth on my carpet!"

"Sister, get on your knees and get hold of God! We have only twenty-five minutes to get this man saved."

"God can't do anything with a drunkard!" she exclaimed.

"Sister, pray!" I exhorted her again. I dropped on my face with my feet against the door and began to intercede with my entire soul. Looking up at the clock, I cried, "Oh, God, only eighteen minutes left."

23

The woman was becoming quite frustrated at me. "What do you mean by only eighteen minutes left?"

"Get hold of God for this man and I'll explain later," I urged her.

Very soon the drunk raised his head and said, "Where am I? What am I doing here?"

"You're reaching God here," I told him. "God is going to make a sober man out of you."

"Well, I believe He has now," said the man. He raised himself up and announced, "I have religion now."

"No, you have not," I said.

"Yes, I have," he insisted as he rubbed his face.

"Get down now and repent and cry mightily to God for salvation as you only have that demon drink cast out of you so far."

We had some trouble getting him to see as we saw, but the sister was now working with me and she and I prayed earnestly to God to show him the truth. God did and the man began to pray for mercy. I looked at the clock again and said, "Lord, only eleven minutes. Father, bring him to terms with You. Take this case on through, please!"

As I lay on my face pleading with God, the glory struck us. The woman began to shout when she felt it. The man jumped up and grabbed and carried me all over the room. The assurance came from God that the work was complete at just three minutes before midnight. Amen!

It pays to trust God. That man remained sober for three years and then God took him home to Heaven. This was my first venture on that definite line, but God has never failed to meet me. Through His answers, several such feats have been accomplished in His name for He always will do as He has promised.

Another such incident occurred in the work in Cincinnati where I was receiving and distributing clothing to the poor. While at Mt. Lookout, a suburb of Cincinnati, I noticed that one of our strong members had not been seen for a week or so. She was a poor woman with three children who struggled with meeting her rent and living expenses. She had never allowed us to help her even though we aided many others in similar circumstances. I went to her home and found her doing the washing. I reminded her that several services had passed without her presence, a most unusual occurrence. As she seemed loath to give a reason for being absent, I noticed she had on quite shabby shoes. I gently asked her, "Sister, are those the best shoes you have?"

Blushing, she turned her back on me. I believed I had guessed correctly. Finally she said, "Brother Bevington, I have to admit they are, but I am expecting to get another pair soon. I must keep the children clothed and fed regardless of my own need."

I returned to my room that Thursday evening and began to plead for a new pair of shoes for this good woman as I had none good enough for her. I prayed earnestly and held on for an answer. Looking at my watch, I realized I had been praying for more than ten hours. I dropped face down again and continued my prayer. Within thirty minutes I saw a pair of ladies' shoes—brand new ladies' shoes at that!

Satisfied that all was settled for her new pair of shoes for our regular evangelistic Friday night meeting, which was just over twelve hours away, I went to my breakfast. Later that morning, after being detained with other details, I finally arrived at the mission and went directly into the prayer room. One of the kindergarten teachers came and said, "There is a lady wanting to see you."

I went out into the main hall where a woman promptly began her story. "Brother Bevington, I bought a pair of shoes this morning, but one is at least two sizes larger than the other one. They look like mates, but they aren't. I only tried on one in the store and it fit fine, so I bought them. Coming near the mission, I wanted to come in and see the kindergarten children at work. While waiting to see you, I decided to put my new shoes on to wear them home, but the one is entirely too large."

"Praise the Lord," I said. "I prayed all last night for a pair of new shoes and I guess these must be the ones."

She frowned slightly and said apologetically, "They may be, but it seems a shame to give such a pair of shoes as this to anyone. But I don't want to take them back to the store." I did not ask her why she did not want to return them, but I think perhaps she was a bit too proud to do so.

I told her, "The woman who needs these is a poor woman and she can probably put cotton batting in the larger one. The smaller one looks just like the right size."

"Well, here they are, you take them to her," the lady said.

But I insisted she take the shoes to the woman as I felt she might be able to help in other ways. I reminded her that she would have to go right past the woman's home on her way to the street car and there wasn't any reason for her not to deliver them in person. She wasn't happy about my suggestion, but finally she picked up the shoes and started for the woman's home.

Arriving there, she introduced herself and said, "Brother Bevington sent me here on a rather embarrassing errand. These are for you." She set the shoes before the woman, not telling her that one was larger than the other one.

26

While she rambled on about other things to keep from speaking of the shoes, the poor sister stood there thinking to herself, "What will I do now? I can't wear those shoes as my right foot is nearly two sizes smaller than my left and I don't want to tell her that. She's already too embarrassed as it is." The sister concluded that she should just accept the shoes and then try to exchange them.

The lady finally took her leave with great relief and started home. However, her discomfort only grew and she felt she must return and reveal the size difference to the sister. The poor sister, upon hearing the woman's confession, laughed aloud as she asked, "Which one is larger?"

"The left one."

Now the poor sister laughed more than ever. Finally she caught her breath and exclaimed, "Well, well, well! God surely understands all things. My left foot is nearly two sizes larger than my right and here are these wonderful new shoes, just exactly as I need them. Oh, praise the Lord."

Now I knew nothing of the difference in the size of the sister's feet, but God certainly did. He worked a very exact answer in order to meet my all-night prayer. Isn't that enough to convince us that God fully understands His business? I say yes! What do you say? Hallelujah!

While my main desire in this volume is to set forth God as our healer, so many other instances have found their way into these pages as an incentive to trust God as the Provider in all matters. If healing is to come to us or another, we must believe the whole Bible. We must believe God for healing as set forth in the atonement. I feel impressed to share the following passages of Scripture on healing and the conditions before and after.

1. God's covenant with His people: Exodus 15:26, 23:20-25; Numbers 21:8,9.

2. Obedience vs. disobedience: Psalm 107:17-21; Deuteronomy 28; Hebrews 10:28,29.

3. God's will is to heal His children: Matthew 8:1-17; Mark 1:41; Luke 5:13.

4. Healing in the atonement: Psalm 103:3; Matthew 8:17; Isaiah 53:4,5.

5. Miraculous proof of Christ's Divinity still needed today: Mark 2:10; Matthew 9:28,29; John 4:46-54.

6. The children's bread and their right: Matthew 15:22-28; Mark 7:29,30.

7. Christ's testimony to Himself: Luke 4:16-21, 7:19-23; John 6:62,63, 19:12-24.

8. Peter's testimony of Christ: Acts 10:38,39.

9. Christ's commission to His church: Matthew 9:35, 10:19, 28:18-20; Mark 16:14-20.

10. Christ's direction to His church: James 5:13-16.

11. Faith in God: I John 5:11-16; Mark 11:12-26; Psalm 4:5,6.

12. Believing prayer: I John 3:18-24; Mark 9:14-29, 11:24; Matthew 21:22; James 1:6-8; John 11:22.

13. Faith, not sight: Matthew 8:5-13; Romans 4:17-25; Hebrews 11.

14. His earnest of His resurrected life:
    Romans 8:11; 1 Corinthians 3:16,17.
15. Rejoice and act your faith: 2 Chronicles
    20:20-23.
16. Your faith will be tried: James 1:2-4; 1
    Peter 1:7.
17. Those who have failed to retain healing:
    Mark 4:17-25; Luke 8:13.
18. A safe shelter: Psalm 91.

The tendency in many quarters during this age is to rule out the supernatural entirely and to ascribe events to a natural cause. This rationalism goes under the heading of scholarship attributed largely to the human intellect and barring the Holy Spirit. I hope that studying the preceding passages thoroughly will cause you to ask if you have the right to ascribe miracles to the apostolic days alone. If you, as the reader, cannot believe the Scriptures and the witnesses of these days, then I say as Jesus tells us Abraham said to the rich man, "If they hear not Moses and the prophets, neither will they be persuaded, though one rose from the dead."

The existence of false teachers who stand against Divine healing is no argument against Divine healing, itself. There are false prophets today just as there have been in all ages. But, thank God, for those who can see even beyond their own vision and catch the truths of the Gospel and actually get healed in spite of such opposition.

I remember being called to a home to pray for a sister who had been on her bed for nine years. She was blessedly saved, but her husband was a radical unbeliever. While visiting with her, he came in from his work in the fields and ordered me to leave at once. I left, but unbeknownst to him, I slipped up into his haymow where I remained in earnest prayer for the next seventy-two hours.

God did not fail to answer. He raised that sister up so that within twelve hours after He touched her, she prepared dinner and called her husband into the house. She went out to the spring with an empty water bucket so as to meet him and when he came face to face with her, he broke down and wept. Then he came looking for me, realizing someone had obviously touched God for his wife. He found me in the haymow. He dropped to his knees and prayed his way through to glorious salvation.

There is an important principle in this story. Healing is not only for the benefit of the recipient, its influence is far reaching as in the case of this recalcitrant, old unbeliever. The doctrine of Divine healing stands eternally solid and true in spite of objectionable professors. When our Savior was on earth, He said that false Christs and false prophets would arise to seduce, if it were possible, the very elect (Mark 13:22). Our Savior also told us that false prophets would also heal the sick, cast out devils and do many amazing works.

We must remember that just because what seems good is done, such as devils cast out and bodies healed, this is no certain proof the person doing the work is a true prophet. There are such false prophets today who may bear all these marks and have the audacity to flaunt them in the face of Christ. At the day of judgment He will reply that He never knew them (Matthew 7:22).

One example of such false works as prophesied in Scripture is being fulfilled in the so-called Christian Science movement today. Christian Science takes the stand that there can be no such thing as sin. All reality is in the mind and therefore there is no pain, no suffering, no sorrow, no sickness. What might seem so is only in the mind. To the sick, to the suffering, to the sorrowing, Christian Science says only to think all such evil out of existence.

"How is your grandfather this morning, Bridget?" said one Christian Science practitioner to an Irish child.

"He still has the rheumatism mighty bad, Mum," was the child's honest reply.

"He only thinks he has the rheumatism. There is no such thing as rheumatism."

"Yes, Mum," responded the child.

A few days later they met again. "Does your grandfather still persist in his delusion of thinking he has the rheumatism?"

"Oh, no, Mum. The poor man now thinks he is dead. We buried him yesterday."

So you have it. Christian Science and Divine healing are not related in any way. Divine healing is not imaginary, it is not simply the exercise of will power. It is not a mind cure. It is not spiritualism. It is not immunity from death or from sickness, for those who believe in Divine healing do get sick. When their work is finished here on earth, they also die. Divine healing is not mere presumption nor a disregard of God's will. It is the direct power of God upon the human body. In spite of all the false doctrines and teachers, people are being healed through Jesus and He is getting the glory.

One man said some time ago, "Well, Brother Bevington, I suppose from your teachings that you are never going to die, for you say God heals and that He answers prayer. So all you have to do is pray and He will heal you of whatever and you will never die."

I reminded him of an incident that occurred while I was working in the carpentry trade near Michigan City,

Indiana. As I and a friend were returning home in a buggy one Saturday evening, we noticed a man and his wife walking around an old log house. They seemed to be scrutinizing the frame quite closely. As we came near, the man shouted, "Hey, Jerry, come in here."

When Jerry got out of the buggy, the man began to speak, "My wife and I have been examining our old house where we have lived and raised our family of eleven. They are all gone now, married off. You know how you have been fixing this old place up for us almost every year for several years now. Just look at the sills and those posts and the roof and that gable end. They are in pretty bad shape. We were just saying that we believe this old place is not worth repairing any more. We want you to build us a new house."

So Jerry and I built them a new house. We watched them vacate that old log house and move into their new home. They left almost all the old furniture in the old house. I said, "Sir, that is exactly the way it will be with me. Christ has promised to repair this building I am now living in, but the time is coming when it won't be worth repairing anymore. I expect soon to see Him come down, take a walk around this old frame and say, 'Well, Bevington, this old thing is not worth repairing, so now just vacate it and move up into the new mansion we have waiting for you. Leave all your old furniture behind for we have your new mansion all furnished in gold and diamonds.' "

Satan hates Divine healing and does all he can to prevent it. When someone does get healed, Satan tries to keep that person from telling about it and often succeeds in doing so. It is then that one gets in darkness over their

32

healing and Satan will do all he can to obscure their way.

Divine healing is the fulfillment of promises that cannot possibly be explained by those who take the position that miracles ceased when the apostles went to their reward. In spite of this obvious discrepancy in their theology, a long list of promises are ignored in most of our public teachings. It almost seems as if some revelations have been set aside by common consent. When the thoughtful Christian meets with the wonderful promises made to believers during his daily reading of the Bible, he often pauses to ask himself, "What can these words mean? If I am sick, can I ask God to heal me? Is prayer really a power with God?"

It is not merely power, but it is a transcendent power that accomplishes what no other power can, overruling all other agencies and rendering them subservient to its own wonderful efficiency. I feel impressed to jot down some of these promises for the reader's consideration, for study and for meditation, as we must be governed by the Word of God. We must draw our conclusions only from the Word, not from people's opinions or from the failures of others.

We must see what the Word says about Divine healing. Start with Acts 2:39. We can really make a plural out of that promise. It would be justified by so many other passages that these promises are for us. Next read Matthew 7:7-11, 18:19, 21:22; Mark 11:24 and John 14:13-14. I do not claim that all of the foregoing promises apply literally to the physical realm, but I do claim that some of them apply directly, and others indirectly, to healing.

Many promises reach beyond the spiritual realm into the physical realm as well. See James 5:16-18. The apostle illustrates what he means by prevailing prayer through the example of Elias, a man subject to passions such as ours, as he prayed for rain and it came.

We must forever settle the Bible's authority on healing. We must see it in the Bible as in Isaiah 53:4,5. Then read verses 2-8 and settle the fact that if God's Word means anything, it means healing is in the atonement. If this is settled in your spirit, then why not have it for yourself? Yes, why not? I, for one, am going to hold onto that chapter as long as I remain in this frame.

In connection with verse 4 of Isaiah 53, read Matthew 8:16,17; Hebrews 9:28; I Peter 2:24; Hebrews 13:8. The Bible says Christ is the same yesterday, today and forever. I believe that the aforementioned Scriptures give warning, invitation and proof enough to Biblically justify accepting the following as being possible.

Jesus said, "And ought not this woman, being a daughter of Abraham, whom Satan hath bound, lo, these eighteen years, be loosed from this bond on the sabbath day?" (Luke 13:16).

I know of no stronger statement of the Lord's willingness to heal His trusting children than this verse. The word "ought" expresses much more than willingness—it expresses obligation, right, something that would not be wrong to do. It places Divine healing on a high and solid plane not only as a possible and actual intervention of God for the help of His suffering children, but as His normal provision for believers.

Divine healing is something that has been included in our redemption rights; something that is part of His Gospel grace; something that is already recognized as within His will; something that does not require a special revelation to justify us in claiming it. If God expects us to do what we ought to do, surely we may expect as much from Him. There is something startling in the positiveness and force of the expression "ought not..." Surely this proves no child of God should ever doubt His perfect readiness to help and heal.

There is another important fact to notice in this verse. I firmly believe all sickness comes from Satan, either directly or indirectly. Note here that Luke identifies sickness with the direct route from Satan. He says, "...whom Satan hath bound..." So you may rest assured when you undertake to see healing done, you have to walk right in on Satan's own ground and demand his own property of him as he is the author of all sicknesses. Thus you have a real task on your hand, for he claims a right to his own property the same as you and I claim a right to what belongs to us. He has met me several times at the threshold and positively forbidden me to enter his domain. He has called me a usurper many a time, but I have credentials from God and never cease to push my claim to the limit.

3
First Light on Divine Healing, Evangelism

I went to Hamilton, Ohio, to hold a meeting and, as usual, took my small drug store with me. This consisted of four quart bottles of medicines, a box of pills and two plasters. That was my regular outfit. I think this took up more room in my suitcase than my Bibles and books.

I was assigned to a fine room in a hospitable home. I settled in and set my medical outfit on the mantle so as to have them handy, as I took of all of the remedies every day.

In this precious home there were several dear children, including one little girl of four summers. Shortly after my arrival, she came into my room and spied that outfit on the mantle. As it was something quite new to her, for her parents used no medicines, she ran out into the kitchen and said, "Oh, Mamma, come here." She began to tug at Mamma's apron.

Mamma, busy kneading bread, paid scant attention to the little child's appeal. But the tiny tugger was determined to have a hearing, so she kept pulling and jabbering.

Finally Mamma said, "What do you want? Mamma is busy now."

"Mamma come and see what the preacher's got."

So, to please the child, the mother followed her to my room. As the child came in the door, she pointed up to the mantle at that curious outlay. The bottles and such were strange looking things to the child, as I suppose she had never seen a bottle.

Well, I raised my eyes just in time to catch the expression on the mother's face. If I had been able to properly read it, this would have saved me much perplexity. That strange look before she turned back for the kitchen set me thinking. Though I could not diagnose the meaning, enough was visible to trouble me. I could not seem to get away from that expression.

However, I kept praying and reading the Word, preparatory to delivering my great message that night. The evening came, the message was delivered and it fell flatter than the first biscuits I ever made. Of course, I had no trouble finding plenty of excuses for the apparent failure. But the next day I was experiencing peculiar feelings that were somewhat alarming. I never felt just like that before, but I was well adapted to excusing myself. I had been sanctified only about a week and had not entirely given up my ability as an excuse maker.

That ability seemed wonderfully revived on this occasion, so I kept at it. But my excuses were failing to produce the desired effect and by noon, I was in a terrible mixed-up mess. The worst difficulty was that I could not locate the trouble. I examined myself carefully and prayerfully and I believe honestly. That I came in on that animal from various angles, getting close but never getting him landed sufficiently to get rid of him.

So I preached again, or tried to, that night. I thought I did better than the night before and gave the credit largely to a man and wife who sat down front where they seemed to be praying for me the whole time. So I thought, "If I can get that couple to come every night, I can preach all right." So God removed them and that prop was knocked out from under me. I was cast loose upon a tempestuous sea.

The next day I felt still worse, so I helped myself quite freely to the medicines on the mantle. But they, too, seemed to have gone off with the crowd and were quite useless. So I went to my usual resort, the woods. I spent all day out there examining myself, thinking maybe I was deceived and had never been sanctified. But God showed me I had been. Then I wondered if maybe I had lost out.

So it was a reconnoitering and digging and boring and blasting all day long, yet I could not get the thing landed. Finally, I felt defeated and went to the house to say, "Brother, you will have to take the meeting tonight. I don't know what is the matter with me, but I can't preach tonight. I will tarry here before God and see if I can get it located."

So he said, "I will help you out." They well knew what was the matter with me, though they never even hinted they were praying for me over that outlay on the mantle. They were doing their talking to God and He was doing His best to talk to me. It was a time, for sure!

I did my best at treeing the critter, but it seemed to be just getting further out in the thicket. I put in a restless, sleepless night and the next morning went to the woods. I

39

had not been there long until this sentence came to me, "I am the Lord that healeth thee."

Well, I paid but little attention as that was not what I was after. I was after the thing that brought this heaviness, as sickness had never done that to me before. That Scripture kept coming at me. I was not sure that it was Scripture, though I knew I had heard it or read it somewhere. We are always sure to get caught in the brush when we give Satan the benefit of the doubt.

I persisted in throwing the sentence out, but it would not stay out and just kept coming back at me. I stood this firing as long as I could and then returned to the house to find someone to talk to. Locating the woman, I asked, "Sister, is there such a passage in the Bible as 'I am the Lord that healeth thee' ?"

She replied that there was and got her Bible to show me. She never said a word to reveal that she and her husband were praying for me relative to my medicines.

Finding the sentence was indeed Scripture, I began to wonder if God wanted to heal me. Yet I had heard so many at the mission testify to being healed and then rush for their doctor or their medicines when they got sick. Their testimonies had little effect on me and I had concluded they were fair samples of what healing was.

But all my reasoning still failed to bring any relief, so I began to search the Scriptures further. There were plenty of evidences that Christ and the disciples healed sick people. I found healing certainly was taught in the Scriptures, but surely it had been dropped back there with the disciples. If not, then why wasn't it being preached in our Methodist churches? I felt they were the closest to the Bible of any, yet many of our M.E. preachers had told us that Divine healing was only for the disciples. Of course that settled it, as these preachers had gone through

40

colleges. What they did not know would surely be foolish for me to try to fathom out.

Having settled that in my mind, I again proceeded with the investigation of this dark horse that was causing me so much trouble. But somehow those M.E. preachers, with all of their collegiate advantages, could not keep that matter settled for me. It would roil up again and again and get me all confused. So I went back out to the woods and there came another sentence to confuse me: Asa took medicine and he died.

These are not the actual words of II Chronicles 16:12, but it is the way it came to me. There is no reference to medicine in that verse, but it says he sought not to the Lord, but to the physicians. We all know what that means. I went back to the house and asked about that passage. The sister got her Bible again and tried to help me settle my mind. But it could not be settled and I went into my room all tangled up, saying aloud, "What does all this mean? I am not after the pros and cons of medicines. I am after the cause of this awful feeling." The only thing I knew for sure was that I was a most miserable, mixed-up fellow.

I got down on my face with my head near the fireplace board, just a little below where my personal drug store was located. "Lord, Lord, what does all this mean? What is the matter with me? What does all this Scripture have to do with my case just now?"

"I am the God that healeth thee," came as an answer.

"Oh, God, dost Thou mean I am to give up all these old faithful standbys? How can I ever do it?" Gripped with fear, I cried to the Father, "Here are six different kinds of medicine that have been my guide, my strength, my all. How can I give them up?"

My hard feelings against those people who had claimed

healing, yet when sick took medicine, had affected me in such a way as to render it impossible for me to take Jesus as my Healer and still use this medicine. It seemed that if I was going to take Jesus, I must drop the six great remedies. God had His hand upon me and He had to answer the prayers of His faithful servants with whom I was staying.

I was called to dinner and as I emerged from my room, the husband came into the room holding up a mashed thumb. He said, "Wife, look here!" She just smiled. I thought she was a most hard-hearted wife. Shouldn't she have just dropped dinner and made a great fuss over that awful thumb? But no, she never even paid any attention to it and just went on with the dinner, smiling all the while. To me, it was a most sickening sight!

The man worked in the tool factory at Hamilton and had somehow caught his thumb between two heavy stones. There it was with two-thirds of the nail gone and the other third just hanging. I hurried to my room and got my bandage paraphernalia consisting of soft rags, castile soap and so on, and rushed back to minister to his injury. I announced to him, "While your wife is getting dinner, I will take care of that for you." He gave no sign of turning his case over to me, instead he just stood there laughing at my supplies. I was a little offended. "Well, maybe you think I am not an expert at this, but I have worked at it several years among the poor in our mission locality and I am good at it."

The wife came in with a steaming dish of mashed potatoes and she, too, was laughing. I was standing there wanting to show them a kindness by demonstrating my efficiency as a wound dresser and they were just laughing! My explanations and references to my ability only seemed to add fuel to their merriment, but I continued to recite the great healing properties of my salve, my soap and my soft rags. All this failed to make any impression upon them.

When they had laughed themselves out, the wife said kindly, "Brother Bevington, we never use any of those things."

"You don't? What in the world do you do? Don't you wrap up a wound with something to heal it?"

"Oh, no," she said.

"Then what do you do?"

"We just trust Him," she said as she pointed upwards.

For the first time it dawned on me what all of my inner wretchedness meant and where it had come from. I just turned and went to my room without eating any dinner. I fell down as before, with my head toward the mantle, and wept great tears. Finally I said, "Lord, Lord, oh, for such a faith as theirs! Give me some evidence, Lord, that I can live without these six remedies. Give me some unmistakable evidence, something that I can and will rely on." Dear reader, I was in a state something like Elijah—I wanted to die. But I was not yet fit for translation.

That was a memorable day, marking one of the grandest landmarks in my life, after sanctification. Glory to God! Hell had put up a stiff fight in those three or four days of intense darkness, but the light finally shone through, bless God. I have been walking in that light all these years and they have all been years of victory over that question of healing. Not one drop of medicine has ever entered my mouth since then.

To finish my story, there I lay fighting out one of the greatest battles of my life as I waited for some evidence. I suddenly heard a noise, but never raised my head. Then I actually heard a voice and down the mantle came those bottles on long legs just like I had seen them

43

in advertisements. They walked down the wall, turned and walked between my head and the mantle and out of the window. Then came the plasters and then the box of pills. I heard the pills rattle as plain as I've ever heard anything.

When all had disappeared out the window, I took that as the evidence I had wanted. I got up and took all of the four quart bottles outside and smashed them. Then I took the pills and the plasters into the kitchen and consigned them to the flames in the kitchen stove. Thus ended the years of slavery to those medicines. I returned to my room and glory flooded over me! I just wept and shouted and laughed. The sister peeked in to see what was happening and I told her the whole story. She rejoiced and laughed with me and we had an old Methodist camp meeting right there.

One additional point that may be worth something to others—when the brother would not allow me to dress his hand, Satan came in and said, "He is just fooling you." So, as the brother was due to return home from work that evening, I went out into the back alley about half an hour earlier and hid behind a coal house to spy on him as he came. I thought he would surely have a rag on his thumb, but would take it off before entering the house so as to fool me.

I lay there for three-quarters of an hour with the sun pouring down on me, waiting for my chance to catch him. By and by he turned into the alley some fifteen rods away. He was swinging both hands and singing a song I had taught him. There was no sign of a rag on his thumb and I was quite ashamed of myself. I slipped back into my room, feeling condemned, where I pleaded for forgiveness and got it.

I love to think of that memorable hour when my soul

flooded with glory and I just walked the floor. I was totally willing to abide by the results of God's answer. I didn't know whether I was to be healed or not, but took it for granted that all that had been done was for my good and God's glory. If I was to suffer, He would give me grace to bear it.

Yet, I also remember that I was not out of my room more than ten minutes until I was accosted by Satan. He came as an angel of light, informing me that I had just made a terrible mistake. He said so earnestly, "It was Satan who had you do all that. You should have had better sense to do what you did, for you haven't money enough to replace all that much needed outfit."

Being quite young in the work, I questioned if it was really God talking to me. It seemed it surely must be, for how could Satan be so interested in me?

Seeing that he had me on the run, Satan reminded me of what the good old Methodist preachers had told me four years earlier. I had ignored their noble efforts to keep me out of fanaticism and now I seemed to have gone straight into it, trampling right over their counsel. I looked the word up and was terror stricken at its definition. Now fanaticism had penetrated my very being, pulled me into its maelstrom and engulfed me by its power. I was astounded it all seemed to have happened so quickly.

I rushed to the kitchen and told the sister what I had just experienced. She reassured me that I was going to be fine, stating, "You have done just right and all this afterclap is of Satan." Then she got the Bible and showed me that healing is for us. She shared of many of their experiences with healing and I began to feel better. Then she said, "When my husband comes in to supper, you will find that his thumb is healed."

"What? That terribly smashed thumb healed?"

"Yes, it will be healed."

"Without a rag on it?"

"Yes, without any remedies. I told you we never use them," she reminded me. I wondered.

Sure enough, when we sat down to eat supper, the man's thumb was not a bit sore although it was red and tender. He had never experienced any inconvenience with it unless he hit it and even then the pain lasted only briefly. That night at family prayer I said, "I want you to anoint me and pray for my healing."

"We haven't any oil," the sister said, "but God understands and it will be just as well." So we got down on our knees. The little girl who had led her mamma in to see what the preacher had was sitting under her papa's chair. Her mamma said, "Now, honey, you lead us in prayer."

The little child said, "Dear Jesus, I am so glad Papa 'mashed his thumb and the preacher saw it, 'cause it'll help him to trust You. Amen."

Well, it was a very short prayer, but its length has never yet been fully explored. Over thirty years have passed and I am not yet to the end of the giant prayer of that little, four-year-old tot. At her amen, the couple came over to me, laid their hands upon me and prayed the prayer of faith for my healing. While I had no evidence of any kind that I was healed, I just took God at His Word. They said, "Brother Bevington, we believe that you are a healed man."

On the last night that I had preached before getting swamped, a young lady had come to the altar for sanctification. The meetings, of course, had been postponed until the preacher could get shaped back up. Now, following the prayer of faith for my healing, I was ready to preach the next night which was Sunday. The same

46

young lady came up to the altar again, but still did not manage to get through in prayer.

I closed the meeting, expecting to go to Cincinnati on the next day. She came to me on Monday morning and said, "Brother Bevington, I want to get through. Can't you remain over and have a meeting at our house tonight? I do believe I could get through then."

"Why, certainly," I agreed.

We planned the meeting at her home for that night and then I accepted a dinner invitation at another home. About 3:00 p.m. in the afternoon, I felt the old symptoms coming on me. Of course Satan was there and within thirty minutes I was as sick as I had ever been. I kept standing on the promises of God, but kept getting worse. As meeting time drew near, two young men came to escort me. As they entered my room, they both stood speechless with amazement at my condition. I was as silent as they were for I was deathly ill and the house seemed to be spinning about at a tremendous rate.

Finally one young man said, "Brother Bevington, what is the matter with you? I am a doctor's son and I'll go at once for my father. He's only two blocks from here."

"No," I said.

"But, you're as white as a sheet. You are in grave danger."

"Well, boys," I said, "I took Jesus for my Healer last night and I am going to leave my case in His hands."

"Yes, but you are dying now."

"Well, I am ready for the translation and I don't want to interfere with God's plans. No more doctors, boys. Can you lead me out onto the porch?" Since heart trouble was my problem, I wanted some fresh air to help my labored breathing.

They helped me out and it was all they could do to hold

47

me as this was one of those times when I was shaking violently. They again insisted that I must have a doctor. Just as insistently, I told them no. Still struggling for air, I asked them to lead me down the steps into the open. Right then a man came out of one of the houses and helped them lead me down the stairs. He also urged me to see a doctor, but as I continued to refuse, he snapped, "I have no time to fool with fanatics!" and walked away.

I was rapidly losing my vision and soon was quite sightless. In my long fights with a weak heart, I had only gone blind three times in my life. I gasped out, "Can you lead me to the fence?" Upon reaching the fence, I grabbed it and held on. Unbelievably, I still seemed to be getting worse.

The doctor's son said, "I will run and tell them there will be no meeting tonight."

"Don't do that. There will be a meeting," I said.

"Man, you just don't know the danger you are in."

"There will be a meeting—God told me to remain over for that purpose. Lead me out into the street and hang on to me. Whatever you do, don't let me go."

I was still shaking violently and we had some real tussling out there, but they managed to hold me well enough to keep me from getting hurt. I began to plead the promises of the Word and felt that Jesus was going to deliver me. I begged "Boys, pray!" as we staggered and plunged down the street—a very unpopular sight on that street at that time of day. After going one block, I announced, "Boys, we are going to have the victory." I could see a little again, although I was suffering greatly.

I began praising God. One of the boys told me I didn't look much like a subject to be praising God, yet I was feeling better and my sight kept returning. So I praised God all the more. People stopped and listened to me praising God in my condition. Some thought I was a drunken man, others thought I was off in the upper story. But I just allowed them to have their opinions and kept praising God.

After going one more block I could see the house we were to meet in, so I began to holler even louder, "Boys, let's go!" I raised my right hand and praised God for real victory. Though still reeling some, I held on to the victory and in ten minutes, I was completely well. Hallelujah! That was my last attack of rheumatic heart trouble for nearly fourteen years.

We went into the house and had a most blessed meeting. The girl prayed through and received the Holy Ghost in all His fullness. Afterwards, she sat down beside me and said, "Brother Bevington, this is most wonderful. It far surpasses anything I ever dreamed of. I had a vision—oh, such a sight—of hundreds of little faces. They were not as our children's faces are, but there were so many of them. Every child had his or her little hands out beckoning to me to come and teach them. There was a great long arch with huge red letters on it that spelled Fiji."

"What did you say?" I asked excitedly and she told me the vision again. I grabbed her and said, "Why, that is a call to the Fiji Islands to go as a missionary and teach them about Jesus."

She rose to her feet with both hands lifted towards heaven and, as tears of joy slid down her face, she said softly, "Glory, glory!" Fourteen months later she sailed for the Fiji Islands after dear Brother Gamble helped us get her there.

She spent sixteen years on that field and then went to Heaven there. But many times before going she would say, "Brother Bevington, what if you had given up and taken that medicine? Where would I have been?" She firmly believed that if I had taken my medicine after accepting Jesus for my Healer, I never would have recovered from that sickness and she never would have been sanctified. Let that be as it may, but I praise God that He enabled me to take the stand I did on that memorable night.

Now, reader, this volume is meant to set forth the power of God as might be manifested in these days of doubt and skepticism. Its intent is not to set forth again what was done in Christ's day. Not having names in reference to exact dates and incidents, I may get some minor details slightly mixed up. But every word recorded here will stand the scrutiny of Heaven whether they run the gauntlet of the critics down here or not.

We are not living in Christ's day nor the apostles' day. Let us fully grasp from the Bible the possibilities of our day. The manifestations of the power of God all come through consecrated prayer. What is consecrated prayer? Real, earnest, believing, solicitous prayer. Prayer that will not take no for an answer. Prayer that moves mountains.

I did not always find it easy to obey God in regard to my call to the evangelistic field, as some others have found their calls. I saw my defects as standing out far greater than the power of God. I had quite a time before I felt secure in venturing out to fully trust God. I had an equally difficult time getting to the place where He could trust me—definitely the more essential of the two. My healing was a great boon to me, however, for it removed many hindrances that had stood like mountains before me. These mountains had seemed to engulf my every effort to obey God in going out.

Thereafter, dear Brother Nichols, a blind, sanctified preacher took me up to West Virginia and gave me some valuable lessons on trust. He gave me the boost that has enabled me to lift many people out of a tangled wire net. I spent one whole winter in West Virginia in cottage prayer meetings with many, including Brother Ails. The power of God was manifest in these meetings. I had definitely moved to a new spiritual plane again.

I remember being out in the woods in prayer one night in the spring. Having wrestled nearly all night for that locality, I prayed, "God, I must have some evidence that I am in the center of Thy will." Wave after wave of glory began to flood my soul and I cried out in great rapture. I shouted and laughed and cried until I just had to get up and give vent by running and jumping over logs and brush piles for the next three hours.

In the meeting that evening, the glory fell unmistakably and I did not have to ask anyone to come to the altar that night. It was filled before I was half through preaching and the seekers were in earnest. No one had to tell them to pray, it wasn't necessary to lift up their hands, either. We didn't have to shake religion into them for that all-night prayer had knocked off their scales. They had a vision and they walked right up to it. Understand this if you understand nothing else of what I am trying to communicate: it is prayer—not money, not congratulations, not large crowds—it is prayer that brings victory.

Later I was in a meeting in Ohio and a man in the lumber business came to me to say, "You ought to hold a meeting down where I live."

"Well, sir, where do you live?"

"Twenty-two miles from here."

So I prayed over his request and felt somewhat inclined to give the matter further consideration. I asked him for the names of the leaders and he gave me two. After the meeting closed where I was, I went to the woods again and curled up inside a hollow log to get the mind of God. I was impressed to go, but as I seemed to be running up against some pretty hard problems in my log, I decided to wait before God to be definite and sure. I spent forty-eight hours longer in that hollow hotel—making it a total of one hundred and twenty hours to get things straight from headquarters. Amen!

It pays to know what we are doing when it comes to dealing with God or minding Him. That is where the trouble is with so many—they jump to conclusions when they should proceed slowly. Brother Knapp taught that nine times out of every ten we get our impressions from Satan. So we need to wait, get still and get where God can actually talk to us. So I searched for the mind of God and He gave me clear assurance He wanted me to go to this place.

After I had finally gotten real still, free from everything else, He showed me the road I was to take. I saw a clump of trees and a little-traveled road running off to the left and down to a schoolhouse. Between the main road and the branch road was quite a grove of small trees. The schoolhouse stood down a slope in front of a creek with a large corn field beyond that. Farther back yet stood a large farmhouse, a big barn, some outbuildings and a windmill. I said, "Amen, Lord, that is good enough."

I backed out of that hollow log and went down to the house to tell the family where I was going. I ate some dinner and started out on the twenty-two mile walk, carrying two heavy suitcases filled mostly with books to sell. I traveled until sundown and stopped at a house to ask the owner for a drink. I gave out some tracts and talked about salvation to that man and then told him where I was headed.

We talked about salvation until after dark for I had

become very interested in his soul and that of his wife. I did not yet know where I would spend the night and was relieved when he said, "You stay with us tonight."

The next morning he said, "See here, you are going down there on uncertainties. I know that man you will have to deal with—he is a hard-headed German. Now right down this road there is a church, but we have no services and no Sunday school. If you will stay here, I will give you the best room in the house and you will have all the time you want to pray. Give us a meeting and then go to this other place since you don't have any definite dates anyway."

Well, that sounded pretty reasonable and seemed to be good logic—a great trap Satan sets. He has little trouble getting lots of victims to fall into it. This was a case where it paid to pray through, for Satan would have stood a pretty good chance of sidetracking me if I had not spent those hours in that log getting everything straight. Yes, it pays to get plain, definite orders even if it does take one hundred and twenty hours.

So I said to the man, "I can't stop now, but maybe I can come back." He still felt I ought to stay, knowing the obstacles and failures of the place where I was going. But I went on.

I gave out tracts all along the road and when I got within ten miles of the schoolhouse, I told people where I was going and what for. One woman looked very doubtful as she said, "Oh, I do wish you could get a meeting and a Sunday school at that place because the people are getting desperate there. They are so ungodly and so wicked that they go into the woods Saturday night to play cards, gamble, drink beer and have rooster fights until Monday morning. Oh, I wish you could, but..." Oh, how many get stuck on that pesky "but"!

I went on and when I was within four miles, I stopped to get a drink. I gave out tracts and told the family of my mission. The woman of the house sighed and said, "I do hope you can get something started, for they are very wicked down there. Their wickedness reaches all over the country."

She paused and then continued, "You see that girl in the garden? She is thirteen and my only living child. Every Saturday my husband goes over to the rock houses in the woods where they gamble, swear, chew, smoke and tell all sorts of smutty yarns. He takes that girl with him to do the cooking. She, being innocent of the danger, rather enjoys it. I have done everything I can do to prevent it.

"I have even tried to get the neighbors to help me break up their hellish work, but the men are all in it. They like to have my girl there to do the cooking for them. I am nearly distracted over this. They leave here about one o'clock on Saturday and don't get back until Monday. Often they do not come back before night and I have all the stock to look after."

I kept on going along, praying and handing out tracts. At another place I was asked to stop and have a meeting in a forsaken Baptist church. But I kept going.

My burden was increasing as I came nearer the end of my journey. I soon met a man and wife and gave them some tracts. They asked my business there and shook their heads when I told them. Starting to pass on, they stopped and called back, "You had better stir up some of these hollows instead, for I tell you that you will be fooling away your time in that awful neighborhood."

"Those are the ones that Jesus came for," I replied.

"Yes, yes. But if you knew what we know, you would never stop there. There have been many attempts there and all of them have failed and left the place worse every time."

So I jogged on along, thinking and praying, "God, this is Thy work. What does it all mean?"

"What's that to thee, follow thou Me," was all the consolation I could get. Well, that was enough. Hallelujah to His dear name!

The man wasn't yet satisfied and he turned around and overtook me. He stopped me and said, "I live over the other side of that hollow. We will give you a good room and all you can eat and you have a certainty there. But up at that schoolhouse is a dark prospect. If there is any place on earth that needs a meeting and a Sunday school, it is our neighborhood. And we will see that you get some money, too. You will get none where you are headed."

That was quite an inducement, but it was not the right place. So I thanked him for his kind offers and said, "I may come back when I get through out there."

"You will be of no account when you are through there, even if you come out alive." Ominous words, indeed, but I had received my orders back in that hollow log. I preferred to obey God and run my chances with Him rather than accept the man's invitation.

I continued on towards this unknown "dark prospect" before me. Soon I saw a faint road branching off to the left with a diamond-shaped clump of trees and a schoolhouse. I knew at once that this was the place and I had arrived at my destination. Behind the schoolhouse I saw a creek and a corn field. Beyond them sat the large farmhouse, the big barn and the windmill.

"Well," I said, "this must be the place." I made my way down through the clump of trees to the schoolhouse. I tried the door and found it locked. So I pushed my way through weeds higher than my head around to the back of the schoolhouse. Then I got down on my face in those weeds and praised God for landing me right at the spot He had shown me in my hollow log twenty-two miles away.

"Father, I am so thankful I escaped the enemies I encountered on the way who tried to get me off Thy line. Dear Lord, I am so glad Thou madest it possible for me to pray clear through and get my orders direct. I am glad Thou has fixed me up so I am able and perfectly willing to run the gauntlet though facing some muscular giants who have been swinging their clubs, aiming to scare me off. I am confident Thou wilt enable me to run through without a scratch."

I lay there for some time, praising God and thanking Him until He let the glory pour right down into my soul. I had to get up and run again. Then I began to return to dealing with the practicalities of my mission. I set off for the nearest house to hand out tracts and inquire where Mr. R--- lived. "In the second house on the right," the woman of the house explained. As I thanked her and started on, she said, "Say, aren't you a preacher?"

"Yes, ma'am, I am."

"Well, are you going to hold a meeting in the school-house?"

"I expect to."

"Oh, I do hope you can, but..." her voice trailed away. There it was again, that "but." I had learned to ignore the buts, so I turned in the direction of the house of Mr. R---and walked away. Soon I came to the house and a large barn, second on the right just as she had said. I saw a very big fellow out in the truck patch cutting down weeds. There had been a great deal of rain and he could not plow his corn yet.

I set my suitcase down and offered a friendly greeting to

him. He looked up and responded cordially. Encouraged, I asked, "Are you Mr. R---?"

"Yes, what of it?"

"Well, I am a holiness evangelist."

Before I could even finish the statement, he had straightened up on his hoe handle and said, "A what?"

"A holiness evangelist."

He repeated the phrase to himself and then said, "I have seen all sorts of evangelists, but I don't believe I ever saw one by that name."

"Well, sir, just come out here and look one right in the eyes!"

Intrigued by now, he came closer to the fence and asked, "What do you want of me?"

"Mr. R---, I want to get in that schoolhouse you have control of and hold some meetings, get someone saved and organize a Sunday school."

"I personally would be delighted to unlock that door and let you in for that good purpose. But I've been notified, all the way from the wiggle tail in the puddle up to the giant of the throne, that I must not unlock that door for preaching. The benches are all just about whittled up, anyway. I am real sorry, though. I know it would make my wife real glad to have you hold a meeting, she would take hold and help you all she could." He really did seem sorry for rejecting my request. Then he said, "It's about dinner time. Why don't you come up with me and have something to eat?"

So we went. It was a somewhat strained meal, for his wife obviously felt very bad that her husband would not open that door. It was not clear what his authority or power was in the situation, it was just clear that unless he unlocked that door, there would be no meeting. That door was to become the all important item over the next nine days.

When dinner was over, he finally spoke, "Mister, I was down at the mill three or four weeks ago and a friend of mine, a trustee over on the other road, told me they have just finished their new schoolhouse. He said if I should meet a preacher, to send him over. They would like to have a meeting there and have a Sunday school started."

With that he led me out onto the porch and said, "Pumpkin Hollow. You go back down the road until you come to the first pair of bars on your left. Turn there, cross that bottom, go up a hill and follow that road down across another hollow through a strip of woods—about three miles, I guess. I've got to get on now, but I hope you have a good time over at Pumpkin Hollow." I had been dismissed.

I picked up my grips and started off down the road thinking to myself, "Pumpkin Hollow, huh? That is not what I came for. Well, Lord, where am I going now?"

"What's that to thee, follow thou Me," came as my only answer. So I kept going until I came to a long hill on my right. Then the voice said, "This path is the way." So up that great hill I began to climb, lugging my two suitcases.

"Well, Lord, where in the world am I going now?"

"What's that to thee?" came the reply.

So up I climbed, asking no more questions. Finally I reached the summit of the hill and dropped my suitcases under a large oak tree. The same voice said, "This is the place."

"This, Lord?"

"Yes."

I sat down under the oak tree and examined my situation. Since the most obvious hindrance to having the meeting was the locked door, I felt that was where I should begin. I stayed under that tree nine days and nights. I had nothing to eat, but that was not of concern to me for I knew my burden was to get that door unlocked. God had sent me there to hold a meeting and Satan was trying to hinder the meeting.

My business now was to pray that door open. Breaking the door down would not solve the problem, nor would giving up. That would be disobeying God and disregarding His orders. So I embarked on nine days of prayer. Why did it take that long? Simply because I could not get still enough any sooner.

After the first twenty-four hours, Satan came down and argued the situation. I had a conflict with him almost every day. Then he brought up Pumpkin Hollow as a much better site than where I had been lying, as it had rained on me three days and nights. He stressed the fact that because I was so damp and shivering under that tree, I would contract a cold that would probably break up all my meetings for the rest of the year. Not only that, he gloomily continued to inform me, such an illness would surely land me in the grave prematurely.

And so it went for eight days and nights. On the morning of the ninth day, I began to sense that I was becoming still before the Lord. At the fifth hour of that day, I rose from my face and held up the Bible while I praised God that the door was going to be opened. I cried out, "Well, Mr. Devil, if you have any more material down there in hell, just bring it on up here!" I had met every objection he had offered with the Word and he could not rake up another proposition. He had exhausted all the resources of hell on me and was completely whipped.

I dropped back down on my face, feeling sure I was near the opening of the door. At noon I knew I was

59

becoming totally still and, oh, how desirous I was to keep that state. I did not even want to breathe, several times holding my breath until I could hardly get any air. Many times when I was so close to the object of my desire, I would hold my breath and just barely touch it.

So I kept getting smaller and smaller, smaller and smaller, until I saw myself as a little worm not over an inch long. I began to whisper "Glory!" very softly. I repeated the word again and again, ever so softly for fear of losing ground in my efforts. But seeing that I did not, I felt assured that victory was near.

In a couple of hours, I was very still, oh, so still, when I said, "Now, Lord, Thou wilt open that door." I heard a key go into that lock, heard it turn and saw the door swing open. As the door opened, it left a mark where it rubbed on the floor. I cried, "Oh, glory, it's open!"

Inasmuch as this meeting had been such a hard pull from the start, beginning with the many hours spent in that hollow log, I felt I had the right to do as Gideon had done—ask for a second witness. So I dropped on my face again and whispered, "Lord, Thou didst answer twice for Gideon and I believe Thou wilt for me."

I held very still and in fifteen minutes, I was as small as before. In five minutes more, I heard the same sounds as before and saw the mark quite plainly once more. I jumped up and praised God for the wonderful victory after the nine days of conflict. Then I picked up my suitcases and marched back down that hill.

I saw Mr. R--- out in his truck patch again. Seeing me as well, he hollered, "Well, well, and how is Pumpkin Hollow?" When I did not reply, he said, "You've had a good time, I reckon."

"I have been having a fine time."

"Well, I knew you would. Say, we just got through with

our dinner. Why don't you go up to the house and get something to eat. You look like you could use a bite."

I went on into the house and was greeted warmly by his wife. "I am so glad to see you. While we were eating dinner just now, my husband had to get up three times to answer the phone regarding the meeting here." She seemed surprised, but I wasn't.

Please remember that I had been doing my duty all along by giving out tracts all along that twenty-two mile trip and telling everyone what I wanted. This had given God a foundation to work with. Then as soon as I reached that tree and began to pray, God began to first work on all those people and then work through them by having them phone Mr. R--- concerning the meeting.

As I was beginning to get still under that tree, God had three of those people call him up and remind him that they ought to have a meeting there. He soon tired of that and after answering the third call during his dinner, he suddenly said, "Wife, how is Nance?" Nance was a bald-faced mare that had been crippled for about two weeks.

"She must be all right, I guess. I saw her running and kicking up her heels just before dinner. Why do you ask?"

"Just get Frank (their ten-year-old boy) and tell him to bring her up, saddle her and go over to Pumpkin Hollow and tell that preacher to come here as soon as he gets through."

That was at the very time I heard the bolt turn in the lock and saw the door open to rub the mark on the floor. God had given me that witness, the evidence that my petition was answered after nine days of praying for that door to open, and He gave me the witness as soon as Mr. R--- gave his consent. We can rest assured that God will give us a satisfactory witness when we pray through and wait for Him to respond.

After doing justice to Mrs. R---'s fine meal, she gave me the key to go down and unlock that schoolhouse and air it out. She promised that they would phone around and inform everyone about the meeting that night. As I passed Mr. R--- in his truck patch, he said, "You go on down. There will probably be some women and children out to your meeting tonight, but we men are going off after the foxes that have been killing our chickens. We got together and have organized a fox band and I was put in as captain," he said proudly. "We have invested quite a lot of money in about twenty hounds and we are all going out every night, about thirty men, until we get rid of those foxes. So, there will be no men at your meeting, but there will probably be some women and children."

"All right, Mr. R---, I have the key and that is the main thing right now." I hurried towards the schoolhouse, quite anxious to open the door and see that mark caused by the door. I held my breath as I unlocked the door and then pushed it open. Sure enough, it rubbed on the floor and made a mark just as I had seen it. I cried out, "Oh, glory to our God!" Then I just stood there and wept and laughed and shouted for joy. I had a blessed time, nearly an hour, rejoicing to know that God would take such pains to show me so many things, all of which were to assure me of the right way.

Finally I returned to the next order of business. I closed the door and got down on my face on the floor and proceeded to begin a spiritual stampede on that organized fox club. I prayed for nothing else for the next three and a half hours. I just stuck to that club of thirty unsaved men with souls that God had sent His Son to save. About 7:30 p.m., I heard quite a racket outside with barking of hounds and the voices of many men. Then I heard their captain say, "Well, boys, let's go in and see what the fellow is doing." They all dismounted, tied their horses and filed in.

I got up off my face and shook hands with everyone, placing a new songbook in each hand after I released it. "Let's have a few songs," I announced.

"Well, now, we are just staying a few minutes," said the captain.

"That is fine, but for whatever time you are here, let us sing." Then I quickly bowed my head and asked the Lord what song I should sing first. I felt everything would hinge on that first song.

The Spirit said to me, "Will There Be Any Stars In My Crown?" I was surprised, for that was not a song I would be partial to choosing to sing in the presence of so many sinners. But I did not dare question the voice of the Holy Spirit, so I called for that song.

"That's it exactly!" said the captain. I was amazed that this song was what they all wanted. And, oh, how they sang it out. I had called upon the captain to lead and he sang very well. In fact, he was quite enthused about leading the singing. Before the song was over, the schoolhouse was packed. So I ventured a second song title and it proved to be another great favorite of them all. I gave out seventy-five books to adults and children and how they did sing! That song service was the answer to my prayer that broke up their great fox club.

I was not able to preach for nearly an hour. After bringing forth my message, we had another song service with the captain leading it. "Captain, I believe you should select all the songs and take charge of the singing for these meetings. Can you meet me here before the services and go over your selections?" My words so met with everyone's approval, I never heard another word about those chicken thieves—the infamous "foxes."

Those blessed meetings lasted nine weeks. On the fourth night, the captain stepped out when I had closed my message and, with tears in his eyes, said, "Boys, we want and need this kind of salvation. Come, let's have it." The whole thirty of them came and began to pray in earnest. The captain was the first to pray through and by midnight he bounded to his feet and proceeded to jump and shout elatedly. Then he began to preach as he walked back and forth through the other twenty-nine men who wept and prayed until nearly 4:00 a.m. in the morning.

Three prayed through. Seven women had also come forward and three of them prayed through. The captain's wife, the only regenerated person in the whole neighborhood when the meetings began, was among those seeking sanctification.

During those meetings, over two hundred knelt at the altars and most of them prayed through. The wonderful stories are too many to relate here, but so many said, "What if Bevington had failed to pray through under that tree!"

Yes, it pays to obey God even if the way is somewhat befogged with conditions we do not understand. A huge holiness hall was built there and many wanted me to take charge of the work. I might have done it except I had so many other calls to answer. I said I would come back often and I did. Sadly, a few years later a shrewd preacher got in there and organized his church. In three years not a sanctified man or woman was there except the dear captain's wife who stood straight all her days. That wonderful handmaiden of the Lord died preaching sanctification.

Later I was holding another meeting in Ohio when I received an invitation to yet another place. When I completed the meeting I was in, I went to the woods to settle this new call. It was late in the fall and quite chilly, so I crawled into a hollow log to pray. God met me there and told me to go. So I went. I had preached three nights when I was abruptly notified I could not preach any more in that schoolhouse. Knowing that God had told me to come, again I went out to the woods and into another hollow log.

I lay there praying for five days and then came a puzzling circumstance. I began to get hungry, a sign that usually meant my fasting and prayer was over. Yet I knew I did not have the victory I was seeking. A decision had to be made and in short order, I chose to remain there praying until I heard my answer from Heaven or died right there inside the log.

My hunger kept increasing and I felt weaker and weaker. These had generally been the evidences that a fast was either called off by God or I had gotten through. I bring up this point to caution the reader that there is a danger in getting in a rut for God works entirely apart from ruts.

About twenty-four hours after I had begun telling the Lord that I was very hungry, but not yet satisfied, I was six days into my watch. My log was somewhat smaller than I generally holed up in so I was a bit cramped and I occasionally stretched as best I could by extending my arms over my head. As I stretched this time, I touched something with my hand. I gathered up several small objects in my hands and found I was holding six acorns.

I had never been fond of acorns, but I felt impressed to eat these. Oh, my, those acorns tasted wonderful. As they were quite fresh, I could not imagine how they had gotten into that log. Also, I wondered how long they had been there since I had not felt them all of the other times I had stretched my hands out in exactly the same way. I asked God these questions and waited for His answer. After eating the acorns, I felt refreshed.

After laying there in prayer all night, I found six more acorns when I stretched out my hands the next morning. I carefully felt as far as I could, but found only the six of them. I found six fresh acorns in that hollow log three times a day for the next four days. The acorns appeared right on schedule until I had finally prayed the matter through—ten days in all.

As the appearance of those acorns was still quite a curiosity to me, on the last day of my watch I crawled from the log and left my shoes at the entrance as a pretense that I was still inside. I moved some distance away to a hollow tree and concealed myself in it. Within a short while, six large gray squirrels appeared. Each one jumped up on that log and dropped his acorn down a knot hole and then disappeared back into the underbrush. "Oh, my wonderful, wonderful God. Thou hast been feeding me through these six squirrels."

I wept for joy to realize He was so mindful of me that He had these small animals faithfully toiling, right on schedule every day, to meet my needs. I cried out in delight, "Elijah isn't the only one who was fed by Your animals, Father!" I was once again humbled by my amazing relationship with this mighty God. I have wished so many times that I could always live feeling as humble as I have felt at times like this.

I crawled back into my log and after another few hours, I looked out and saw several men and women down praying just outside of the schoolhouse I had been put out of ten days before. They did not know I was nearby, so I started down the hill towards them. The man who had put me out of his home and the schoolhouse looked up and saw me and began to rush towards me. He was bare-headed and looked completely wild-eyed and reckless. I was not sure what his intentions were, but I held steady in the faith that this was in order.

As we met, he shouted, "Oh, Brother, please pray for us. I am so glad to see you. Pray for us. I have been in hell for these past ten days."

So we knelt down right there and he prayed as earnestly as I have ever heard any man pray. We stayed on our knees, pleading his case for the next two hours. He finally prayed through in fine shape and then begged me to come into his home again, promising to open the schoolhouse back up that very night.

So the meetings resumed and we had a blessed time there for the next three weeks. Many sought and found God all because I had stayed in that hollow log in spite of the confusing aspects of my intense hunger. Oh, how I wish that folks were not so ready to give up so quickly! They are all too willing to fold up and give in to whatever Satan says. That man allowed Satan to drive me out of his home and then out of the schoolhouse. If I had done as many easily would have—given up and gone off to more inviting places—where would those souls have landed?

During those meetings, one man found out I had been in that log those ten days and that I claimed squirrels had fed me. He caught up to me as I was walking the road to my lodgings. "Mr. Bevington, I understand you have been up on the hill in a hollow log and that you claim the squirrels fed you acorns while you were in there."

"Who told you such stuff as that?"

"I heard it straight and I want to know whether you say it is the truth or not?"

"I would still like to know where you heard it," I calmly replied.

"Never mind that, just answer my question, please."

"All right. Yes, sir, I did and I do claim that six squirrels fed me three times a day."

He stopped right there in his tracks and said, "Mr. Bevington, do you know you are a thief?"

"No, I don't know that."

"Well, you are and I can prove it. Those squirrels were putting up their winter food and you stole it and ate it all up." With those words, he walked away with a satisfied look on his face.

I must admit that such a statement staggered me for the moment. Was it possible he was telling the truth? I went on to my apartment considerably worked up about that transaction. The next day, for a better understanding, I returned to the woods in the late afternoon and crawled back into that log. I did not find any acorns. I kept that up for three days and never found one single acorn. That settled the question for me. It was clear that God had made caterers out of those squirrels for this special occasion. I felt like lying low at Jesus' feet once again. I knew He would work everything out as He always does when we do our part and then give the outcome to Him.

I am pretty well convinced that a large portion of all our troubles and sickness come upon us because we allow Satan to put them there. For instance, when our Wednesday night meetings come, Satan knows that all he has to do is afflict us a little. He also knows that there are only a few who will not allow him the room to do this. He deals out his aches and pains in abundant quantities to any who will allow him to so they will have an excuse to stay home.

God wants us to get to the place where we will believe the promise in Exodus 15:26, "I am the Lord that healeth thee." He wants us to take a firm stand against Satan's bold attacks, a stand for our "blood-bought rights." I have often fought Satan face to face on this line. You will produce no effect at arm's length and he is too great a swordsman to tackle him that way anyway.

I was called to conduct a tabernacle meeting in Ohio and, after praying over the invitation, I decided I should accept. I went by train and was met at the station and then escorted to a hotel. In the afternoon I was visited by six of the leaders, four men and two women. "Brother Bevington," they queried me, "when do you want your money? Do you prefer it now or at the close or in installments? We are prepared to pay you all you want."

That was a great surprise to me as I was not generally troubled with much money. Often I just walked away at the close of my meetings. I replied, "Well, what are you in the habit of paying?"

"That depends upon the number of singers the evangelist has. As you are going to lead the singing, we will give you eighty dollars."

"Eighty dollars? Whew! Where do you get this money?"

"Oh, that isn't for you to think about or discuss. You are just to conduct the services and we are to see to the paying. We don't want evangelists to be encumbered with any of the expenses."

Eighty dollars was more than I had gotten at times in a whole year. Their liberality set me to thinking and I asked again, "How do you get this money?"

"Brother, we don't want you to be bothered with that at all. The evangelists who have been here just leave that to us. You just say whether you want it now or at the close."

I was standing my ground, "Well, brethren, I feel like insisting on knowing how you raise this money."

So one of the sisters spoke up, "In the first place, we have gate fees. Then we have stands on the grounds and we get quite a bit of money out of those."

"What do you sell at these stands?"

"Oh, candies, cigars and tobacco, soft drinks, popcorn and so on. Some offer lunches, meals or whatever we can make money out of."

"And you have been conducting this camp on those principles—allowing all that stuff?"

"Why, yes. How would you expect to make such expenses from any other source?" they asked in surprise.

"My people, you have the wrong man," I told them. "I could never allow such as that at any meeting I preached."

"Why, you don't set yourself up as better than those other grand evangelists who have been running this camp for years, do you?" they all exclaimed. "Our camp stands out second to none in the great state of Ohio!"

"Well, I will have nothing to do with that kind of operation. This is a personal matter with me and I cannot do anything here for you unless you are willing to change your methods." With that, we parted company.

That was Thursday evening and on the following morning about twenty of them came to see me. "Now see here, Bevington, we have advertised these meetings extensively and at great expense. We can't afford to have them fail. Why, it would ruin our camp. We won't be able to meet any of the expenses unless we do as we have always done. And, I might add," one of them said defensively, "everything we have done has been perfect right and legitimate as any reasonable person would admit!"

They were positive about their position and I stood firmly on mine. Finally one woman on the committee rose to her feet and said, "We don't want this crank here as he would not preach to suit us anyway. We would meet with failure on all lines. Let us send and get our old standby." I knew this person and his fondness for getting drunk almost every time he held a meeting and got his hands on some money.

They rose to their feet as one and informed me, "You will have to pay this hotel bill and walk out of this town unless you have the money to pay for your own transportation. Good day, Mr. Bevington!" They left somewhat roiled up.

"I am quite a good walker," I called out after them. With that final closing remark, there seemed to be nothing left to do but pack up and leave. So I paid the hotel bill, pocketed my remaining eighty-four cents and headed off towards my next destination, some thirty-six miles away.

I was packing a heavy suitcase in each hand and after walking about a mile and a half, I sat down under a tree. "Lord, I am able and willing to pack these cases the distance, but I feel like asking you to give me a lift." I felt the need to have a little more extended prayer, so I stepped some five rods farther up from the roadside and had a wonderful time of praising and rejoicing and fellowship with God. Feeling pretty well muscled up for the task ahead of me, I rose and started back down to the road. A man and a woman were sitting in a two-seated wagon watching me.

As I came up to them, I reached out and heartily shook their hands, giving them some tracts. The man said, "Isn't your name Bevington, the one who is going to hold the camp here this summer?"

"Well, you're part right. My name is Bevington, but I will not be holding the meeting."

"What are you doing out here?" the man asked.

"Well, I have been having a prayer and praise service up there," I pointed back up the hill.

They laughed pleasantly and the woman remarked, "Yes, we heard you praying up there and thought we would stop and hear what you were praying about."

Then the man said, "We stopped at the store as we came through and heard them talking about what a crank they had engaged to conduct the camp. They were setting you out in great shape. We drove on up here and my wife said, 'I think I believe in that crank. Let's stop and meet him.' So, here we are wondering about any fellow possessing all those remarkable characteristics. I'm a little disappointed, though, because you don't look much different than any of the rest of God's children."

His wife inquired, "Where are you going?"

"I am going to L---."

"Well, we are going right through there, so jump in and we'll give you a ride." Little did they realize what would begin with that simple offer. Before God was through, the man and his wife and daughter and many more were regenerated and sanctified in the town of L---.

God's intentions for the whole situation were different than anyone had guessed. He obviously wanted this man and woman and their daughter to work for Him and He decided that a most circuitous route was in order to bring them into line. That little family went into a most fruitful evangelistic work. If I had compromised my understanding of holiness, who is to say if they would have been saved or not. I have seen and heard all three of them testify on the platform at that very camp many times.

If God had undertaken to tell me all that He wanted to accomplish, He probably never could have made me understand it. So He just sent me first to this noted camp and then out on the road to meet with this man and

72

woman. Because I knew His standards, I ended up being exactly where He wanted me to be. I set off when the work was finished and started down the road to Louisville with little change and no visible encouragement, but a joy and peace in my heart.

4
Work at Cleveland and Chattanooga, My Rib Experience

While at the Ironton mission, we had a nice baby organ, but there was rarely anyone who would play it on the street. One night a nice-looking man came up to me and said, "Brother, if you can get someone to pump the organ, I will play for you every night and start each line in the songs. I haven't enough strength to pump the organ myself, as I am consumptive."

"Well," I said, "I think I can get pumpers and good ones at that." So I did and he played for several weeks.

One day, with a sad expression, he came and told me, "I am getting no better here in this climate. I was so much in hopes it would prove helpful to me." His home was in the South and he had decided to return there. He was gone in a few weeks.

The next turn in affairs came when it appeared I was to go to Cleveland and open another mission. Well, I fought that hard. I was very attached to those dear, poor children at Ironton—a labor of love I had wrestled with for sixteen months. So I gave little attention to this Cleveland impression at first. But somehow it kept coming up nearly every time I prayed until it overwhelmed nearly all the petitions I sent up.

Finally I had to give in, although through many tears. I don't know if I ever had such a time giving up a place as Ironton. I had overcome so many swamps and quagmires just to be there in the first place. When I could deny the call no longer, I said, "Lord, send someone to take my place and I will go." Within two days, a man and his wife came to take up the work. With a heavy heart I removed myself and headed for Cleveland.

I left everything at Ironton. I had no money, but I had never run up any debts, either. The first thing to do was to get still and pray down a mission. I went to the home of the only person I knew in Cleveland and was given lodging. I entered right into six days of fasting and praying and on the seventh day, I found myself ordered out. I set off to search for a meeting place. Finding one, I engaged it and began cleaning out the dust and cobwebs.

A man came along and asked if I was opening up a saloon. "No, it is to be a holiness mission."

"Well, well," he remarked as his face brightened up, "when are you going to open?"

"In two days, on Saturday night to be exact."

"Got your seats, I suppose?"

"Well, they are not here, but I have them," I said, smiling to myself.

"Where are they? I have a team and might draw them for you. The cost of drawing by cart is pretty high here in the city, you know."

76

"I will let you know if I need your help. Just give me your name and address."

As he was doing so, he said, "Now, tell me your name and where you are staying."

I gave him my name and told him the address where I had been residing. I went back to my work as he boarded a street car and left. I did not know it at the time, but he went straight out to the address I had given him. The man of the house was at work, but the wife was more than willing to talk to him when he asked if they knew the man named Bevington.

"Well, I don't know anything about him. He came here about ten days ago and said he was acquainted with my husband. I bid him to come in until my husband came home. We assigned him a room, wanting to be hospitable and all, and he went in there and began groaning something terrible. I suppose he was praying, but he went on at it for six days. He had not eaten a thing all week and then he emerged on the seventh day and said he was hungry. While he was eating, he told me he was going to open a mission by Saturday night."

"I suppose," said the gentleman, "that he has plenty of money. He said he had his chairs and an organ and songbooks, but he would not tell me where they are. I could have drawn them for him this afternoon."

"Well, if he has money, I would like to know where he keeps it," she said suspiciously. "My husband got a little uneasy about his actions, so we pulled out his outfit and went through all his grips and belongings. All we could find was twenty-nine cents in his pocketbook."

"But he told me he had the chairs and the whole works," said the man.

"Well, he sure is a funny person," she sniffed. "We didn't understand him at all."

77

With that, the man left and returned to where I was busy cleaning. He approached me and offered his help again. "My team is now idle, why don't I draw those chairs and the rest of what you need?"

I saw at once that I had better explain myself. So I quoted I John 5:14 and 15, "And this is the confidence that we have in him, that, if we ask any thing according to his will, he heareth us. And if we know that he hear us, whatsoever we ask, we know that we have the petitions we desired of him."

He shook his head and said, "I don't understand you at all. You said you had those chairs."

"I do have them according to that verse, as I prayed through on them and I am expecting them to be here when I open on Saturday night."

"But there aren't any chairs anywhere," he gestured around in frustration. "How are you going to get them?"

"By standing on the Bible."

I saw he was genuinely puzzled now, so I left him thinking and resumed my cleaning and looking through the stuff on the floor. I had put out my sign that said "Pentecostal Mission" so whoever was to bring the chairs and whatever else God would send could locate me.

Satan certainly found the sign. He showed up as usual as he is always interested in any work for the Lord. He began reasoning with me, "You are a stranger here and are going to have to make your wants known. That is the way all missions do. They go out and solicit help. You will never open here until you do."

But I had tried that once before and had failed at such an approach, so I rejected his suggestions. I stood my ground in spite of the fact that I might face great reproach if I opened Saturday night and there was no place for anyone to sit down. I believed the Lord knew exactly where my seats were. He did and, in fact, He used the brother where I had been staying to acquire them. I received several fine benches and songbooks and an organ. I never went after a thing nor told anyone of the needs. I just laid it before God and let Him attend to it. He did just fine!

First He sent a brother from the First M.E. Church of Ironton. He came and expressed great interest, "What is opening up here?"

"A holiness mission, a work among the poor people," I replied.

"Well, if you haven't chairs, I am sure I can furnish you with some good benches."

"If the Lord leads you to do that, I will be very glad," I smiled.

In five hours here came fine benches with good backs. While they were being unloaded, a sister came along and said, "What is going on here?"

"I am expecting to open a holiness mission Saturday night."

"Oh, my, I have an organ I would like to put in here. I will even play it if you want me to."

"Send it down," I urged her.

The next morning it arrived with forty good songbooks. She proved to be a good organist, too. It is wonderful how, when we get out of the way, God will get His work done. The reason He doesn't work in some situations is that we get in His way. If we can just tuck ourselves off in the corner when God is ready to move, He will always do His part!

After I had been in Cleveland for quite a while, I received a letter from Sister Allen of Chattanooga. Her husband, Brother Allen, was the man who had played the baby organ for me at Ironton. I can well remember his playing while someone else pumped the pedals for him.

Mrs. Allen wrote, "By the time you get this letter, Mr. Allen will be buried. The doctor has just left and said there would be no need of his calling again. Mr. Allen has bled over a quart and is now barely alive. I can scarcely discern any life in him anymore. What I will ever do, I do not know."

I took the letter into my prayer room, telling the brother who was with me not to allow anyone to come into that room and bother me. I lay down on the floor on my face and began to intercede for the next eleven hours. I had much going on at that time of my life, so it took me some time to get still enough to hear the voice of God.

After eleven hours, I saw Mr. Allen lying as a dead man, white as a sheet and perfectly still. I thought he was surely dead. Not permitted to break the vision, I lay there for five minutes more when I saw him raise his right hand and smile. "Thank you and amen, Lord. Now, I will pray for his healing." I put in another nine hours of prayer to be certain whether or not the Lord wanted to heal him. Twenty hours on my face had passed, but I knew I was now on the right track. I had laid the foundation and could proceed intelligently. It was just a matter of time.

After another forty-six hours, I saw him raised up as a healed man. Then I saw him sitting in front of a baby organ pumping and playing with all his might. So I said, "Praise the Lord, that is good enough for me!" I had laid prostrate in a dark room for fifty-six hours, but I came out a conqueror in the name of Jesus.

After treating myself to a meal, I sat down to write Mr. Allen and tell him that he was a healed man and he would be working in two weeks. I told him the exact time I saw him at the organ, a totally healed man.

Shortly after that, I saw him in a vision again. He got up and sat on the edge of his bed and began to rub himself. Then I saw him feel his arms, pinch himself and rise to look in the mirror. I heard him say, "Yes, this is Allen, no doubt about it. Pretty poor, pretty poor, nothing but skin and bones. But it's Allen."

Before he had ever received my letter, Brother Allen and his wife wrote to me again. In this letter he detailed every act just as I had seen it some several hundred miles away. He had risen from his bed and walked out to surprise his wife on the porch where she was doing her early morning clothes washing. His poor wife almost fainted from the shock, but managed to hold her poise. She insisted that he go back to bed before he dropped dead right there on the porch.

He refused, saying he was hungry and wanted something to eat. "Why, Mr. Allen," she had replied, "you are out of your head. You ought to know that the doctor would not allow you to eat anything as it would be sure death if you did."

The letter continued with his next words to his wife. Oh, those words brought me great joy! "Well, I am out of the doctor's care now. You must have written to Bevington, didn't you?"

She nodded her head as he continued, "I can tell you this, he has prayed through for me and I am healed. Give me a square meal, wife. I can eat anything now." Mrs. Allen kept repeating that he would drop dead if he didn't get off that porch and she would not be guilty of murder by having any part of feeding him. He kept insisting on having something to eat.

My amusement grew as the letter continued to unfold the story. His neighbor was coming in from his nearby barn when Brother Allen hollered out to him. The man

81

was thunderstruck when he saw who it was. "Say, brother," Brother Allen called out, "I am hungry as a bear and my wife won't give me anything to eat. You tell your wife to bring me over a good breakfast, will you?"

The neighbor went quickly into his house and urged his wife to come out and see. "Such a sight—Allen is up and out on the porch begging for something to eat."

She rushed outside to see if her husband was correct and was amazed to hear Mr. Allen calling to her for some food. He pounded on his chest to show his soundness. As Mrs. Allen was in a state of shock, the neighbor's wife ventured over with a soft boiled egg for the recovered invalid. Mr. Allen swallowed it down and asked for more. Since he did not fall down dead, she returned again and again with small offerings of food until he finally had acquired a strong man's meal for himself. In two weeks, he returned to work just as I had told him. This all occurred in the spring.

In the fall, I began to get some inklings that I needed to go to Chattanooga. Believing I was only thinking that because Brother Allen lived there and it would be pleasant to see him, I didn't give the thoughts much attention. But they did not subside, rather kept growing until it seemed I nearly had a monster by the tail. As a trip clear to Chattanooga was a large undertaking for my limited faith at the time, the Lord decided to head me for Cincinnati first. That did not seem such a hard problem.

I was attached to Cleveland and did not want to leave there, so I did not listen very well to the Cincinnati call, either. Yet the call was quite loud and incessant. I finally said, "Lord, if Thou wilt send someone to take my place, I will go." Though for the life of me, I could not see why I should. I was making such good headway there in Cleveland. But as so often happened when I finally surrendered my will and said I would obey, in three days a man and his wife came.

As soon as they saw me, she burst out laughing and said, "That's the man. Yes, he's the one."

Her husband agreed, "He certainly is. This is the place."

Though I had prayed and asked for someone to take my place, I could think of no former acquaintance with this couple and must have appeared somewhat bewildered. Sensing my confusion, they proceeded to explain the vision they had seen, which included me, two nights before in Rochester, New York. I believed their story and assented they must be the people God had sent to take my place. Then, excusing myself, I went into my room and fell across the bed. I broke out in sobs as I tried to accept my departure. I was not ready to leave my beloved work there and I soaked my bed with tears of remorse.

Finally I said, "God, I cannot doubt these people came from Thee. But I cannot leave in this condition. Oh, God, if it is really true that You want me to leave, relieve me from this work and remove this burden." Soon the tears were dry and the cloud had lifted. The sunlight of Heaven broke upon me with such a beautiful mellowness that I felt all desire to remain melt away.

It was settled. I was prepared to go, but I had no money to go on. While praying in my room about railroad fare to Cincinnati, I heard a knock at the door. I opened it and there stood a Salvation Army sister who had helped me much in my work.

"Brother Bevington, we just learned that you are leaving us," she said. "These people who have come to take your place have a baby organ and won't need yours. I want to buy it."

I had opened fourteen missions, equipping each one fully. I had never taken anything with me or sold anything from any of them. "I have never done such a thing," I told her.

Just then the dear brother who had come from New York stepped to the door and spoke up, "We won't need the organ and we both feel you need the money. So, please, sell it to her at once."

The sister promptly asked what it was worth. "I paid fifteen dollars for it and used it for four months. I reckon it is worth about ten dollars," I told her.

"It would be cheap at twelve dollars. I'll give you twelve dollars for it." With that, she laid down the money and took the organ.

I took the money and departed. First I bought three dollars worth of clothing and then purchased an eight-dollar train ticket for Cincinnati. I had a dollar left and some twenty cents in pocket change. I arrived in Cincinnati and spent the night in nearby Constance. The following morning, I was walking around the downtown streets when I passed a very large storefront window on Fourth Street. Looking inside I noticed a bulletin board with the words, "Your Last Chance."

I continued on, but the words "Last Chance" kept tugging at my curiosity. Finally, I returned to the window to peer in again to see if I had read it right. I had, but that still didn't tell me what it meant—so I opened the door and looked inside. It was a railroad office. I pointed to the board and asked the attendant, "Sir, what does that mean?"

"Just what it says," he replied with little enthusiasm.

"What is it saying?"

Sighing, he said, "Haven't you heard of the price reduction in the excursions to Chattanooga?"

"No, I haven't."

"Well, Chattanooga fares are greatly reduced and this

is the last chance, the last day, you can use them."

"What time does the last train leave?"

"Nine this evening."

I started back out and then remembered I had not asked the price. "What is the cost?"

Peering over his spectacles in disgust at so many questions, he said, "Round trip is three dollars and seventy-five cents. Round trip means clear to Chattanooga and back. Anything else you want to know?"

I slipped back out on the street and began to walk away. Chattanooga kept ringing in my ears. I approached the intersection where I would board the street car for my lodgings of the night before and the voice kept repeating Chattanooga over and over in my head. Then a voice said plain and clear, "Will you or will you not go to Chattanooga?"

I was startled, but quickly replied, "Yes, Lord, I will, but..." There it was again, that little word that has stranded so many. I was not about to be sidelined by those three letters, so I boarded the street car, made my goodbyes, retrieved my suitcases and returned to the downtown area. I struck out for the railroad depot with only thirty minutes left before the final "Last Chance" train. Noticing a man was eyeing me very closely as I approached the depot, I thought to myself, "He won't get much money if he plans to waylay me."

As I came nearer, he broke out in a smile. When I reached him, he threw his arms around me and said, "At last, Brother Bevington."

"Yes, but I am in a hurry. I want to make a train in twenty minutes. Who are you?" He fell in beside me as I hurried toward my destination.

He laughed as we entered the depot, saying, "You prayed for my wife four years ago and Jesus healed her.

She said, 'Since we don't have any more doctor bills, let's give Brother Bevington our doctor's money.' In one year, we had five dollars for you and I have been carrying it around for the past three years waiting to see you again."

God had brought him in from the country just to meet me. Oh, how it pays to let God do His work. He understands His business far better than we do. God, will we ever learn? Will we ever learn?

We got to the train just in time for me to be shoved onto the last coach. I collapsed in my seat and thought, "Well, here I am, Lord, at your command. Now what are you going to do with me?"

As was often the case when I questioned God, I got the answer, "What is that to thee, follow thou Me."

Arriving in Chattanooga, I did not feel it right to arrive on Brother Allen's doorstep unexpectedly since they were very poor and had a family. So I spent twenty cents to check my two heavy grips and splurged my last eighty cents on dinner. How I lingered over that meal, but finally I stood out on the street—penniless, homeless and among strangers. I decided to walk awhile and think about my situation.

Passing along a high board fence, I noticed a sign. "At 2:30 p.m. Sunday—every Sunday." I paused and looked around to see what the sign might be indicating, but could see nothing. So I walked slowly on, wondering what the sign had meant. Then I heard a call and looked back to see a black man with such a glow to his face, I knew he had to be a real child of God. He started toward me with a great big smile on his face.

"Lord bless you, man," he exclaimed. "You're the man, you're the man!"

I hardly knew what to think, so I just replied, "Well, what about it?"

"You're the man I've been looking for. You're going to preach in the mission down here on the corner. The man who was there has broken down. I was down to see him three weeks ago and he told me he was of no account and couldn't go on. He asked me to pray for a man to come and give him relief. So I went into my home, got down and laid the case before the Lord. He showed me just as you are now except you had two big suitcases, one black and one yellow. Brother, where are those grips?"

I laughed, "I guess you have the whole thing pretty straight."

"Oh, I know that. Yes, sir, I've got it straight all right." He pointed the way I should go and asked for the two baggage checks. "I will bring the grips to you in my cart."

As I went on, another man called to me, "You're the man Joe told me about, aren't you? Come on into my house and get a drink of cool water."

I followed him in and after I had enjoyed a long, refreshing drink, he said, "Now, let's have prayer." That suited me fine and we got down on our knees and prayed. I don't believe I've ever had freer access to the throne in my life than I did there in that modest home. As I left, he gave me a dollar bill. Then he showed me to the mission where I was to preach.

The man of the mission was sitting at the window on the second floor where he could see down to the road. He knew who I was instantly from the description Joe had given him three weeks before. He came down quickly and welcomed me heartily, then introduced me to his young wife. I began preaching that night.

The mission was run by different churches, the M.E. one night, the Baptist the next and so on. There were five meetings a week, with a different church coming in each

87

night. I soon saw that some of these meeting house folk didn't take to my way of preaching very well.

The M.E. folks took me all right. On the second night, M.E. night, three fell at the altar and we all had a good time. On the fourth night was the meeting for another church. As I was preaching, in came a drunkard and as was their custom, he was signaled to go back out. But he didn't seem inclined to go. So the head man of the church said to the leader, "Put that man out at once."

I called out, "Hold on there. Don't put him out."

But the man in charge motioned the leader to obey his orders. So I jumped over the railing, rushed to them and implored the leader, "Please don't put that man out. Jesus came to save just such poor creatures as him."

The boss said, "You don't know this man. He is the lowest down creature in town. He has to go out."

"No, please don't," I begged them.

"Put him out!" he ordered.

I sprang between the leader and the drunkard and stood my ground. They dropped back and the drunkard dropped down on a seat. The odor emanating from him soon cleared him plenty of room. The boss and his crowd all got up and left, taking some fifty total with them. As the leader went out the door, he turned and said, "Brother Bevington, I know what Jesus came for, but we have been dealing with this man for ten years. There is no hope for him."

"My dear brother, you will never make me believe that. Jesus can make a difference and He will if we give Him a chance."

The leader called back over his shoulder, "Then you and Him go for it. I'm putting out all the lights but the one by the pulpit and we're leaving." And they did.

I ushered the drunken man up to the front of the

platform and began to lay hold of God for him. He did pretty well until about 2:00 a.m. and then he began to get boisterous. He said that he was burning up and had to have some whiskey. "Just get me a pint and I will be all right. I would like to be a Christian, but I am in hell right now."

I kept trying to reason with him, but he was getting the best of me. Being much stronger than I was, he kept backing me toward the door in spite of all I could do. Within a couple of hours, he had pushed me to within eight feet of the door. Near exhaustion, I knew something had to happen.

I wanted to call out to the man sleeping upstairs, but the Spirit rebuked me. So I held my peace and began to intercede at the throne more intensely. Unable to hang on any longer, I finally let go of the man and threw up my hands, crying out, "God, what did you send this man in here for? What did you send me here for? Oh, God, come, come, come!"

At the third "come," the man fell prostrate on the floor. He actually crawled around under the chairs just like a snake. Then I began to plead to have the demon cast out. "God, cast him out, cast him out," I cried.

In thirty minutes the man was quiet as a lamb. He sat up, rubbed his face and said to himself, "Is this really Tom? Why, I believe I just got religion."

"You may have religion, but you do not have salvation yet," I warned him.

"No, I know better. I have religion for sure."

"Come up to the altar and get saved," I invited him.

"I'm saved right now."

"No, you are not saved. You just had the whisky demon cast out. Now you are a candidate for forgiveness."

He kept insisting that he was already saved, but I finally

got him to the altar. He got down and prayed earnestly until he began to see that he did indeed need salvation. In a little over an hour, he prayed through. Of all the capering you have ever seen anyone do, old Tom did it there.

The young wife came downstairs about then and she was delighted. She called her husband down and both seemed satisfied that Tom was really a saved man. I was thoroughly worn out from wrestling all night with that ferocious man and needed some rest badly, but I said to the couple, "Get me a tub, a broom, a bar of soap and a scrubbing brush. Then go get some good clothing. I'll take Tom out in the back yard and scrub him up."

The wife sanctioned that suggestion and even brought me some assafetida as a preventative. I tied it on and went for him. I used three tubs of water and a bar of soap and actually succeeded in getting him fairly clean. They furnished me with some good clothing and soon we had him looking entirely different.

Whiskey may have floored him, but he was a well educated man. God gathered up the fragments of his life, polished and put them back in place and he was in pretty good shape by the time we were through with him. He looked at me and said, "Will you go down to my cousin's? I used to be his foreman in his lumber yard, but he hasn't allowed me around for years."

We went down just as the cousin was preparing to eat his dinner. Tom had me stand in front when I knocked on the door and we were invited inside. The cousin looked at me and then at Tom and did not recognize either one of us. I did not readily make our business known and after some suspense, I asked, "Mister, did you ever see this man before?"

At that, Tom smiled. The cousin said, "This can't be Tom, can it?"

Tom sprang forward saying, "Yes, it is. I am a new man, Bill. Jesus saved me and this preacher has cleaned me up. Then the mission man gave me this nice suit. Bill, I want to go to work again. I will join the M.E. church with you if they will have me."

After a time of rejoicing and a wonderful meal, Tom took me outside and asked for one more favor. "Brother Bevington, Jesus has sure cleaned me up on the inside and you cleaned me up on the outside. Now I want you to go with me to see my wife."

"You have a wife?"

"Yes, I have. At least I did. I haven't seen her for eleven years. They say she is worse than I was. She is down on Pokey Row with the very poorest, most onerous people that are in Tennessee."

I said I would and back we went to the mission. The leader saw us coming and met us. When I had told him of our mission, he asked me to go upstairs alone with him. He looked at me very seriously as he said, "Brother Bevington, I think I can work things out with the manager of the mission now that Tom is so different. But whatever you do, please don't go near that woman. It is unmistakably evident God has undertaken for Tom, but that woman is a thousand leagues lower than Tom was. If you have anything to do with her, it will kill any aspect of getting him back in here. They'll probably throw me out, too. I am too old and my health is not sufficient for me to make a living anywhere else. Please, Brother Bevington, listen to me."

I was listening and his dear, young wife was, too. She joined us, setting down a cool glass of lemonade for each one and said, "Husband, I am young and strong and

91

willing to take in washing to make our living. I believe Brother Bevington is on the right track and he knows His God better than either one of us. If God could save Tom, He surely can save Lizz. I say let Brother Bevington alone and keep your hands off. Let him and God and Tom do their best. If it comes to our having to get out of here, I will work our way through."

I said, "Amen!" and took her by the hand, weeping for joy at her noble stand. "God bless your dear, good heart."

The husband finally agreed and kissed his wife, saying, "My dear, you are the better of us two."

I went back downstairs, calling out, "Come on, Tom!" We headed immediately for the worst vicinity of town. After a distance, we turned into an alley where all of the combined poverty and ignorance and filth I had ever seen did not approach what was before us. I was somewhat taken back, but I said, "We have started and we will trust God." Realizing I still wore the assafetida, I took it off and threw it down. "Jesus doesn't need any help from that."

Tom said, "You better keep it on. We are not there yet. It's much worse where she is." I shook my head. Holding our handkerchiefs over our nostrils, we kept going. Finally we reached our goal. The greater obstacle now loomed before us. We were there, but where was she? We had no idea even of how many times she might have changed her name.

We ventured into a yard and began to make inquiries, but we could find no one who would involve themselves in our quest. Their only interest was in whether or not we had any tobacco, whiskey, beer or opium. Spying a staircase going up to the roof of one shanty, we climbed some twelve feet above the filth thinking we might escape some of the awful stench. There on that roof we began to call on God for information.

Soon a huge man, very filthy, came out and saw us kneeling. He was curious and wanted to know what we were doing there. We told him and he said, "I know who you are after. I will bring her out."

In all my mission work in Cincinnati, St. Louis, Louisville and Cleveland, I had never seen such a vile-looking, evil-smelling, hopeless case as the wretched woman this man brought before us. I told her what her name had been some fifteen years earlier and she acknowledged she remembered using that name. Oh, how even I wondered if Jesus could do anything for such a creature as stood before me. After attempting to talk with her further, I finally brought Tom forward to present him to her.

She grunted in surprise and squinted up her eyes, peering at him with great suspicion. "Is that you, Tom?" she finally asked.

Tom assured her it was and began to tell her what God had done for him and how he believed He would do as much for her. She swore at him. Feigning complete disinterest, she turned to smoking an old pipe she clutched in her dirty hand. She only stopped to swear at him further. I don't know what was in that old pipe, but the stench was almost unbearable.

But Tom kept on telling her about Jesus. Myself, I was getting faint and almost wished I had the assafetida back. Finally I began my way down the filthy stairs as I said, "We will come back tomorrow morning at 10:00 a.m. Make up your mind that you believe Jesus can do as much for you as he has done for Tom and that you can live a respectable life again."

Then we hurried out of that malaria-infested pit as fast

as we could. Tom went to his cousin's place and I went to the mission where I fell into my bed. I slept over twelve hours and awoke the next morning at dawn. I went down to breakfast and related our previous day's trip to my hosts.

The young wife was very interested and immediately began to gather up many of her own clothes for Tom's wife. "They are going to get her and she will need these," she said confidently. The husband still tried to persuade us not to bring her there to the mission. His wife said, "We will take her down to my Uncle Ben's coal house then and fight this thing through with her. He is a man of God and he will let us go there."

Tom showed up at the door after a short while, full of hope and faith for his poor, emaciated wife. Back we went. Praise God, there she was bundled up in filthy rags, standing out at the head of the first alley waiting for us. The first thing to do was get her cleaned up, so we took her back to the mission and Tom led her into the same yard where he got his cleaning up. He used five tubs of water and two bars of soap to get her clean enough to put on the nice clothes waiting for her.

The leader of the mission was not able to go, but the wife went with us to her Uncle Ben's coal house, a nice and clean enclosure. If I had thought I had a terrible time with Tom, I found it was nothing compared to what we were about to go through with that wild, unreasonable woman. We wrestled with her there for eighty-four hours, day and night. It took all of us to exert any kind of control for she managed to bruise Tom all up first and then she turned her fury on me. She was pounding and pulling on me so roughly, she tore my clothes almost to pieces. Tom had to extricate me from her clutches, but together we managed to hold her inside the building. We fed her coffee and good food and prayed with her until the eighty-fifth hour when she was knocked down by the power of God.

She lay on her back cursing God and man alike. Froth was foaming out of her mouth, but she was powerless—perfectly helpless and exhausted. She lay that way for nine hours until at last she was completely quiet and still. Then she raised her hands, weeping, and asked us to help her up. Her clothes and Tom's were in complete shreds and we sent for more clothing before we could even take them out of the building.

When the clothing arrived and they had dressed, we took her to Tom's cousin's house. The next morning she prayed through most gloriously. She did not caper like Tom did, but simply walked the floor with her right hand help up towards heaven for the next two hours, laughing softly and saying, "Oh, glory!" Finally we all went in to sit down for a wonderful, family dinner with Tom's cousin.

The next day the cousin outfitted a three-room cottage with new furniture for them. Then he gave them both new clothes and other necessities. Once those needs were met, the cousin gave Tom his old job back. I had the privilege of marrying Tom and his wife over again before they set up housekeeping. Then, upon our insistence after they were installed in their new home, Tom and his wife prayed through to getting the Holy Ghost. That created quite a stir in the many who knew of them and their past. Neither one of these two ever went back into sin. They had three sweet children with them the last time I saw them at the Cincinnati camp.

God is really in the saving business. That was what Jesus came for and He made sure this purpose of saving souls was within the reach of whosoever would believe. I saw Tom and his wife three more times at the Cincinnati camp where they gave their glorious testimonies on the platform. They were a most blessedly saved and sanctified couple.

The mission managers did end up giving orders for the leader and his wife, who had stood so faithfully by me, to pick up their belongings and go. The story of Tom and his deliverance and salvation was being told about everywhere. Two days after he had prayed through with me in the mission, I was preaching a meeting on Sunday (the M.E. Church day). Some twenty of those involved with the leader's dismissal came and fell at the altar. Several of them prayed through and after God adjusted their thinking further, they decided to allow the former leader and his wife to remain at the mission.

I felt it was now time that this man went after the Holy Ghost, so I went after him. He was somewhat scared of that, but God shored him up and in a couple of days, he was truly seeking. Then the wife came seeking for the same blessing. With these two and with Tom and his wife, it was a busy week. But glory to God, the Lord got them all through!

During the time this man was down at the altar seeking the Holy Ghost, several of the leaders came to break off the proceedings and ordered us to leave. They threatened to discharge him again, but he had gone so far in his seeking, he could not turn back. He pressed on through. When his wife prayed through, also, the leaders again rescinded their orders and allowed them to remain. What a time we were having! Some of the meeting house folk pulled completely out at this time, but the M.E. people stood by him.

They all decided that I should not preach anymore, so I quietly stepped aside. I was allowed to use a spare room and take my meals until I could determine my next assignment. I was not upset, for I knew that God had accomplished exactly what He had wanted to through my time there.

Another incident occurred during my time at this mission. As I previously related, I had seen a vision of Brother Allen sitting at the organ playing and singing with all his might while I was still in Cleveland. When I answered the Allens' letters and told them of this, I also told them I expected some day to see him just that way.

The first Sunday I was at the mission in Chattanooga, there was no morning service. So I was sitting up in my room by the window, watching the people passing on the street. As I sat there praying, reading and meditating on the Word, I looked out and saw a man singing as he walked down the street. He was carrying a baby organ in one hand, swinging it like a suitcase. I looked more closely at him and spoke out loud, "I declare. I believe that is Brother Allen."

I called out to him and looking up to see me, he began jumping and waving his hands. I knew it was definitely him and I ran down to meet him. I had not seen him or written him that I was there in Chattanooga at the mission.

He seemed truly delighted to see me and quickly told me, "Brother Bevington, I am holding meetings every Sunday in the jail house. Last Sunday I told them I had heard you were here and that I was going to bring you with me today. Come to the meeting, won't you?"

I was delighted to say yes and made arrangements to meet him there shortly. When I arrived, I heard the organ going in the hall. I looked in and there he sat, looking exactly as I had seen him in Cleveland so many months before. I threw my hat in the air and gave out a whoop. You see, God doesn't give us visions on uncertainties. We all had a most rousing time. I went back again the following Sunday and five claimed to pray through.

After I was out of the mission and looking for direction, I went to a businessmen's prayer meeting in a rented meeting room. After dinner, someone would read a short lesson and give requests for prayer. Then they would all get down and pray for about thirty minutes. With some fifty or sixty attending, it was a beautiful time. The leader of the mission took me there the first time, introduced me and then told of the story of Tom and Lizz.

The next meeting they handed me the Bible and I read Romans 4:14-25, especially emphasizing the verses that tell of Abraham. They all seemed delighted with that and invited me back to read another lesson. I went and read and talked on faith and obedience. We had twelve minutes to read and speak.

When they had all turned in their requests for prayer, the man who led the group told about a long-standing trouble he had. He had related it to the others often, but said he wanted me to hear it. When he finished, I stood and spoke for about ten minutes. Then I said, "Dear brother, I am sure Jesus can heal you and I believe He wants to."

"I wish He did," was his reply. He said he had not walked to his office for thirteen years and had to hire everything done for him. He kept the hire of two girls and a doctor full time. He had also not slept a natural sleep for ten years.

Feeling we should pray for his body right then, I knelt down and got real still before God. Our faith began to take hold for this man and I laid my hands upon him, receiving a real blessing from God when I did. Praising

God, I said, "Brother, you are a healed man. Didn't you feel the touch of Jesus?"

Meekly he replied, "I am sorry, sir, I have to tell you the truth. I felt no change whatsoever."

"Well, it doesn't matter, you are a healed man and you will sleep tonight as good as you ever did. And you will do it without any remedies. That's not all—you will walk to your office tomorrow morning." I noticed after my words that there was a general exchange of doubtful looks, even some jeering ones. Nothing was said as the men all quietly walked out. They were usually given to shaking hands at the close of each daily meeting, but this day everyone walked out with bowed heads. No one shook hands with me and I returned to my room.

Satan was waiting there and promptly began to tear at me, "You go too far down here among these Southerners. You are not up north, you know. These people cannot take so strong a diet as you gave them this day."

I had to go down on my knees to ascertain the source of this admonition and felt a confirmation it was definitely Satan. I went back to the meeting the next day, but as I was slightly late, I took a seat near the rear. The singing was finished and the leader stood for a short message. Then he called for requests and several were given. Satan whispered, "See, it is just as I told you. You went too far yesterday. He isn't healed, for if he was, he would have said so. He never mentioned a thing. If you hadn't brought up the walk to the office and the good night's sleep, you might have gotten away with it. But you went entirely too far!"

I said, "Satan, you are a liar. I did not go too far and if I had it to do over again, I would go even further!"

We all prayed until the closing prayer. The leader never said a word about what had happened and what I had said

99

to him the previous day. So Satan reminded me again that I needed to learn discretion and common sense in my dealing with Southerners. I stood my ground, "He is a healed man."

"You really don't have any sense, do you?" Satan shot back. "If he was healed, he would have told everyone." And we went at it in that back seat.

We finally all stood and the leader began to give the closing remarks. I lifted a prayer, "Lord, make him confess it. Break him up so he has to do it."

The man tried to talk, but his mouth began to quiver. I saw he was determined to be a coward about speaking out the truth, so I pressed my claim all the heavier to the Father. The man broke out crying when he finally spoke, "Brethren, I have a confession to make." Raising his right hand, he pointed to me. "That man's prayers were answered last night. This morning I must admit that I am a healed man. Last night I never thought about my medicine until I was almost asleep. I was too sleepy to get up and get it and I was reminded of what that brother had said about sleeping well without any remedies. The next thing I knew my wife came in saying, 'What is the matter with you this morning? Breakfast is ready and waiting. You are already going to miss the first trolley car, you know.' "

He went on to tell how he realized he had slept just as I had said he would. He hurried and dressed and got outside to see the street car hurrying off. He knew it would be another hour before he could catch the next car. When I had made the assertion that he would be walking to his office that morning, I had never dreamed he lived so far from it. I was under the inspiration of the Holy Spirit and just said what the Spirit gave me. Had I known he lived over three miles from his office, the Spirit no doubt would have had a great deal of trouble getting me to make the assertion I did. But as I was ignorant of this fact, the Holy Spirit was able to work through me. It is sometimes best to not know all the facts.

When the man saw the car was gone, he decided to walk down the street a way as he did feel quite good. He didn't even think about what I had said about walking all the way to his office that morning. He just kept going slowly, gaining strength every foot of the way. Several times, he said he thought, "I must be healed. I feel so well."

He was beginning to warm up to his story now. "I just kept on walking and all the while speeding up a bit. When I got within five blocks of my office, I looked back and saw the trolley car coming. I thought I would get on it then, but I suddenly remembered what Brother Bevington had said. So I just walked on. Upon entering my office, I discovered one of the girls had not come into work. I took her place and have been working all morning thus far. I phoned her to tell her she might stay home all day. Brethren," he said with both hands lifted in praise to the most high God, "I am, without a doubt, a healed man." The glory of God fell and what a time we had!

They tore loose from all conventionalities, programs, time and everything else. It was an hour past our normal departure time when we finally left that room. Everybody shook hands with me that day and no one had their heads bowed. Everyone's heads were raised up as they sang and shouted their joy on the way out.

We need to learn to take our stand and then remain standing right there. We need to find where God wants us to stand and stay there. How Satan tried to get me to back down that day! It surely looked as though I would have to, but I knew God. He had satisfied me the day before that I had not gone too far for Him.

I will now proceed to tell you about my three broken ribs. Some time later, still being out of a mission, one dear brother came to me with an invitation. "I have been going out in the suburbs for several years to hold services. I have a Sunday school out there and I believe the Lord would be pleased to have you go out with me. I will take you with me tomorrow which is our regular night."

So we went and the brother preached to the people in a home. The meetings went on for several nights and there were four saved, two sanctified and three healed. Soon no home in the area could hold all of the people who came. Three sisters came to us and said, "We have rented a storeroom near here and will fit it up for you to hold these meetings in." We agreed and went to help them prepare the room. This was in the fall of the year and it was quite chilly. On the second day of work, I was polishing the stovepipe while standing on a cloth-bottomed chair. Not wishing to soil the cloth, my feet were on the outer edges of the chair.

I was rubbing with all my might, stretching and reaching as high as I could, when the chair turned over. I fell heavily, striking my side on the chair. The poor chair was completely smashed and I just lay there among the bits and pieces for some time. I don't know how long it was. When I regained my senses, the building was spinning around at a tremendous rate and I felt very sick. I tried to get up, but could not; so I fell back on the floor and tried to pray. I was in such misery I could hardly even do that. Finally I did feel a little better and with the aid of three other chairs, I pulled myself to my feet.

The pain in my side had me gasping in agony. I

wondered what in the world was the matter. I found that putting my hand on it and pressing hard helped a little bit, so I kept the pressure there. I even preached that night with my hand pressed to my side. I didn't tell anyone what had happened or how the chair got smashed.

The following morning I found myself in difficulty. I had rigged up a way to keep the weight of the covers off me during the night by propping a machine cover up at my side. I spent the night praying, getting some relief and sleeping briefly. But at any move, I would awaken feeling as though a thousand needles were pushing into my side. Then I would pray, get some relief and doze off again. What a night.

Brother Allen heard of my fall and came to see me that first day. He worked only five blocks away and had meals sent to my room so he could be at my side as much as possible. At night he slept in my bed as I was now down on the floor for firmer support, no longer able to abide the bed. He would get up and go to his work every morning.

"Brother Bevington," he finally said, "I know that God healed me, but this seems to be a different case. There is surely something terribly wrong with your ribs. You must have a doctor."

"No, no doctor for me," I replied. But by the fourth day, I seemed to be impressed to see one anyway. "Lord, I don't want to see a doctor, Thou art my Healer." I stuck it out another day, the sixth day since the accident, and finally decided to go to a doctor. I had not had anything to eat all during this time, although women came daily to bring me food. I couldn't eat a thing or even swallow water without being thrown into a spasm of pain.

I pulled myself up with the aid of two chairs, holding my side. I packed cotton batting under a belt and wrapped it around me for some relief. Using a stick for a cane, I ventured out to search for a doctor. After hobbling three blocks, I saw a medical sign and went in. I stood against the wall near the door and soon the doctor entered to call his next patient and urged me to take a seat. I knew I would have a terrible time getting back up, so I remained standing. His southern hospitality would not permit him to leave me standing, so he kept insisting that I sit down. Finally, to appease him, I did and suffered for doing so. I sat there for forty minutes waiting my turn. Finally he motioned for me to come in.

"Doctor, I don't think I can get up alone," I responded. Three men came to my aid and assisted me inside.

"Well," said the doctor jovially, "you seem to be somewhat crippled up." He put his hand on my side and as I was not prepared for that act, I hollered out loud and almost fainted from the pain. The doctor reconsidered his approach. "Perhaps this is something quite serious. I'll give you something for the pain so I can examine you."

"No, doctor, nothing of the kind, please. Just go ahead and make your examination."

He poked gently at my side and then looked at my face. "You cannot undergo such an examination as I will have to do without some kind of pain medication." I refused the medication again. "What happened? Did some mule kick you?"

"No," was all I said. I didn't want to tell him what was wrong, I wanted him to find out.

"What is your profession?"

"I am a holiness evangelist," I replied.

"Do you live around here?"

"No, I'm from Kentucky."

"Oh, you're from up north then. Were you holding some meetings here?"

"Some, yes," I replied, wishing he'd quit asking questions and start giving me some answers.

"Whereabouts?" he asked.

"I started first in the Wilcox Mission."

With that, he stopped and looked at me most critically. "Are you the man from up north that saved old Tom and Lizz?"

"I never saved anyone," I replied.

He eyed me with suspicion, "Well, I heard that story pretty straight from a friend of mine. What's your name?"

I told him and he repeated it slowly and then said, "That sure sounds like the name to me. You must be the one he told me about."

"No, you're mistaken."

"I got it pretty straight and it was in the newspapers, too. Your name sure sounds right. Didn't you hold a meeting at the Wilcox Mission?"

Finally I admitted I had, but then explained to him that I had not saved Tom and Lizz. It was Jesus who had saved them.

"Well, well, so you are the party who fasted and prayed and stuck to them until you got them saved and re-married. I hear they are both doing quite well."

"I guess they are," I replied.

"How much money do you have? I'd like to take an X-ray."

I knew they charged ten dollars for that in Cincinnati, so I quickly said, "I am not able to have an X-ray." Still, I felt that somehow an X-ray was exactly why God had wanted me to come there. I was unsure what to do, except wait for God to move.

Finally the doctor said, "I have to put in a silver dollar each time I use this X-ray machine, because it isn't mine. If you just have one dollar, I'll go ahead and use it on you."

I knew I didn't have a dollar, so I bowed my head and waited for a moment. Then I said, "I have a friend who will give you a dollar. So if you will go ahead and do it, I'll have the X-ray." He positioned me, blindfolded my eyes and slipped in one of his dollars.

Upon one look at the X-ray, the doctor pulled the blindfold from my eyes, exclaiming, "My good man, you are all torn to pieces inside! I don't see how you have lived these six days in this condition. Your first rib is separated three-fourths of an inch, the second one a half an inch and the third one a quarter of an inch. There is a piece of bone about the size of a horseshoe nail torn from your first rib laying right across your other ribs. That is what is causing you so much pain." He shook his head in amazement.

"I can't do anything for you, but I have a cousin in Nashville who is in charge of the finest hospital in Tennessee. He and I were talking over the phone the other day about Tom and Lizz. He said he really wanted to see that 'northern fellow' and I am sure I can get you in there real cheap. Ordinarily it would cost you five hundred dollars and take about seven months. But tomorrow I will see what I can do for you."

I went back to my rooms, saying, "Five hundred dollars and seven months? Lord, Thou canst beat that." I went into my room and resumed my position on the floor. Every movement caused great suffering, but I believed I would soon get victory. The floor was getting harder and harder.

Night came and so did Brother Allen. I told him what I had done and where I had been. He said, "What doctor did you go to?" I told him the name. "Oh, he is a dear friend of mine—a saved man. He is the one who bought the baby organ for me to play at the jail and on the streets. He does all the doctoring at the foundry where I work and everyone recognizes him as a Christian. He always gets down on his knees and prays at the foundry before examining patients. I see him as I pass by his office."

Brother Allen gave the doctor a dollar for me the next morning. The dear doctor worked faithfully all that day for me. That night, when Brother Allen came in, he was covered with perspiration after having run three blocks to break the news to me. "I just stopped in at the doctor's office to see what he had been able to do. All things are planned out. There will a stretcher with four men here at 9:00 a.m. tomorrow morning. They will bear you to the depot where a special train has been chartered to take you to Nashville. You will be cared for at the remarkably low price of just what the material for the artificial ribs will cost—it won't be more than eighty dollars. All of the work and care and board will be donated. You're going to have nearly seven hundred dollars worth of medical help donated to you! That doctor is such a good man."

"Brother Allen," I said, "that is a great favor, indeed, and I do feel thankful for what the doctor has done. But I can't go to a hospital."

"What! You won't go to the hospital?"

"I can't." I felt helpless to explain.

"Brother Bevington, you must remember that you are not in the North now. You are in the South where gangrene springs up in cases such as you have and spreads so rapidly, it risks infecting the whole city. The Board of Health will have to interfere and you will be sent to the pesthouse. I will never endure seeing you sent to that place!"

"Didn't the Lord heal you down here in this very city?" I reminded him.

"Yes, but your condition is altogether different. In the

107

first place, you are older than I am and I didn't have any ailments that would cause gangrene."

"Perhaps not, but is God circumscribed to conditions or places? Is God's power conditional? Must all of these earthly facts be analyzed before God can operate?" I questioned him quite firmly.

Still he tried to reason with me. "Brother, you must exercise judgment here. You are not dealing with Northerners now, you are dealing with hot-headed Southerners."

"So, according to what you just said, you believe God's power is limited to places and people. You may believe that, Brother Allen, but you will never make Bevington believe it. I will not, under any conditions, go to that hospital. I cannot turn my back on my heavenly Doctor. Never! He has done too much for me to fail me now."

"But you might infect the whole city which they will not allow for millions of dollars," he pleaded. "You will have all the officers in town after you and the pesthouse is where you will land. That will be the result of your refusal and you will not have anyone to blame but yourself." With that, we retired for the night in complete silence.

The next morning, he set off for work only to meet the doctor along the way. "Well," said the doctor, "I suppose Brother Bevington is delighted with what has been done for him?"

"Doc, that fellow is acting like a crank for sure!"

"Why do you say that?"

Brother Allen was frustrated to the point of sharpness as he spoke, "He doesn't want to go to the hospital. He has it set in his head that the Lord is going to heal those broken ribs!"

"Nonsense," replied the doctor.

"He has said that he absolutely will not go."

"Are you telling me," the doctor asked incredulously, "that he is turning down all I have done for him?"

"I am sorry, yes, that is what he is doing."

Off stomped the good doctor with his Southerner's blood dancing to a dangerous beat. About 10:00 a.m., three officers showed up and raked me over the coals quite briskly. They gave me twenty-four hours to reconsider my decision, leaving me well informed as to the pesthouse.

The time limit was to be up at 11:00 a.m. the next day. I went to praying the best I could. The next day they returned right on schedule, ready to take me to the pesthouse. I prevailed upon them to give me until 7:00 a.m. the following day. They had a doctor with them who said, "Gentlemen, there isn't any sign of gangrene yet—a most remarkable exception. Strangely enough, there is no sign of inflammation, either. It is a really clean wound. Grant him his wish." The officers left for the time being.

Brother Allen came in expressing great desperation over my obstinacy, especially upon seeing I still could not sit up or lie except in one very limited position. I told him to just keep quiet as I was trying to compose my own feelings. I was getting somewhat weak and nervous and I had never been troubled by those feelings to any alarming extent. "Brother Allen, you just stand still and you will see the power of God," I finally told him. I was well-nigh convinced God was arranging to give the people there an object lesson they would not soon forget. My suffering seemed to increase, but I held on.

I continued to struggle in prayer. Just before dawn the next day, I saw myself actually shrinking down, getting smaller and smaller. I felt a glimmer of a hallelujah for I knew I was on the Lord's trimming lathe—I was being trimmed down. So I began to softly praise the Lord. I did

109

not dare to exert myself, nor did I want to for fear of breaking the bond that was being woven round and through me. Neither did I want to awaken Brother Allen. I just kept quietly saying, "Glory, glory, glory." At each utterance, I would see more shavings fly. I knew I was getting the victory. The "glories" just kept coming out, whether Brother Allen was sleeping nearby or not. They were getting louder and louder.

Once I knew it was time for him to get up, I did not hesitate to open my mouth even more. I was getting excited to realize my efforts were not hurting in the least. I had not taken a long, deep breath in days and I had wanted to so bad. So, I tried it and rejoiced that it didn't hurt. Brother Allen had now awakened and was staring at me.

I raised my right arm in the air and nothing hurt and I just shouted as loud as I could, "Glory, it is done!" As I said those words, I heard the ribs come back together. I jumped to my feet and began pounding on my ribs. Frightened by my actions, he bounded out of bed and grabbed my arms.

"Brother Allen, I am healed!"

"Brother Bevington, you will kill yourself if you don't stop."

"No, I am healed!" In spite of his trying to hold me, I kept pounding those ribs and feeling no pain. Brother Allen did not believe me—he actually thought that the suffering, the possibility of not getting healed and the prospect of the pesthouse had so worked on my mind that I had gone crazy. But it was done—a complete, wonderful work of the supernatural.

As I relate these words, I can still feel the glory, the same power I felt back then. I rejoice in a Christ who heals. Hallelujah to His dear name. May that name always be magnified as we exalt Him above all other agencies and powers!

I felt hungry right away, so I went and had a good, early dinner. I had not eaten but one meal during those eight days of struggle. When I came back to the room, how different everything looked! I fell on my face on the very spot where I had been healed and sent forth the contents of my heart. A great landslide came into my soul and I laughed and shouted for about three hours.

Finally calming down and becoming somewhat "normal" as I adjusted to the change, I thought I should let the doctor know what had happened. I went to his office, took a seat and waited for him. When he came to the door, I spoke to him, but he just grunted. He had been insulted and the "old man" in him was making a fine display of what he felt on the inside.

When it came my turn, he stepped to the door and motioned for the next person, ignoring me. So I jumped up, feeling he could not fail to see the difference in my movements. It had the desired effect and he looked at me in amazement. "What has happened to you?"

"Doctor, I am a healed man."

It was readily apparent he did not take much stock in that statement, but the facts were staring him in the face. He couldn't reason them away as I stood there pounding on my ribs and shouting. That Presbyterian doctor just stood there looking at me with a wild look in his eyes. I didn't care that all his other patients were staring, either. He finally laid his hand on my side. "Go ahead, pound on my ribs, doctor."

He did and then he dropped his head down on my shoulder and began to weep and tremble until he shook my whole frame. He reminded me of an aspen leaf in the wind. After weeping for several minutes, he said, "There

111

must be something in this healing power. I have never seen anything like this. You say Jesus did this without any other kind of remedy?"

"Yes, sir. Now here is another dollar, for I would like you to turn that X-ray machine back on."

"Oh, I will gladly do it. I am very interested in that sliver that was laying across your ribs." I informed him that the sliver would be in its place. When he turned on the X-ray, he just stood speechless while I laughed. He laid his head on my shoulder again and wept and trembled as he said, "There is no splinter to be seen and no trace of it ever having been there."

Again the glory fell and I had to walk the floor. I didn't dare be too noisy in that office, so I just paced back and forth. I felt that I actually was flying, for it seemed my feet were not touching the floor.

"Brother Bevington, I want you to come to our Presbyterian church on Lookout Mountain and give your testimony tomorrow morning. I will vouch for it. I will pick you up in my car."

"I will," I said.

So we went. There seemed to be no objections of any kind to my testimony. It took me an hour to tell it all and I felt it seemed awfully dry. No one seemed to be interested in it except the doctor, his wife and his son and daughter, aged twenty-three and nineteen respectively. The doctor wanted me to preach that night and the pastor finally agreed, although somewhat reluctantly. I did preach, touching lightly on holiness, but in such a way that they all knew where I stood and what I claimed. At the close, I said, "I feel there is someone here who would like to get saved—saved with old-time salvation. But I see there is no altar here."

The word "here" had scarcely left my lips when the

doctor had two chairs put out. His son and daughter fell to their knees there and began praying. This did not suit the pastor and he soon pronounced the benediction and had the lights extinguished, leaving almost all the congregation in the dark. We had to feel our way out of there and go home.

The next day I was happily surprised to see the doctor at my door. He threw his arms around me and said, "Brother Bevington, the children want to get through." So in they came and knelt down and by the middle of the afternoon, they both got saved.

I went back to their Wednesday night prayer meeting where the son and daughter gave their testimony of the experience. Then the doctor stood up and said, "I move we invite Bevington up here to hold a meeting."

That is one move that never got a second. It was kicked out of there before it even had a chance to show itself. But the doctor was not to be denied. So the next morning, he showed up at my place and said, "Brother Bevington, I want that blessing you preach about."

"Doctor, are you sure you do?" I asked him.

"Yes, I am."

"Do you want it bad enough to get down here and die out?"

"Yes, sir!"

"Then die out to that Presbyterian church!"

"I already have. Last night's action settled the Presbyterian church with me."

"Can you die out to the proud wife of yours," I asked him next.

"Yes, sir, for she will be after the same thing." And down he went in my bedroom. He remained there three days, groaning and pleading and wrestling. Then I heard a knock at the door. It was his wife and I was somewhat concerned about her reasons for being there, but a second look at her allayed any fears.

"Is the doctor here?" she asked in a more meek and humble attitude than I had ever given her credit for being able to have.

He called out from the bedroom, "Come on in, honey." In she went and fell into his arms, crying and kissing him. That was a happy surprise to me, for I had feared just the reverse.

She rose to her feet and said, "Brother Bevington, I want this same blessing." So after it she went. She stayed there all night and the next morning proposed to go to their home and fight it out. I was a little scared about that until she said, "We will take Brother Bevington with us." So I agreed and went with them.

We were on our faces forty-two hours in their home with no one eating a thing. In fact, neither the doctor nor I had eaten anything for nearly six days. That night the four of them went to their Tuesday night prayer meeting, all on fire and testifying of what God had done. They were quickly sat down and at the end of the meeting, their membership letters were handed to them. God had delivered them from that ice chest.

Very soon thereafter the doctor came to me and informed me that he was praying over a certain matter. His wife was impressed to make a radical change which he found himself a little afraid of. So he and his wife put in three days waiting upon God. His office had now remained closed for over a week. At the end of the three days, the two of them came to see me and said, "We are impressed to sell our place here, get a rig and drive through to California, preaching the old-time Gospel all the way there. Would you give us an idea as to what we

114

will need? We will want to eat, sleep, cook, travel and preach from this wagon."

I made a list of the things needed and they sent to Studebaker at South Bend, Indiana, and ordered their outfit at a cost of over twelve hundred dollars. They sold off everything else they owned and were on the road eleven months, preaching and distributing tracts. Their children, as they called them, were sanctified three weeks after they left. I heard from them periodically all the way through their journey. They have sent money for my ministry from time to time.

5
Important Truths

Divine Healing: What It Is Not

1. It is not healing by remedies.

2. It is not imaginary healing.

3. It is not the exercise of willpower.

4. It is not the power of magnetism.

5. It is not mind cure or metaphysics.

6. It is not spiritualism.

7. It is not faith cure or prayer cure—faith and prayer simply being the avenues leading to healing.

8. It is not immunity from death, but strength for life.

9. It is not presumption and insubordination to God's will.

Divine Healing: What It Is

1. It is the direct, supernatural power of God upon the body.

2. It is in accordance with the Holy Scriptures and founded upon them.

3. It is founded on Christ's sacrifice and work of redemption.

4. It is through the resurrection life of Jesus Christ.

5. It is through the personal indwelling of Jesus Christ in the body.

6. It is through and by the Holy Spirit.

7. It is through the personal faith of the sufferer or his faith united with the faith of others.

8. It is submission to the Divine will, requiring our repentance of any disobedience and consecration to God.

9. It is for the service and glory of God.

10. It is a fact of church history from the apostolic age to our age and is confirmed by innumerable testimonies in our own day.

11. It is a sign of our Lord's approaching advent.

12. It is a testimony to the Word of God and the truth of Christianity in this day of unbelief.

It is not our business to save people, it is our business to lead them to Christ. So it is also not our business to heal people, but it may and should be our business to lead them to Jesus who has promised to heal them. Divine healing is not the most important teaching in the Bible, but it is truth and God has shown it to me. We cannot avoid it without detriment to our spiritual development.

Divine healing is not doctrine or theory, but a living fact. It is thoroughly established in the Word of God. Divine healing in its deepest, truest sense is a life of utter abandonment to God and an incessant dependence upon Him. It is a dependence on the power beyond ourselves in the most trying places. Here is our source of strength if we keep our eyes on God at all times. Amen! May God help you to see Him as He really is and what He will be to those who meet the conditions.

I want to give you some more evidences and facts. While holding a meeting in Hopewell, Kentucky, I was called to Brother Jim Felty's to pray for his wife's healing. She lay as a dead person, having been in bed for nearly three weeks. She was not expected to live. I asked Jim if he could pray with me for victory for her healing in the name of our blessed, compassionate Christ. He said that he could, so we got down and prayed.

We were some three hours when her brother, Less Bradford, came in. He got down with us as well. We stayed perhaps two hours longer waiting on God until I felt the confirmation. "It's done!" I said.

"I know," Brother Less said. We got up and went outdoors. In less than five minutes Mrs. Felty was out of that bed, reeling like a drunk woman, but healed. We all felt the power of God. She dressed, assisted in getting supper and went to the prayer meeting with us that night. She set the congregation on fire with her testimony.

The point I am wanting to make is sometimes it takes much waiting on God, other times not so much. God alone makes the determination.

Another woman from near Grayson, Kentucky, had been confined to her bed for several weeks. She was almost an invalid, being unable to walk unless assisted by her husband and son. I was invited to pray for her and the following morning at church I was told she was out of her bed and walking without any assistance. That night she came on horseback some two miles to get to the meeting. She got down from the saddle by herself and walked into the meeting which set the congregation to rejoicing.

There was another case several miles from Grayson where I was called to pray for a certain woman who had become weak minded through her great suffering. I prayed for her, pleading the promises and believing that God, without assistance, was able to heal her in the face of every darkness. I left feeling somewhat bothered over the conditions there, as I did not have the liberty I felt I should. But I stood my ground for her healing.

The next night we had a cottage prayer meeting. Quite a large crowd was there and Satan showed up, too. He informed me the woman wasn't healed or she would have been there. Several had shaken my hands as they came in and one sister had given me an especially hearty handshake. I noticed it, but did not think much about it. As soon as all were in and seated, I slipped over to a brother and said, "I expected the sister we prayed for yesterday to come."

He burst out laughing and called over to the woman,

"Sister, Brother Bevington doesn't know who you are." She hurried up to me and grasped my hand in the same hearty handshake she had given me earlier. It was the woman I had prayed for, but I would have never recognized her for there was such a radical, instantaneous change. That is the way God works, praise His dear name!

If Brother Black were still living, he would gladly tell how God answered prayer in his remarkable healing while we were holding a meeting at Honeywell. He came through on his way to Cincinnati where he was to be operated on for a complication of multiple diseases of several years' standing. He thought he would stop over Sunday where I was as we were having quite a good meeting.

When he told me where he was going and why, I said, "It might be that we could get a better shortcut than you having to go all the way to Cincinnati—one by way of the throne." We went to prayer and I had no trouble at all in reaching the throne in his behalf. That very afternoon God wonderfully healed him. He was a living witness in all that community to the healing power of God.

Brother Tom K---, from back of Anglin, is another case. He was so crippled with rheumatism that he had to use two canes or a crutch and a cane. He came to this same meeting in Honeywell. It took three of us to get him upstairs to my room, but when we had prayed through, he came down alone and that without the use of a cane. He went home to work on railroad ties, which meant first getting down on one knee and then on the other. He never had one bit of trouble. He was an unmistakable witness to the mighty power of God to heal.

121

I think there were seven or eight cases of healing in that county, all persons given up on by the doctors. To Jesus be all the glory! He is no respecter of places or diseases. All He asks of us is obedience and faith. Hallelujah.

I wish to chronicle one more marvel of how God brought me from death to life. I was painting a house for Reverend John Fleming and stayed there three weeks. It was in the fall of the year and quite cool, so I slept on feathers and between blankets during that period. I am recording this for people who entertain evangelists as a warning against any thoughtlessness in putting them in unhealthly beds.

Being quite accustomed to the feathers and being past sixty, I found it somewhat hard to make changes in my sleeping habits. But, I went from this feather bed to a quite different one when I accepted an invitation out near the Michigan line to hold a meeting. I got there on Friday night and preached in the M.E. church to a good crowd. One girl came to the altar.

I went back to my lodgings to sleep and got up the next morning feeling very bad physically. I was sore and ached all over. I went into the kitchen and asked, "Sister, about how long has it been since anyone slept in the bed you gave me last night?"

"Well, let me see now. Grandpa died in that bed some sixteen years ago and I guess no one has slept in it since."

"Has it been aired or have the sheets been changed? I am afraid I have caught a terrible cold," I asked, trying not to sound ungrateful.

When she evaded answering me, I returned to the room and looked more closely at the bed. Then I wrote my whole name in capital letters on the sheet and called the woman up to show it to her. She seemed surprised and somewhat mortified, so she put on a clean, dry sheet. That didn't help the mattress, so after preaching that night with some difficulty, I slept what little I could sitting in a chair.

Sunday morning I could not speak above a whisper and, oh, I was so sore all over. There was no preaching that day. Sunday night I remained in the chair and a dear, faithful nine-year-old boy kept the fire going for me as I could not move without severe pains. Monday morning I was still worse. The man of the house, John, said he was going to send the doctor up on his way to work that morning. "I don't think Brother Bevington believes in having a doctor," his wife cautioned him.

"I don't care what he believes. I am not going to have an old crank die on my hands and have to pay seventy-five dollars for not having the doctor come," he stated emphatically.

As this severe cold had seemed to completely stop up my ears, effectively deafening me, the sister wrote down everything for me so I would understand what was going on. I immediately set to praying as best I could that no doctor would come, for I knew I would not take any of his medicine. But I was so sore and having such severe pains, I could make little headway in my praying.

I believe the wife was saved, but not sanctified. John belonged to the meeting house, but that was about all. When he returned from work that night, no doctor had come yet. I was getting worse, now unable to move any of my limbs. But my faithful young friend, the nine-year-old boy, kept a good fire going for me as it was quite cold. Although I was running a high fever, my legs and feet were ice cold.

John told his wife he was too tired to make a trip back after the doctor that night, so my feeble prayer was answered up to that time. But the doctor did show up the next morning at 5:00 a.m. As he stepped into my room and looked at me, he threw up his right hand and hollered. He turned to the sister and began to give her what appeared to be quite a tongue lashing—I suppose for not sending for him sooner. I still was having trouble hearing anything, but I did hear him shout, "That man won't live forty-eight hours."

He never came close to me, but stood there eyeing me closely for about ten minutes. Then he stepped over to the table and left five kinds of medicine. One was the strongest he ever gave and was to be taken every ten minutes for about five hours. Three others were to be taken every forty minutes until used up. He said, "If he isn't better in four hours, he is a gone man. He has typhoid in its worst stage and at his age, everything is against his favor."

As soon as the doctor left, the sister came in with a glass of water and a dose of the ten-minute concoction. "What is that?" I said weakly.

"This is what the doctor left to help you." She handed me the instructions she had written down for everything the doctor ordered.

I read it all carefully and then looked her right in the eye as I said, "I cannot take that medicine. Just throw it outdoors."

I could see she was much disappointed and quite frustrated with me. She promptly proceeded to tell me why her husband was so set against holiness preachers. "There was a holiness preacher here four years ago who preached holiness as straight as you do, but when he left, he took another man's wife with him. She left three children behind, all under ten years of age. So John has no use for holiness preachers, though he did consent to allowing you to come here after much praying and coaxing. If you die, we might get in all kinds of trouble and John could have to pay seventy-five dollars for not having a doctor medicate you. So please, Brother Bevington, please take this medicine for my sake."

Well, I tell you, to resist man or doctor was a small thing. To resist such a plea as hers was about the hardest thing I had met in a long time. So I tried to reason with her, "I don't believe I am going to die. If I was, I would have gone before this." But the fact that I was getting worse all the time was poor encouragement to convince her I was going to get well. She believed I was alive at that point only through my willpower. I persisted until I finally persuaded her to take all that "truck" outdoors, live or die. The doctor had ordered her to phone at a certain hour and when she didn't, because she had no good news for him, he phoned her.

"Well, doctor, I guess he is worse if such a thing is possible. He refuses to take any of the medicine and I don't know what to do." That infuriated that doctor and he went right to the officials. The best he could do was get them to come after me the next day as their Maria was being repaired. So he phoned back to say that if I did not take the medicine at once as he had prescribed, the officials would be out the following day and take me to the pesthouse. The sister informed me as to the probable conclusion if I would not give in.

I knew I would never survive a mud road on a twelve-mile jump to the pesthouse if I was scarcely keeping warm sitting in that room with pillows and blankets and a huge fire. I tried to rally to pray, but it seemed I could not get myself still. I said to the boy, "Get me that chair and then if your mamma can spare another comforter, put it on the chair." He did and I readied for the effort of raising my legs up onto the chair. The boy tried to be as gentle as he could, but I fainted the first attempt he made to raise my legs. His mamma came in and helped him and they got one leg raised up. I fainted again while they were trying unsuccessfuly to get my other leg in place. It was nearly an hour before I came to and the mother had already pronounced me dead.

After I rallied again, I had some trouble convincing them to renew their effort. I said, "I must have both legs up there for two reasons. First, to lay my Bible on, and second, it will be warmer for me."

So they worked with a board under my leg and finally got it up. "Now, lay my small Bible carefully on my legs and draw my right hand down on it." I fainted again when they moved my arm. All in all, it was nearly two hours before everything was in place and I was conscious. I kept my hand on the Word of God, pleading the promises I knew it contained—all night long. The boy slept in a chair beside me, faithfully keeping a fine, coal fire burning. I could see but little, but I kept pleading the promises, saying over and over, "Thou art my Healer."

If anyone reading these words does not believe in a personal devil, I want to say right here there is one. I saw a dark form and heard a voice saying, "Yes, you have a fine Healer, don't you? I would like to have such a fine Healer as you have. Here you are and can't move an arm or leg. You have pneumonia in its worst stage and you're getting worse all the time. You can't even move your head."

That last word, "head," impressed me. I had not tried to move my head. I yelled out with the last of my strength, "You are a liar!" and undertook to move my head. I fainted again and was as dead for an hour.

When I rallied, I could see better out of my right eye, though the left one was still useless. I was reminded that this was the last day I had to get the victory. The officials

126

had not said what time they were coming to take me to the pesthouse and I prayed it would not be until after dinner.

Well, Satan certainly had me in pretty close quarters. I could not move my head, but I coaxed the boy to work my fingers. I noticed as he raised them an inch, it hurt scarcely any. I felt I was getting the victory and I could see really well out of my right eye. About 10:00 a.m. the officials phoned and said they would be there by 2:00 p.m. to take me to the pesthouse. While I could not yet move a muscle and was in great pain still, I could plead the promises better. So I just stuck to it until noon when I managed to take some soup with a goose quill.

About 1:00 p.m., while pleading the promises without any pain, I asked the boy to raise my hand. He did so slowly—one inch, two inches, three inches. I shouted, "Hold on!" and began praising God. The sister rushed in and I yelled, "I am getting the victory. Let go of my hand, son." He let go and it dropped, but there was no pain.

"Raise it up again," I told him. He did so—one, two, three, four, five and then six inches high. I shouted, "Oh, glory, raise it higher." Up to twelve inches it went. "Now, put it back on the Bible," I cried as I felt the power of the blessed Lord coming through my body. My left eye opened and I could see as well as ever. I raised my right arm, but fainted dead away. Again the woman pronounced me dead. She seemed determined to have me dead!

I revived in less than half an hour and began pleading the promises with greater energy than any previous time. Satan came to me with the same words as before. I told him he was a liar because I could move my neck. Then I offered up a prayer, repeating I John 5:14 and 15, "And this is the confidence that we have in him, that, if we ask any thing according to his will, he heareth us. And if we know that he hear us, whatsoever we ask, we know that we have the petitions that we desired of him." I moved my head and it didn't hurt. I raised my left arm for the first time and then my right arm, shouting, "I am healed!"

I kicked the comforters off my legs and was out of the chair, leaping and yelling. Still weak, my exuberance quickly exhausted me and I would have fallen to the floor if the sister had not caught me and pulled me back into the chair. She looked out the window just then and said, "There they are."

I urgently began to plead the promises so my strength would return. It did not come as rapidly as I wished, but I kept repeating I John 5:14 and 15 over and over. The officers were coming through the kitchen and if I ever saw a demon, the man leading them looked just like one— unsympathetic, crabbed and hard looking.

He stopped in the doorway and the sister was talking to him. As I now had my hearing back, I heard her say, "He claims to be healed. He was just up and out of his chair, but he over-exerted himself. He is very weak, not having eaten anything for six days."

I could not speak, but I saw the fiendish look on his face. Just behind him was another nice-looking man who looked both pleasant and sympathetic. I longed to get to him, but I couldn't move. The main officer shook his head and said, "I take no stock in that nonsense," referring to the former man who had preached holiness. It turned out that his brother's wife was the woman who had run off with the holiness preacher and his brother had ended up in the insane asylum from the grief and pressure.

I rallied and attempted to reassure them that I only lacked strength, but I was indeed healed. "I am a healed man," I stated. The officer said he would not go without me as he would only have to come back and would have to pay the cost of the second trip himself. "Here," I said, thrusting my watch towards him, "this watch will sell anywhere for twenty-five dollars. If I am not at your office tomorrow morning at 10:00 a.m. and you have to come back after me, sell the watch. It will more than pay for your second trip."

Then the pleasant-looking man stepped up. I offered him my hand as I wanted very much to connect with him. He said to the officer, "Go ahead, take his watch and try him. I believe he will be there." The officer finally was persuaded to go without me. Then they walked out and stood talking in the living room until I heard the pleasant man say, "You don't want that man's watch, let me take it back to him. I really believe he is all right. Let me take it back to him for I think he has had a hard struggle and needs some sympathy and love and encouragement."

If ever a man spoke the truth, that man did. I felt I would give almost anything to have some sympathy and caring extended to me right then. Then he said to the officer, "If you do have to come back, I will pay the extra twelve dollars for you."

So back in he came with my watch. I felt all melted up from the confidence he was placing in me. I got hold of his hand and kissed it, then squeezed it as best I could to express my gratitude for his faith in me. Everybody else had been against me, even the sister who wanted to be kind and help me. Because she had never seen anyone healed and her husband was opposing me, she was so fearful of trouble that she was absolutely miserable. This man's act of confidence was a great stimulant to me.

I rested all day and slept good that night. The next morning I started out for my 10:00 a.m. meeting, but still being weak, I felt very sensitive to the cold. I put on two overcoats which loaded me down and I was glad to have the boy accompanying me. We stopped sixteen times to rest in the three miles to the man's office, but we arrived outside his building just before 10:00. Then I saw we had nine steps to go up. Now quite tired in body and mind, I said to the boy, "How can I ever make it up those nine steps?"

I will never forget how that boy looked up at me with such faith. "Ask Jesus," he urged.

Well, I did. The nice man was sitting at the window and seeing me, he came right down. He called to two men who were passing by, "Gentlemen, will you please help us get this man up these steps?" God was right there to see me through.

Inside, they had a doctor who examined me quite thoroughly. Finally, he pronounced, "There is nothing the matter with this man except he is very weak."

So I was given a clean bill of health and released. The kind gentlemen stopped me on my way out and said, "When I got home yesterday, I told my wife about you. She was very interested and told me, 'I believe that man will be there right on time. Take the horse and buggy down to the office with you and bring him back up here for dinner!' "

I gratefully climbed into the buggy with him and we started up. I asked him, "Are you a saved man?"

"No, I wish I were." He began crying. "My wife is a backslider, too. We have tried and tried and tried, but have not been able to get back to the Lord. We heard of your meeting and we were planning to come out."

When we came to their house, the wife came running out to the buggy to offer her hand and help me down. She practically carried me right into the house. "I knew God would answer your prevailing prayers and heal you. I am so glad. I am a miserable backslider, but I felt God would heal you and then you could prevail for my husband and me to get back to God. I have a sister living just half a mile from here and when I went to see her yesterday, she just broke up crying as she said, 'Bring him over here, too.' "

Though I was very hungry and weak and the steaming dinner was already on the table, I knew there was important business to be conducted first. "Do you want to get back to God badly enough to fall down right here and stay until you meet the conditions?"

"Yes," she cried and down she went as her husband and I dropped down with her. We pleaded the promises all afternoon until he arose with shouts of victory. He grabbed me and began to carry me all over the house, shouting and yelling all the way. Then she got the victory and began to jump and dance about. We had a real blessed time, believe me. Then we had dinner—the first meal I had eaten in six days. After everything was cleaned up, we got into the buggy and went over to her sister's house.

As the wife jumped out the buggy, she was shouting, "Hallelujah! Hallelujah!" and kept it up until her sister came running outside. The sister threw her arms around us and begged us to come right in and pray for her. We all dropped down on our faces in the nice, warm kitchen and went to praying.

Two hours later her husband came home, all black from digging coal in the mines. The wife jumped up and threw her arms around him, saying, "I am trying to get back to God. Help me, help me!"

He broke up and dropped right down with us. They both began to do some real good digging, meeting conditions. He got through first in just two hours. Then he positioned himself at his wife's side and pleaded for her as few have ever pleaded for another person.

We prayed all night and she got through right early the next morning.

I was feeling much stronger and I walked the floor and praised God for all He had done. Oh, how precious the Savior was then! He had not only healed me, He had reclaimed four inside of fifteen hours. We all magnified Jesus. The woman had prepared breakfast, but when I sat down to the table, I couldn't even eat. I had to get up and walk again, my whole being bathed in tears of joy. Jesus was so real and precious, I was feasting on His presence.

We all fell back on our faces in great adoration until each one had poured his or her heart out in praise. It was a most wonderful praise and prayer service. Finally our hostess said, "Brother, you must eat something. You had nothing this morning at breakfast." So I did, even though there was a continual bubbling up inside of me—the spirit of praise rising from my heart. I was beginning to fully realize what God had done and as my strength continued to return, the volume of the praise increased also.

Thus began some very remarkable workings of God. I remained at that house over Sabbath and preached that night. There really wasn't much preaching, though, for everything kept turning into a praise service. The four who had been saved were seeking sanctification all day Sunday. We finally retired at midnight, or I thought we all retired. When I arose the next morning, I found all four still in the kitchen where they had been wrestling throughout the night. The young girl who had been saved in the first meeting just before I fell sick was there seeking sanctification, also. I remained and wrestled with them through that night and by the next morning, the five had swept through to complete victory.

After we had our dinner, I felt strongly impressed to return to John's house. Upon informing the others of this, they protested with pleas for me to remain with them. "Brother Bevington, we want you here for a month at least." The M.E. preacher had come to the house earlier and now joined with them in pleading for me to remain. He offered his church for as long as the Lord would lead me to occupy it.

Well, that was somewhat perplexing as these five who had been reclaimed and sanctified had relatives there who were backsliders. Their plea seemed to be based on good reasonings, but when I went out to the barn and weighed the matter carefully and prayerfully, "Go back to John's" was all I could get.

The M.E. preacher said, "Let him go. When he gets through out there, we will have him come back here with us. In the meantime we will circulate what God has done and be in better shape for God to work."

So on Wednesday morning this nice man took me back to John's and we gave out tracts and advertised the meeting along the way. We got out to John's just as he was coming in from work and, of course, he had to admit the power of God in my healing. He said, "You are not expecting to hold any more meetings here are you?"

I said, "Yes, I want a meeting tonight."

He asked with some skepticism, "Are you able to preach tonight?" Now, here came an opportunity to use a little strategy. He had told his wife several times that he would never go to hear another holiness preacher. That evening he told her, "You may go, but I will not." She told me what he had said.

So I went to him and said, "John, I am somewhat weak. While I don't contemplate any failure in my attempt to get there, you know there are a lot of sightseers and sport-seeking boys around. With three-quarters of a mile to walk over a rough road..." I let my voice trail off. Then I

133

made my move, "Now, John, I want to ask a favor of you. Will you go along and take my arm and make it possible for me to have more strength than I otherwise would have?" I assured him he would not have to go inside, though that was my objective in having him go with me. Being a kindhearted man, he could not very well refuse.

Well, I prayed all the way down to know how to get him into the church. At the door I said, "Now, John, we have gotten along fine and I feel quite strong enough for the service. But I worry I might fall on the platform, which would have a tendency to break up the meeting. Being such a cool, level-headed fellow, you would know how to catch me and prevent a commotion."

He scratched his head thoughtfully and finally had to submit to my plea. I had him wade through all the obstacles of holiness preachers and mourners' benches to the meeting and set him right down on the front seat at the side of the platform.

The next night, I got him to do the same thing. The following night I didn't even have to ask him and before I was half through preaching, he was at the altar. He prayed about as good as any man I had ever heard. The following night, Saturday, he and others were at the altar and stayed there until 4:00 a.m. Sunday morning, some of them getting through. John's wife was among them, seeking sanctification.

We remained there all day Sunday and clear on into Monday evening, making about thirty-six hours of praying, praising, preaching and shouting. Someone told me that the souls who actually had prayed through had averaged one per hour during the whole time. So you see, it was a pretty fair meeting.

And now I come to another way that God has of leading His people. On Sunday and Monday, I felt I must go, but said nothing. I preached, or rather tried to preach, on Monday night. But the meeting was all prayer and praise and all the time I felt that voice saying, "Go, go, go." Well, I supposed of course the "go" meant to go to my next meeting.

The next morning I told this to John and those who were there. John said, "Oh, no, Brother Bevington, your work has just begun here. We are all planning for the greatest meeting that has ever been in this community."

Well, I retreated to my usual place for solving problems (the haymow), but from the first there was still that "go," After three hours, I had to give in to it.

The next morning John hitched his horse up to the jolt wagon to take me, as we supposed, to the depot some twelve miles away. I bade the wife and dear, faithful, young Frank good-bye. The wife kept insisting, "I cannot believe your work is done here," and would not bid me good-bye. I was a bit confused, myself, as I had only had about a third of my anticipated railroad fare—but off we went.

We had gone about three miles when John looked back and said, "I declare, I believe that is Jim."

I said, "Who is Jim?"

Now I have left out some things that will need to be entered here. When John's wife first wrote to me to come out and hold a meeting, she stated that there were fourteen sanctified people there, the father and mother of each of seven families. So on that first Saturday night— the last night I preached until after I was healed—I thought inasmuch as there were fourteen sanctified people there, it would be safe to venture on a testimony meeting. So I turned the services over to their class leader.

I could hear some then, but not sufficiently enough to clearly get all their testimonies. I could not settle myself with the ensuing proceedings and finally said to little Frank, "Who are these people who are testifying?"

"Why, they are all members here—the superintendent, the class leader and the officers of the church. Oh, they're all sanctified," Frank assured me.

By the time the seventh one got up, I was in doubt as to their having a right to testify and noticed a woman laying a quid on the bench as she got up. I suppose she felt the quid might bother or hinder the display she had planned.

I endured until the ninth one and could not stand it any longer. So I said, "Mister," (I did not feel clear in addressing him as 'brother') "you just sit down."

"I don't have to sit down for you," came his hot reply.

I rose to my feet, pointed my right index finger staight at him and ordered, "You sit down right there." I tell you, he dropped like a shot calf. He struggled back up to his feet, grabbed his hat and started for the door. All but eleven followed him—all told about some eighty going out. The girl who had gotten sanctified in that home back of the village and ten more remained. Well, I did my best at preaching and then dismissed them.

As we were going out, John's wife said, "Now you keep behind me as that crowd is all out there and I don't know just what for."

We stepped off the porch and up rushed the man I had called down. Out of all the tongue lashings a man ever got, I got one of the strongest right there. I did not reply to him and just said, "Come on, let's go," and we made our way on through. He and several others followed for some distance, calling me about all the names in the catalogue of vengeance.

Now I want to return to where John and I were in the wagon and he had just said, "I believe that is Jim."

When I asked who Jim was, he answered, "The man

you called down at the testimony meeting. He is my cousin. I can see he is bareheaded and looking kind of wild, yelling for me to stop. But Brother Bevington, you need not fear as I have this loaded whip stock here. I will protect you even if he is my cousin."

Well, he was a sight indeed. Here he came on horseback, yelling like a cowboy chasing a renegade calf, "Stop! Stop! Wait!" So John stopped. Jim leaped off his horse, rushed right up into the wagon and threw his arms around me. "Oh, Brother Bevington, pray for me. I have been in hell ever since that Saturday night."

I said, "Do you really want God?"

"Oh, yes!"

I could tell he was serious. "Drive up along the fence," I instructed John. We did so and John got down on one side of the wagon and I on the other. Jim began to pray with us, still up in the wagon.

In about an hour he burst out, "Oh, God, oh, God—have mercy, have mercy! Oh, God, save me from this awful hell that I am rushing into!" Then he cried out, "Brother Bevington, come over here! Come over here! Take my hand, for I am slipping into hell right now. Oh, come here quickly!"

I said, "No, I won't come up there. You repent!" I stayed at my post beside the wagon.

"Brother, I am going to hell!"

"If you had what you deserved, you would have been there long ago. Repent! Repent!" I was determined he would pray it through. We were there by that fence all day long.

Three times some of his relatives came along, but they could not get him out of that wagon. One of his cousins, a wealthy farmer, came along with a flock of sheep and called out to John, "Who is that in the wagon?"

"That is Jim."

"What in the world is he doing in there?"

Jim yelled out, "I am getting God." The cousin made all sorts of threats against me and John, too, but Jim stayed in his place until he prayed through. Then he jumped out hollering like a coon dog, grabbed me and landed us both flat on the ground. He got right back up and carried me all around there for nearly an hour. Finally he got on his horse and left, rejoicing as he went.

"Well," I said, "I can't make any train now, so I guess we will go back to your house." That is just what John was expecting.

Now many will say, "Why, Brother Bevington, I thought you were going to the depot. Now how would God lead you for the depot and then not get you there?" Pay attention for here comes an important lesson for all. We must remember that we are only human beings and God does not always reveal His plans ahead of time, instead He just leads us as He sees best.

God knew He couldn't undertake to explain to me that He would have to get Jim out there in that wagon on a public road—subject to all the embarrassing scenes it would be necessary for him to go through—in order to knock his churchianity out of him. Only God knew what it would take to shake Jim loose from his long membership, the testimonies he had been giving for ten years, his antipathy against the holiness preacher who broke up that peaceful family, his good standing in the M.E. church and all arising therefrom. If God had undertaken to explain all this to me, He would have landed me in the brush.

Consider His wisdom. He told me to "go" and allowed me to interpret the "go" as I saw fit, as that would make no difference to Him as long as I did "go." Then He just took a shortcut to make the many points necessary to getting

138

Jim saved. God was well aware that I was nowhere nearly done in that vicinity, but He knew it was necessary to get that leader completely transformed and broken all to pieces so He could use him.

Now as Jim was on horseback, he could make better time than us. When we drove back into John's barnyard, here came Jim and his wife rushing up. She jumped off the horse and sobbed out, "Oh, Brother Bevington, forgive me. I have been in hell ever since that Saturday night." We went right into the house where we all fell on our faces in the dining room.

Thus began one of the most remarkable seven weeks of my life, right there in that man's house. I never took off my clothes and never preached a sermon. I just lay day and night on my face, praying, weeping, groaning, pleading, imploring, beseeching and besieging the throne in behalf of that M.E. membership of three-hundred people. Some would get through and strike out for their relatives and friends. They would come back in wagon loads, bringing provisions, feed and even their cows. They would stay until the whole load got saved and sanctified. Then they would strike out after someone else.

That kept up for seven weeks—day and night. No one ate but one meal every twenty-four hours, yet someone was out in the kitchen cooking all the time. I got such a burden that I could not get up, but just lay there wherever I was praying. They would come in at times and feed me like they would a baby.

Well, they claimed there were over four hundred down there and most of them prayed through. Of all the times I ever saw, this beat anything. Some were praying, others crying, others testifying, others preaching, others shouting, others making restitution. I just lay on my face, bathed in tears. When it was all over, I looked as though I had gone through a right hard six weeks.

I think the most remarkable case was that of Jim's wife who had been of a real boisterous nature or makeup. Before this meeting she would run and shout and yell when giving her testimony. She was the first to get through and she lay under the power of God some sixty hours. When she arose, she was so different. There was none of that bold, hilarious conduct. She was so meek, she just walked the floor, bathed in tears, wringing her hands. Not a word fell from her lips. She was like a little, country girl of eleven summers. I tell you, she lived salvation after that. She and her husband and many, many more lay there until they were sanctified.

Of course, news soon reached the village that I had come back and here the people came. Even the preacher came and got sanctified, as did his wife and many of his members. So you see, it pays to mind God and trust Him.

I love to rewrite these experiences and do hope they will prove the blessing to many that they have been to me. Real, steady, unselfish prayer will move things. We need to mean what we say. Once a little girl said to her papa, who was saying that Jesus didn't mean all He said in the Bible, "Papa, if Jesus didn't mean what He said, why didn't He say what He meant?"

I shouted, "Amen, that's reason."

I have seen ministers get down and pray for Jesus to heal some of their members and seemingly they prayed in earnest. But if their prayers had been answered, they would have been more surprised than those folks were when Peter stood knocking at their door for entrance. I remember one who prayed thus and then I heard him deny that Jesus heals.

I was holding a meeting years ago near Lexington,

Kentucky, where God instantly healed a sister of a disease of eight years' standing. She had not stood on her feet for five years. Her preacher stood up in the pulpit and denied that Jesus had anything to do with her healing even though she walked to the church the day she was healed. (Oh, Consistency, thou art a jewel!)

I was holding one meeting in Ohio, not far from an insane asylum. As I so often did, I went to the woods to pray. Supposing I was out of hearing, I got somewhat noisy, prayed pretty loud and brandished my hands and arms about in gesticulations that looked sort of queer to a passer-by.

It seems that one of the inmates had escaped out of the asylum and a reward had been offered for his capture. Well, two men were going through the woods right then and hearing me, took notice. They immediately pronounced I had to be that lunatic. As the reward was sure, they agreed between themselves, "We dare not tackle the fellow, so let's run to the village and get the officers to capture him." So they hurried away and reported their discovery. Officers were dispatched with three conveyances along with ropes, cuffs, chains, wires and a grand display of safety equipment. Out they came to capture me.

Well, I had gotten through my gymnastic performances and had gone back to the house. As this was a somewhat secluded place, the lady of the house was quite bewildered when she saw seven men in three conveyances drive up to the woods and begin unload all their equipment. She called upstairs to me, "Brother Bevington, did you notice those men going into our woods?"

I replied that I had not and she called me down to see the crowd out there. I didn't know what it all meant and went back to my room. Soon one of the officers knocked on the door to ask the woman, "Do you know of a lunatic who has recently escaped from the asylum and was seen in your woods this forenoon?"

The woman made a few inquiries as to appearance, dress and probably actions of the fugitive. As the officers were describing him, she burst out laughing for she had seen me praying. She said, "Yes, I know where he is—he is in my house right now." With that, she stepped to the door and called me downstairs. As the officer had been out twice to hear me preach, he recognized me and they all had a big laugh. Well, that is all except the two who were planning for the reward—they weren't amused at all.

So our praying definitely has meaning. Taylor was once praying and wrestling and pleading for Africa and finally God said, "Taylor, pack up your grip and get for Africa." Well, my praying came near to getting me into that asylum, but they let me off.

Now I would like to say right here that if any of the parties who attended those seven weeks' meetings just described should get this volume, they will at once recognize the meetings. I wish they would write me, giving the names of as many as possible, as all their names are gone from me. It would be a great comfort to me to write to them. I can remember Jim's and John's given names, but not their surnames. Just write me at Kingswood, Kentucky, and all mail will be forwarded to me wherever I am. That is, if I am still this side of Heaven. If not, then I expect to meet a lot of those people up there.

I went to the Cincinnati Camp one year and was invited to go on down the river to hold a meeting. I don't remember much about the meeting, but I do remember one sister who was unable to attend the services as she

142

was confined to her bed. I went to prayer for her and soon saw there was something hindering, but I couldn't tell just what. Wanting to know if was the same as is recorded in Daniel 10, I went first to the barn and from there to the woods.

This woman had been healed once before through our prayers and, in about forty-eight hours, God showed me that she had never testified to the other healing. So I went to her and reminded her of this negligence. After a pause, she said, "Brother Bevington, who told you that I had never testified to it? Whoever did, told you a lie."

I said "Sister, you never testified to it here in this M.E. church where you are so well known."

"Well, no, I never did here, but I did once at an open air meeting at the Cincinnati Camp."

"Yes," I said, "it was no trouble for you where you were not known. There was no sacrifice there, no danger of anyone pointing a finger at you. Sister, you were too big a coward to stand here and tell what God had done for you. Jesus said, 'Whosoever shall be ashamed of me and of my words, of him shall the son of man be ashamed.' "

She replied, "I would like to know who told you that."

"God told me out in the woods."

"Oh," she said in a small voice. "Yes, it is true. Brother Bevington, will you ask God to forgive me?"

I replied, "If you can convince God that you will stand here amongst these scoffers and tell it, I presume He will heal you. But you will have to convince Him, which may mean much on your part. You might easily convince me, but you are not dealing with Bevington on this case. You are dealing with God now, the all-seeing Jehovah. He has no use for cowards."

So I left her and went to the woods. I remained there about sixty hours, then slipped out the back way from the woods and did not go near her house. I went about four miles away to hold another meeting, while she just kept getting worse all the time. I conducted a fourteen days' meeting in which several found the Lord and two were healed.

She finally heard where I was and sent for me. I returned to her house and she said, "I am in heaps of trouble, even though I have told the Lord I would tell it here in this neighborhood, in this church."

I said, "I think He knows you are lying, just as you did before," and I grabbed my hat and made for the woods again. I remained there about four days as I was very desirous that she should get where God could trust her with such a boon as this healing would be. She had means and talents that God could use if He could get hold of her. Well, she was dumbfounded at my actions and about concluded that there was something radically wrong in my upper story.

Be that as it may, I was up on the hill under a large oak, pleading with God to wake her up and get her where He wanted her. I was doing my part and God was doing His part. On the fifth afternoon, He said, "Go to her at once." I went.

Such a sight met my eyes! She had been crying for forty-eight hours and as I knocked at the door, I heard her sob out, "Come in." When I entered the room, she threw up her hands and cried, "Oh, I am so glad you came! God has answered prayer. Forgive, oh, forgive me for feeling so hard against you and saying so many bad things about you. Oh, I am so sorry. I never knew I was so mean."

That was what I had spent those hours in the woods for—that proud heart had to be subdued. You see, she had never had anything more than a meeting house religion. I was also fully convinced that she had never received the Holy Ghost, for to believe a person could lose regeneration and retain sanctification always was a pretty hard thing for me to buy. So I felt she was an entire backslider, but I did not consider it wise to so inform her right then. I felt wisdom would be best exercised by silence on my part. Finally she spoke up, "Brother Bevington, I believe I have lost my sanctification. If I was sanctified, I would never have felt toward you as I did."

Wisdom prevailed in me and I remained silent. I am quite sure if I had said, "Sister, you are a complete backslider," she would never have accepted it from me. So instead, I went back to the woods and pleaded with God to tell her, for He seems better capacitated for these emergencies than we. Then I spent five hours in the barn after coming down from the woods. I cried, "Oh, God, don't let her be deceived."

That five hours of struggling in the barn caused the X-ray to be turned on. When I went into the house, she said, "Brother Bevington, I am sure you will be very much surprised at what I am going to relate, but I feel that I must tell you. I am an entire backslider, so don't pray any more for me to be sanctified. Pray that I may be reclaimed."

So it is to be seen that perhaps nine times out of ten, we make an awful failure of work for which God is so much more qualified than we. God succeeds ten times out of ten if we let Him. In three hours she was blessedly reclaimed and so happy. "Why, I wonder if I didn't get sanctified when I got reclaimed here. I feel so very happy."

I said, "Did you ever see anyone who was sanctified at the same time he was regenerated?"

"But I am so very happy."

"You ought to be happy. Any woman who is mean enough to slam the door in the face of as good a friend as

Jesus and treat Him as you have treated Him and then have Him tenderly forgive you for that treatment, throw His loving arms around you and restore your former joy, should be happy. Yes, you ought to be a very happy person indeed!"

She said, "I guess you are about right. Now can we pray for my healing?"

"The Book says, 'Seek ye first the kingdom of God, and His righteousness'. Have you His righteousness now, being only a regenerated woman?"

"I reckon not. What must I do?"

"Don't you want to be sanctified?"

"Certainly I do."

"Then why not pray for sanctification?"

She tried to make excuses, "Well, I thought that after I was healed, I could pray through better and get sanctified."

"Well, you settle that squarely from the Word." I grabbed my hat and left her room. It had now been nearly seven days since I had anything to eat, so I went into the kitchen and told her daughter I was hungry. The young woman got up a nice dinner and I ate heartily.

They had a little girl about seven who came in just then and saw me in the kitchen. After listening to me for awhile, she went into the mother's room to tell her what I had said about a little girl in Cincinnati. The mother had not known what had become of me and gratefully said to her daughter, "Go quickly and tell him to come back in here." When I returned to her room, she said, "I have no more bad feelings about you. Do you believe Jesus will heal me?"

"He may—after you get the Holy Ghost."

Well, she drew a long, deep sigh at that. Finally she said, "I want the Holy Ghost all right."

So I went to prayer that afternoon. I remained there four nights and three days, holding onto God for her to die out to herself. Neither of us ate a mouthful during this examination. God answered, but she seemed about the deadest, living person I had seen for some time.

Her husband was an unsaved man, but a firm believer in entire holiness, so he continued to encourage me the entire time. He was also a staunch advocate of Divine healing and told me several times that if we could get her where God could have His way, He would heal her.

On the fourth morning, she bounded out of bed. No one but the daughter was up when the mother started shouting, "Sanctified and healed! Oh, I have the real thing this time!" I saw her twice more after that and it was obvious she was an entirely different woman.

The husband wanted me to stay one more day, so I went back out to the barn where I climbed into the haymow and began to plead for him. When I finally came down late that afternoon, he was in one of the stalls there in the cow barn, praying like a good fellow. That was what I had been pulling for during those several weeks of queer actions, but they all counted. That night he got through. I have heard him, on the platform at the Cincinnati Camp, give unmistakable evidence of having just what he had been advocating for some time.

So listen to me! Is there anything too hard for God? Can't we afford to be talked about, misunderstood, lied about, misrepresented and ostracized if, in so doing, God can bring the people to themselves? It isn't necessary for us to understand all the "whys" and "wherefores," it is our business to just obey God.

While I had not been perfectly satisfied as to the all-around state of this woman, I just minded Him. As time went on, certain revelations were given and I could trust

147

Him for further guidance and developments to bring out all the facts as they became necessary.

God seldom tells us His whole plan when He has specially delegated us to work with certain persons. He wants us to go through one step at a time. He had this woman's entire sanctification and her healing—as well as the salvation and sanctification of her husband—all in view. Everything had been mapped and marked out, but He had to have someone who would allow Him to bring forth some very unreasonable things (from the human stand point) in order to accomplish His designs.

He saw that Bevington could be trusted with that important work. So He assigned it to me, allowing about seven weeks to get it done. Most of that time I spent in seclusion in the woods or the haymow. That is when God accomplishes His greatest feats, you know—when He can get us in seclusion.

6
Personal Dealings Of and From God

I love to think of John Wesley and I wish I could insert so many of his sayings and miraculous doings by the hand of God. Oh, how well he knew that the resources of all Heaven are at God's command when He speaks—the elements are subservient to His will. Wesley truly lived in the knowledge that "All things are possible to him that believeth!" It is so blessed to know that the wonderful instances recorded in Wesley's works were not confined to his day—we have the same privileges he had. If our faith in God is unlimited, we can be assured that "whatsoever we ask for, we receive." Amen.

I once was spending a few months in northern Indiana with my only living brother, R---. Since then he has gone to his reward, leaving me the only one still on probation out of a family of thirteen children.

He had a boy named Harry staying with him who had been brought up a Catholic. One day all of us were going by wagon to Michigan City, several miles away. None of us had any wraps or umbrella when it began to rain.

I said to Harry, "I don't want to get wet, as this wind off the lake here would be too chilly for my health. Now see if it continues to rain as I will offer up a prayer."

In less than five minutes, the rain stopped. "Well," Harry exclaimed, "that is certainly wonderful. My folks all go to church, but I never saw anything like that done there nor anywhere else." God gave me this opportunity to enable Him to display His power there in the presence of that boy.

At that same time I had something growing on the lid of my eye—it had been there about seven years. Occasionally it would draw up as small as a large kernel of wheat, then it would seem to lengthen out about an inch. It had not bothered me much, so I had not bothered Jesus about it. But soon after this miracle of the rain stopping, I was holding another meeting some miles away and on the last Sunday, that growth spread out larger than ever. It bothered me in reading the Word and was quite sore.

I put up with it until I got back to my brother's the next day. By then the growth was so large, Harry was amazed when he saw how my eye was swollen and inflamed. "Uncle Guy, why don't you ask Jesus to take that off. If He stopped the rain for you, wouldn't He do that?"

"Yes, I think He will," I said. So when I went to bed, I knelt down and offered up a prayer of faith that the thing would be gone by the next day and then I fell asleep. In the morning I got up before Harry did and went down to wash. I had not thought of my eye since praying for it the night before. Soon after I got up, down came Harry to see about that thing on my eye. He came bounding out on the porch, saying "Uncle Guy, how is that thing?"

"Well," I said, "look and see." Lo, there was no trace of it, not even a scar!

He called for my brother to get up and see what Jesus had done for Uncle Guy. Harry said, "I don't see why my folks don't do things that way. I had a sore knee and had to stay out of school four months and they paid out a whole lot of money, too."

There was also a sore on my body that had been forming about six years. It had never bothered me much, so I didn't bother with it, either. But that summer at Jerry's, it began getting quite sore. It was about the size of a twenty-five cent piece with rims of different colors around it. After no sense of feeling for six years, it got so bad I could not touch anywhere near it. I could not even sleep on that side. As it grew larger and more sensitive, I finally got tired of it. I went up to my room, called Harry and showed him the sore. He thought it was awful and pronounced it a cancer. I told a doctor about it and he said it was undoubtedly a cancer.

Well, I laid my hand on that sore and prayed the prayer of faith, asking for its removal. In no more than six minutes, the soreness was all gone. I could rub and even pinch it without the slightest pain. The colors were still there, but the next morning they were all gone.

So this youngster had three good lessons given him through faith. He wrote home to his people and asked them if he couldn't join Uncle Guy's church, telling them what he had seen in answer to prayer. It resulted in the conversion of the whole family. Oh, glory, how blessed to have such a God!

After this I was called on to pray for a sister who had been sorely afflicted for eight or nine years. I prayed for her and she went to sleep, so I retired to my room. The next morning she said she had not slept better in years until about 4:00 a.m. when she was suddenly taken again with the malady. She suffered terribly until they finally called me up. I laid my hand on her and prayed and she was soon asleep again. When we had our breakfast, she was still sleeping.

Her husband had little use for a holiness preacher as he had the meeting house for his support. He seemed to think that filled the basket and he believed in letting well enough alone.

I took my Bible and went to the woods until I heard the dinner bell and came in. I found her still suffering, so I resumed praying and she was made free again. After dinner I returned to the woods. The bell rang out in the middle of the afternoon. She was again suffering, so I dropped down on my face in her room and lay there until they called me for supper.

I told them I didn't want any, for I was getting a good hold upon God and He was enlarging my vision of His power. I just lay there pleading the promises and believing God though she was still suffering. Her husband came in and said to her, "I want you to take this medicine. I can't bear to see you suffer this way under this crank's supervision."

I said nothing, but prayed she would refuse. She did, saying, "I am going to take God, as He has wonderfully delivered me three times since Brother Bevington has been here. I believe He will heal me entirely."

"Well, I would like to see some signs," was his response.

I just lay on the floor, praying with all my might. About 9:00 p.m., I rose to my feet and laid my hand on her forehead. Then I raised my right hand with the Bible resting upon it and said, "In the name of Jesus Christ, depart, depart, depart!" I opened my eyes and could see she was still suffering, but I held on to demanding the instant departure. I was still holding the Bible up and pleading the promises when I looked at the clock and it was after 4:00 a.m. While she was still suffering, it was not quite so bad.

I kept holding the Bible up, changing it from one hand to the other, when her husband got up from his bed and came in. He saw that she had been having a hard night for he was so accustomed to waiting on her, he could tell how she was doing just by her looks. He grabbed the medicine, shoved me out of the way and ordered her to open her mouth and take the stuff. She opened her eyes and shook her head with a smile.

I could see he was boiling and determined that she should not suffer any longer when he felt he had the needed remedy. He turned to me and yelled, "Get out of this room. Take your traps and leave this house!"

I went outdoors, still pleading and believing, and she kept refusing to take the medicine. I was out under a tree and actually getting hold of God when the husband came out and gave me a pretty hard kick. He shouted, "I told you to leave this place. I mean it and will not tell you again."

I continued praying. I was getting hold of God and did not want to move or utter a word. I felt sure victory was coming. Although the waters were raging about me, I was still. There was such a sweet, calm, quiet assurance that she was going to be healed. I just lay as still as I could, fearing any move upon my part would break the connection. I didn't want to breathe—in fact, I held my breath for long spells.

Then her husband came out again. I turned over from lying on my face and said, "Let me remain here one more hour."

153

"I told you to leave," he shouted.

"Just give me one hour and you will see the power of God," I urgently pleaded with him.

"Nonsense, that has been your cry for twenty hours." He headed towards the barn to get the large horse whip.

I got up and went into the house with the assurance of victory. As I entered, the woman raised her right hand and a smile broke over her face. "We have the victory, Brother Bevington."

I shouted "Amen," and went back out the door. Before I even left the porch, I heard her feet strike the floor. She ran clear out to the barn yelling at the top of her voice. That was a good thing, for her infuriated husband was coming with his whip to give me a good thrashing. But as she dropped on her knees, praising God and praying for her husband, he just melted. Then he called for me to join them. I went out and we had an old-fashioned prayer and praise service there in the weeds and grass. We had a scene that three worlds were witness to until he prayed through and actually got salvation. Oh, what blessed times we had!

Then she went to their church and set the whole congregation to weeping and laughing—some to shouting. The preacher never did get to preach at that service. It pays to hold on to God no matter what appears to be happening for He works quite differently than we do. Well, hallelujah. Amen!

Today is the twelfth day of April, 1923. I am at South Ashland, Kentucky, and all is under the blood. Glory to Jesus! Jesus hath redeemed me, hath cleansed me, hath healed me and hath taken my sickness with Him on the cross. Glory!

He doesn't want us to suffer as He has delivered us.

Hallelujah! Oh, let us praise Him and hold Him up so the world can see Him through us. The world can see Jesus only as they see Him in and through us.

Another time, after the Cincinnati camp, I was impressed to go down the river to see how the people were getting on at Rising Sun. I went to the depot where I had to wait for at least four hours. As I sat there, a voice seemed to say, "Go out to Mrs. M.---'s," about three miles out.

The voice seemed so plain, I had to give it some attention. I thought, "I can walk out there and still get back for this train."

So I took my suitcase and grip down to a drug store and asked permission to leave them there. I started up the walk, but the voice said, "Go back and get the grip."

That seemed so foolish that I just took it to be Satan. "No," I said, "I will not pack that grip out there and back." I went on walking. But that voice still kept calling me to go back and get my grip. It got so plain, I finally had to stop and consider it. But as so often was the case, my wonderful reasoning faculties were working at their best to carry the day. I had quite a struggle. The voice could not be silenced and I had to turn around and go back and get the grip.

I went to where the family had last lived, but found they had moved and the person living there could not tell me their new address. I was feeling quite foolish as now I faced packing the grip a total of six miles by the time I returned to town. I headed back at a pretty good speed and the voice said, "No, go on out to Mrs. M---'s."

I argued with the voice, "I can't go out there if I don't know where she lives." I never broke my stride heading back for town to catch that outgoing train.

155

"Go back, go back, go back!" It kept ringing in my ears until I suddenly stopped as though a man had grabbed me. The voice said, "Will you or will you not go back?"

I was dumbfounded, but I was listening. What could it all mean? So I turned back and went to the neighboring house and asked if they knew where Mrs. M--- had moved. They gave me directions and I headed there. Upon arriving, I found the woman sitting under a tree and as soon as she saw me, she exclaimed, "Oh, I knew you would come! I knew you would come!"

"How did you know?" I asked.

"I heard from headquarters," she said, pointing upward. "I have been suffering from a running sore on my leg. Oh, how I have suffered day and night trying to do the work here for my husband and two boys on this farm. I heard you were at the camp, so I just began praying the Lord would send you here. Yesterday I saw you coming, so I rested on the matter. But, really, I did look for you earlier than this," she chided.

She had not known, of course, what a time I had in obeying God. I saw at once what it all meant and throwing off my coat, I went into the kitchen to help out. I began by wrestling with the pots and kettles. That night I prayed for her and she fell asleep while I was praying. Her husband whispered in surprise, "She is asleep—this is the first time I have known her to sleep without drugs in a long time."

The next morning I got up to get breakfast and prepared to do a large washing. Upon checking, I found she had been suffering severely since 3:00 a.m. that morning, though she did not completely wake up until I entered her room. "Please, Brother Bevington, I am in such misery! Please pray for me," she pleaded.

I started to pray and in ten minutes she was asleep again. I washed clothes until dinner time and got together a meal for the three men. Then I went in to see what she wanted for dinner and found her suffering again. This kept up for over a week. I could get victory for her every time I prayed, but the pains insisted on coming back again and again.

I got tired of that and went after the case roughshod. I bore down in prayer until I finally struck fire and she was completely delivered. The second morning after the breakthrough, she said, "I have two daughters I have not seen for several years, Brother Bevington. Would you stay here for three weeks and do the work and let me go see them?"

That surprised me, but after praying, I knew I was to remain. This Scripture came to me, "In honor preferring one another." So she packed up and went and had a good three-weeks' visit. She came back a different woman, having never felt the soreness of her leg. To Jesus be all the glory!

The multiplication of man's machinery means the diminishing of God's power proportionately. In many places so much of man's ingenuity has been introduced into the workshop of God's house, there isn't enough power to run it. God will not hitch His power onto the bungling, weighty, clumsy machinery of man's methods and wisdom. It is prayer that tops the reservoir of power. All that is needed is the right kind of prayer.

> It may not be my way,
> it may not be thy way;
> But yet in His own way
> The Lord will provide.

This Gospel of healing is one of good tidings and it is for all people. All hell is turned against the Bible doctrine

157

of Divine healing, so it behooves us to be wide awake—to be at our best—if we expect to get our prayers through.

I was holding a meeting at R--- and a young lady of beautiful character attended all the services she was able to, being severely hindered by a form of epilepsy. When I was informed why she could not come regularly, I went to her home and prayed the prayer of faith for her. She never missed another service while I was there. I have heard her testify several times to her healing at the Cincinnati camp. I magnify Jesus as it was He who did it.

A brother at that same place came to me saying he had suffered for years from neuralgia and asked "If Jesus could heal those two, why can't He heal me?"

I assured him, "He will, if you will allow Him to."

"I will."

So I anointed him and in twenty minutes he said the pain was gone. He has told me since that it never came back. Oh, glory to Jesus! Will we ever learn to trust Him? Stop right now. Ask yourself that question over again. Meditate thereon.

A sister in Ohio where we were holding a meeting was sadly afflicted. She had been forced to take to her bed for the better part of eight years. She had quite a family of children to look after and her lot was indeed difficult. I went to her home and anointed her, though it seemed quite dark and much of an uphill pull.

I had many misgivings and it took me some time to get where I would not allow my eyes to rest on the condition or the atmosphere surrounding us. I finally had to get up and abruptly leave her without any excuse being given. I went to the barn and prayed, laying there several hours. I was then impressed to go back and anoint her again. In about forty minutes she raised her hand and said quietly, "It is done—I am a healed woman."

Then she got up, dressed herself, and got together a fine dinner. That settled all her trouble. So, let's shout amen and see the devil run, for he can't stand Heaven-sent amens.

While at Ironton, I went out to hold a meeting in the country. As I often had done before, I canvassed the homes, giving out tracts and telling the children about an extra Sunday school we were to have. I prayed where I was permitted to.

I went in one house with several children, the eldest being about ten. The house really looked as though it needed a mother's care. I told the children about the meeting at the schoolhouse and the Sunday school.

Soon the mother came downstairs with her head all bandaged up. She had been suffering from acute neuralgia for several days and had been unable to do anything. She told me, "I heard you say something about a Sunday school and children's meeting. Several of my children here need such training, so I felt I had to get up and come down to see what you were talking about."

I said, "So you have neuralgia. Are you a saved woman?"

"Yes, sir."

"Don't you believe Jesus can heal you?"

"I know He can if I have the faith for it."

"Let's all get down and get hold of Jesus," I suggested.

We got still and in forty minutes I saw rags go flying. She tore every strip of cloth off and cried out, "There is not a pain in my body." Then she jumped up and began walking the floor, praising God while tears of joy and gratitude just rolled down her cheeks. She hugged all the

159

children and I had a good time seeing her appreciate what Jesus had done.

"Brother, you go into the other room," she turned to me and said, "and I will clean up and get you some dinner."

As it was still morning, I said, "I will go out for awhile and give out more tracts. Then I will come back."

When I returned, she had the house nicely cleaned up and, oh, how different she looked than when she came down those stairs! We had a fine dinner and then I taught the three girls a new song. Let me say right here that the youngest of those three girls is out preaching holiness now. She went to God's Bible School. Celia Bradshaw is her name and she is a dear, precious girl.

They had a Sunday school up at the school with anywhere from twelve to sixteen youngsters attending. There were hardly ever the same ones two Sundays in succession. I set out and began to meet with several children at a time and taught them new songs. By the next Sunday there were over one hundred and fifty children at the schoolhouse.

The superintendent did not know what to do with them all, as he had no other teachers. So we just divided the youngsters into two classes—I took those under the age of twelve and he took the rest. Everything was just fine. This is a testimony of what a little personal work can do.

Before I left there, that mother got sanctified, as also did her mother. Her mother was delivered of a serious goiter. Both of them have gone through fires innumerable, yet they have been and are still are completely true to Jesus and their sanctification. All glory be to Jesus!

I believe that all of this came as a result of that mother's healing. So the important message here is that blessings don't stop at healing, but go on and spread out. That is why I still believe in and always preach healing.

While holding a meeting in Ohio, I was told why a certain sister did not attend the meetings. She had been in bed several months and her daughter was doing all the work—they were farmers. I am not much in favor of going to pray for the sick, that is to pray for their healing, except when asked to come. Yet I felt impressed to go to see her.

So I went one afternoon and saw her condition. I felt there was a case on hand here, as she had never seen anyone healed or heard of anyone being healed. She found it comforting to just take her four kinds of medicine.

But I knew Jesus sent me there and my God was charitable, so I did not give up the case. I prayed there in the room without kneeling and then I felt I must go somewhere and fight the thing to a finish. I knew it would take some time to get her where God could talk to her. There was no one to take my place at our service that night and the meeting had arrived at a point where I considered it unwise to be absent. Being somewhat confused, I went in and asked her for a private room.

I was shown one where I promptly fell on my face. In about twenty minutes, I felt impressed I must go to the woods. I argued with the impression. What would I do about my meeting? But it was still go to the woods. Since I had learned not to question God's ability, I said, "All right."

I got up, though a little confused, as I had nothing definite as to the night's meeting. I started downstairs, however, determined to obey God whether I was able to understand or not. I went through the hall and out onto

161

the porch, leaving all with God. Glory enveloped me and I just had to stop and weep as I looked up to praise Him, for this was an evidence of approval of my obedience.

I looked down the road and there came a dear brother whom I had not seen or heard of for over a year. He was walking as fast as he could. He was a Holy Ghost evangelist.

I threw up my hat and shouted "Glory!" Then I called out, "Dear brother, where in the world are you going?"

He stopped, stared at me and burst out laughing. "Now it is all clear why God has been talking so strange to me for the last twelve hours. I had planned to be elsewhere at this time, but about ten hours ago God began to try to tell me something. I could scarcely grasp it for it was breaking into my plans. Now I am sure God wants me to preach in your place."

I just threw my arms around him and we both wept for joy to see how God so minutely carried out His plans in ways foreign to our human understanding. The brother said, "I closed my meeting twenty-one miles from here day before yesterday. I intended to open another meeting tonight, but yesterday God began talking to me about going elsewhere. Then He made me walk all night. I did not know where I was going, yet I felt really sure I was in Divine order.

"So here I am. I had been led to a certain text for tonight, though I could not see where it was to be delivered since I was in an entirely new area. I told God that I would preach from that text, but I did want to know why I was being brought here. Now I know."

God did not tell him about that farm or that I was there, but he had obeyed and come at just the right time to fill my place. This enabled me to take up the other case which seemed to be demanding speed.

He went on, "I stopped at a friend's yesterday afternoon and had something to eat. Then I went out to their barn. This text was crowding on me and it was not at all appropriate for an opening service or the place I had in mind." While he was in the barn, he cried out to God, "Where are you sending me?"

The only answer he could get was, "What is that to thee, follow thou Me." So he went out and started down the road, like Abraham, not knowing whither he was going. You see, that was none of his business.

"So here I am, Brother Bevington. Are you willing for me to preach tonight?" I had a hearty laugh as I told him of the struggle I had been going through for the last ten hours. Oh, how wonderful it is to see how God will work when we give Him a chance. Jesus had quite a time in getting me to let go of the meeting, as well as getting the brother to come and take it. What trouble we would save our blessed Lord if we would just relinquish our hold and let God—yes, let God! Here God had opened the way that we both could meet on the plane of obedience. He knew the puzzling features would all be obliterated if we would get out of His way.

The sick woman's husband was a close observer of all the rules of their church, but had no use for holiness preachers. That was why she had not sent for me and why I had to go there much against my rule. With much to be overcome, I was going to the woods and the evangelist was going to the meeting. I cautioned him, "Brother, be sure and obey God. Don't you leave here until you have unmistakable orders to do so. I may be in the woods a week or I may leave there in the morning."

I had no opportunity of notifying anyone of the change or the reasons for it. I only knew God seemed very anxious that I should get to the woods and leave the whole thing in His hands. That is hard for us to do as we seem to feel we have such wonderful executive and judicial properties in us. Sometimes God has a real time getting a chance to display any of His power when we're involved.

I never saw the brother again until camp meeting at Cincinnati. He preached and then walked thirteen miles to the rail station as no one there was interested enough in holiness to invite him home with them.

I was somewhat used to that. Many times I had lived in the woods for days because no one invited me home with them. But when I knew God sent me there, I would go to the woods or to the haymow and live on acorns or sassafras bark until God could get someone saved. Now back in the woods again, I got under a tree and wrestled all night. Finally, early the next morning I saw her sitting up in bed and clapping her hands. I jumped up and ran all the way to the house, for I wanted to get there before she got through. As I neared the barn, I heard the daughter calling from the back door of the house, "Papa, come here quick. Oh, hurry, hurry up!"

He ran out of the barn just ahead of me, but I passed him and ran around to the front door. I found the wife out of bed, jumping and clapping her hands and shouting, "God has healed me! God has healed me!"

She saw her husband and ran to him, crying, "Oh, dear husband, Jesus healed me! Now won't you love this holiness preacher for staying with us until I was healed? I saw Jesus come into my room to the foot of my bed just as the clock struck 5:00 a.m. He said, 'I have come to heal you.' And oh, husband, such a wonderful sight! I never saw such a face—so sweet, so loving, so tender, so sympathetic. Husband, I wish you could have seen Him as I saw Him. Before leaving, He touched my body and I felt

His power go through me like electricity." As the tears of joy fell in great drops, she continued to say, "I am healed, I am healed!"

She did not know where I was, but had supposed I had come home from the meeting and was still upstairs in bed. I have seen her twice at the Cincinnati camp and she had a good testimony. She never took another drop of medicine, at least for nine years that I know of—since then I lost track of her.

All we need is to obey God. I was well aware that God had sent me there to conduct that meeting. What I could not understand was why He wanted to interfere (as we are too apt to say) with His own plans by sending me to the woods with another taking my place. The essential thing is to get where we will know the voice of God and obey Him whether it conflicts with the arranged program or not. But you can see that though He broke into the original plans as I understood them, the work was not stopped or hindered. It resulted in a good revival where some twenty actually prayed through and several were healed.

On the night of the day she was healed, this woman came to the meeting and fell at the altar for sanctification. Her husband fell at the same despised holiness mourners' bench for salvation. Suddenly his meeting house religion didn't seem to harmonize with what he had just seen and realized. He had held every office and position in his church except pastor and janitor, but he knew reality when he saw it.

It took him four days to pray through. We knelt right behind him and held him four-square to the Bible so he could not back out without crawling over us. He said several times in his testimony, "I would have backed out many times had it not been that Bevington was right on

165

my heels. I could not get up without making a display. I do thank God that Bevington had the grit to stick to my back, shaking me over hell until I made a complete surrender. I now have something that enables me to know I am saved." Later he got sanctified. Their daughter, a most vain girl, had to succumb to the prayers of us three as we turned all the forces of heaven on her until she finally yielded, too.

All this came about because I was willing to be a laughing-stock for the whole family which resulted in the woman's healing. I tell you it sets my soul on fire as I write about these wonderful manifestations of God's power.

I had held another meeting in Ohio where several got saved and two years later someone sent me money to come back. As the meeting was progressing, I kept missing one sister who had been such a power after she got saved in that earlier meeting. I kept wondering why I did not see her. "They must have moved away," I thought.

I did not ask anyone about her for several days. It seemed I would think of asking only when I was absent from those who would know. Finally, when I was praying in the home where I was lodging, this woman came to my mind. I got right up and went into the kitchen. "What has become of Sister D---? Why doesn't she come to church? Has she backslidden?"

"Why, Brother Bevington, haven't you heard about her?"

"I guess not, so tell me."

"She scalded her foot and has been laid up in bed for nine months. They got in a doctor for her. Three or four of us went and reminded her of what you had preached on Divine healing, but she clung to the doctor anyway. We wanted her to write to you, but she just held onto that doctor. She is in the hospital now. They have spent seven hundred dollars and the doctors are now talking of amputating her leg above the knee. She has suffered terribly."

Note all I have told you, as I want to show you the difference in doctoring down here (going down to Egypt) and in doctoring with my Doctor. This was a woman who knew that God healed, as her niece had been instantly healed the first time I was in the neighborhood. This woman had greatly rejoiced over that healing, but now she said, "Well, this a different case, a different cause."

How Satan loves to hoodwink God's children by getting their eyes on conditions instead of on Jesus. Do you think Jesus' power is confined to surroundings? Is Jesus confined to certain conditions? I want to record right here for the glory of God that for the last thirty-two years, I have not seen one peculiar case. I do not look for them nor allow myself to look at the peculiarity of any surroundings. I just see Jesus and Him alone. He says, "I am the God that healeth thee."

I want to show you the difference between trusting God and refusing to trust Him. This woman suffered for sixteen months and then had her leg amputated above the knee, costing them nearly a thousand dollars. Now here is the other side.

When I was keeping house about two squares from where I am now typing this in Ashland, I was having some boiled potatoes for dinner. I had a large quantity of water on them to prevent scorching the kettle. As I was pouring out the boiling water, the lid slipped off. Over a quart of boiling water went into my shoe. I had been practicing economy and had on shoes that were good ventilators. These shoes were crisscrossed with openings that allowed the boiling water full access to my entire foot.

It was very painful. I set the kettle down, laid my hand on the steaming shoe, and said, "Now, dear Jesus, I was thoughtless, no doubt. But Thou knowest I did not intend to be." At once Satan reminded me of that sister in the country who had spent nearly a thousand dollars and still lost half her leg. "I have no money and wouldn't go down to Egypt if I did. I can't afford to be laid up sixteen months and then lose my leg." All this time my foot was throbbing terribly and the pains had shot up to the knee.

Of course Satan was there to give vent to his sympathy for me in that sad event. He kept urging, "Get that shoe off quickly or it will burn down to the bone. The shoe and sock are retaining the heat!"

Tears were falling fast because of the intense pain, but I was waiting on God. I was nearer Him than to Egypt. Of course there was logic in Satan's suggestions, but I ignored them as I gave Jesus a chance at the foot. When I had gotten still and fully given the case over to Jesus—committed all to Him—I laid my hand again on the steaming shoe. Sickening pains shot up to my knee, but I said, "Now Jesus, as I take off this shoe, please do not allow any of the skin to come off." And I took off the shoe.

Satan continued his attack, "You have been so slow that it has burned clear to the bone. That is why those pains are flashing up to your knee."

I looked at the sock, laid my hand on it and said, "Jesus, Thou art my Healer and have been for years. This is quite serious and Satan is on hand to remind me that the sister had only a pint of water go onto her shoe. Her shoe was not full of holes, either. Lord, as I pull off this sock, please allow the skin to remain at present." I was to have a street meeting that night and had three-fourths of a mile to walk over cobblestones.

I closed my eyes as I began pulling off the sock. It came off with much pain and before opening my eyes again, I said, "Oh, God, thou art my Healer! Please stop this awful pain." I was still holding my hand on the foot with my eyes closed. I whispered, "Yes, Lord; yes, Lord; yes, Lord." As the last "Lord" fell from my lips, the pain stopped. I still had my eyes closed and I just sat there weeping for joy. I raised my right hand and went to praising God for being my Healer.

Opening my eyes, I found not a particle of skin had come off. The foot looked very red and disfigured, but there was no pain. Satan said, "You better send word to Brother Stapleton to be sure and be there as you can't walk that distance tonight. You won't dare to put your shoes on this week. Give it a chance so that you will be ready for Sunday school next Sunday." (This was Tuesday.)

He continued, "It will be very unwise for you to attempt to put a shoe on and go there and stand on that damp ground. You will catch cold and have a long, serious, painful time." All this was quite logical, of course. I am confident that if I had listened to that plea and believed it to be coming from God, I would have been as bad off as the sister.

Then Satan tried to get me to wrap the foot up with soft cloths around it. I refused all his suggestions, put on a dry sock and put on my shoe. After dinner I went to the street meeting and stood on the damp ground. We had a blessed time—hands went up for prayer and that night was the starting point for two precious souls to find Jesus. Oh, how God did bless my soul as I testified to what Jesus had done!

I went to prayer meeting in our church the next night and testified to my healing there. Oh, the hearty amens

169

that rolled up to Heaven! Reverend John Fleming, the pastor, threw his arms around me and wept for joy. I could feel he heartily approved of all I had said. Sister Walker had quite a spell and a number of others were greatly blessed. All said that it was a glorious meeting.

So that was the end of the scalded foot. I saved a thousand dollars, sixteen months of suffering and my leg. Can you see the difference in the two processes or choices of doctors? Which would you prefer? I will hold to my family Doctor, Jesus, thank you. Hallelujah to Jesus!

I never missed a service or experienced any pain or inconvenience. That old skin did shrivel up terribly and came off, but the skin underneath was clean and new. I never pulled any of the old off, either, just let that be for my Doctor to do. So many times there would be loose skin and Satan would say, "Now pull that off. It will irritate the foot and prevent the new from coming on smooth." But I would not do any such thing.

I did not look at any of the symptoms. I had told Jesus back there in the kitchen, with the potatoes lying on the floor and pains shooting up to my knee, that I would turn the case entirely over to Him. So I dared not interfere or even suggest such a thing. Amen and amen!

I am reminded of something relative to symptoms that I feel should be recorded right here. When I first took healing, I was taught that in order to exercise faith and get direct results, I must deny any symptoms. I tried that, but I would get confused. One time when I had a severe toothache, I was told, "Well, just deny it." I did, but the fact was I knew very well I had that toothache.

Well, there was only one way to find out, so I dropped on my face and said, "Now, Lord, these people here tell me to deny I have the toothache. What am I to do? There must be some better way out of this than that."

I lay there over an hour waiting on God. The answer came and this is it: "You need not deny the symptoms, but you can deny their right on your body."

I saw at once where I had been wrongly instructed. So I jumped up and said, "Yes, the symptoms are there, but according to the Word, they don't belong to me. This toothache does not belong to me. I will not have it. I belong to Jesus. This body, this head and every tooth in it belongs to God. It is His property for He says in His Word, 'Ye are not your own, for ye are bought with a price; therefore glorify God in your body, and in your spirit, which are God's.' "

So I took that stand and in twenty minutes the toothache was gone. I have followed that plan up ever since and always come off the conqueror. Hallelujah!

I will give you one other instance directly on this line. Although I was healed of rheumatism at Hamilton, that does not mean it was impossible to ever have another attack of it. I had been holding meetings under a large tree in the woods down below Portsmouth, Ohio. Despite much rain, the people came out. Several nights someone would hold an umbrella over me while I preached and someone was at the altar every night.

The workers would put in dry straw each night, yet by the time of the altar service it would be damp. We would be on our knees on the wet ground for hours until our clothing would be soaked. My legs were cold and damp each night. I might have exercised more zeal than knowledge, but be that as it may, I got a bad case of rheumatism.

That was several years after the healing at Hamilton. Satan was right on hand with his logic regarding my indifference to God's laws in getting myself so wet. I had

171

quite a time with the pain all night and slept very little. Satan nearly swamped me on the grounds that I certainly could not expect Jesus to heal me after I had deliberately violated what I knew to avoid.

In the morning I was suffering quite a bit and had a difficult time getting out of bed. I ate nothing until late afternoon. I prayed and wrestled as best I could and finally came to the place where I saw that if I was to preach that night, there would have to be something done—and that right away, too.

I began to plead the promises, but made slow progress at that. I said to myself, "I don't have only the symptoms, but the real thing is here. I can't deny that." Just then I caught an inspiration and said, "Mr. Devil, this rheumatism doesn't belong to me. I will not have it!"

Well, I heard him chuckle plainly and say, "Ha! You can't help yourself this time."

"You are a liar, Satan, I can be helped." I got hold of two chairs and pulled myself to my feet.

Again Satan laughed, saying, "You really look like a cripple."

"I will do it," I promised and started moving with the two chairs to lean on. I made slow progress, taking nearly an hour and forty minutes to go from one corner to the other. But, thank God, I made it.

"Now, dear Lord, I believe you inspired me to make that assertion. You will help me just now to put this foot in the corner and then victory is assured." For the first time I felt strong enough to raise my foot without the aid of my hands and I planted that foot in the corner so that the toe of my shoe struck the corner. The moment it did, the pain was all gone and God gave me added strength.

Oh, how the glory did fall as I praised God while the tears flowed freely! I had to contend earnestly for every inch across that room, but I did so though it took an hour and forty minutes. That was about the best hundred minutes I ever put in since I was sanctified! I have never had even a symptom of the rheumatism since. So I repeat, it pays to go through with Jesus and trust Him. Where there is no opposition, there is no advance made.

Now I feel impressed to give this instance of prayer answered and the results of holding on to God. I was holding another country meeting in Ohio. That seemed to be my field of operation among those who did not have big meetings very often. The presiding elder came and preached on Sunday and also preached on Monday night. He gave a good message against the saloons, showing that the majority of fallen girls and wayward boys came through them. It was a heavy blow on the saloons, but of course could not be too heavy.

When he had finished this remarkable message, he said, "Brother Bevington, did I hit them too hard?"

"Oh," I said, "I suppose not."

Well, that answer and the way I said it shocked him. He had thought I was going to pat him on the back. He gave me a surprised and somewhat curious look which made it necessary for me to explain myself. So I said, "You and your people put that man in the saloon and gave him license and authority to sell that hellish stuff. You and your people told the government to let him sell the stuff to make lawless men and women. Then you demanded the government protect him in his nefarious business."

Well, he disagreed with me. But I held that if the professors, even of the M.E. Church proper, would vote prohibition, it would throw out the saloons. I said, "The

173

saloon keeper was put in there by you people. He pays his rights at your approval."

This presiding elder didn't like that very well, but did not allow it to interfere with his mission. He and I were going to the same place for lodging that night about a mile from the schoolhouse where he felt, I supposed, he had just given a fatal blow to the saloons. The next morning he said, "I understand that you put in quite an unusual amount of time in prayer, often going to the woods and spending hours in prayer out there. I was told that you generally remain until God answers. I heartily approve of that and wish I had the time to put in at that kind of work.

"I would like to get you interested in a puzzling case that has baffled all efforts in trailing the matter out. There is a family over where I came from yesterday, a most precious family. They are highly cultured, all very refined, studious, careful, prayerful and quite well off. Yet they are the most humble people I ever met.

"They have one child, a seventeen-year-old daughter of estimable character and loved by all. A year ago she gave birth to a baby girl, but she still is unmarried. This has been a terrible blow on the family, nearly crushing their lives out. They have not been to the church for sixteen months. They will not be persuaded to come, as the calamity seems to be more than they can face.

"This girl is still there caring for the baby. The great trouble is no one can see her and very few can get to see the mother. They keep secluded. The father is trying to sell so they can get away from the scene they believe has brought them down to the lowest plane. People are doing all they can to prevent his selling. Now that I have given you the facts in the case and, as you have been accustomed to ferreting out such cases through prayer by the way of the throne, I came over here purposely to get you to trail it out." Mark in your memory how he used the word trail.

He continued, "Get on the trail, Brother Bevington, and the pastor and his board and I will stand by you. We will be right at your back. You just stick to the trail and don't give it up until you have uncovered the matter."

The whole thing is founded on that word trail. So, as a trail finder and sticker, I will proceed. First, I will take you back about a year to where I was holding a meeting near Chillicothe, Ohio. The man I was staying with had several fox hounds he valued highly. One was my particular favorite—a hound that was very intelligent.

One night I heard a terrible yelping and blow after blow laid on that dog until I could stand it no more. I went to the window and called out, "Who is pounding that dog that way?" When the answer came, I recognized it as from the brother with whom I was staying. "Brother," I called down, "why in the world are you pounding on the poor dog?"

"He is my main fox dog and I get money from others in training their dogs by this one. I was to get five dollars tonight, but this dog got off on a rabbit's track and nothing was done."

"Does he know the difference?"

"Most assuredly he does. That is why I am whipping him so."

"Will it do him any good?" I asked.

"Yes, sir, it will be a long time before he will take up another rabbit's trail." That poor dog got a terrible whipping for getting off on the wrong trail. That elder had told me to be sure and stick to the trail. You see, if I failed to stick to it, I might get what the dog got. Keep these things in mind, for they play an important part in the coming events.

175

Now back to the elder's trail. When I closed my meeting over there, I went to the woods as that is my college. When I got comfortably quartered in a hollow log, I said, "Now Lord, dost Thou want me to take up this trail? You know the father of that baby and all about it. Is the case demanding a ferreting out? What wilt Thou have me do about it?"

I lay there several hours before I could get much light, yet I dared not crawl out of my log domain. "Wouldst Thou be getting any glory out of it if I do?" I asked several times.

The trouble was I had several places awaiting my appearance for a meeting, though no definite dates were actually set. I avoided setting times for a meeting to begin or close. That was always left entirely for the Father to attend to. Many have said, "Brother, where are you going when you get through here?"

I have only been able to say truthfully, "I don't know."

It took me several hours to dispose of these prospective places as some of them would be liberal in their offerings. My pocketbook had been lain on so much it had gotten pretty well flattened out—all of which would be used of Satan to keep me from getting to the point of the issue. After nineteen hours on my face, I was clearly impressed to take up the case.

Well, it was somewhat difficult to get on the trail. To get started right and know that I was right took me fifty-four hours of getting still and small enough that God could handle me. So many of us are so important, so big, so great, so clumsy and so awkward, it takes God quite a while to get us on the wheel so He can trim us up to fit through some of the small places. He has to grind off a lot of this self-importance as He can't use that very well in developing the cases, whatever they may be.

I finally got to the place where He could actually pick me up and set me over there on the trail. I felt disappointed with His placement for I could neither discover any track or smell the presence of one. But having received many thrashings for setting up my own ideas, I just got down until I found the scent and started making good headway.

Going back to what the preacher and the official board had said, "Be sure and stick to that trail," I will now draw on my imagination. This is a right I have always reserved for demonstrating things. In this instance, it will help you in getting the case clearly set up in your mind.

I had to assume these four men had meant what they said and they were on hand to do all they could. Here comes the imaginative help. They had said, "We will be at your back." So, here I am on the trail and now you imagine they are following me at the rear. The trail goes through some pretty dark places where it is somewhat difficult to trace out, so the men occasionally call out, "Bevington, are you still on the trail?"

I answer back, "Yes, still on the trail, making headway, though slow."

"Stick to it, as we are at your back. We want this thing ferreted out."

I will not detail everything that I faced during the next nine days, but I stuck to it day and night without anything to eat. I only had two drinks of water during that period. I would get so close at times that I dared not leave the trail even to get a drink. Occasionally these words rang in my head, "Brother Bevington, are you still on the trail?" Of course I assured them I was.

On the ninth day, early in the morning, I saw a large church. Remember, I was on the trail of the father of that babe. There was a large church with a deep porch in front

177

and steps going up onto the porch from each end—one for the ladies and the other for the gentlemen.

I saw a door at each side of the church on the end and a space in between these two doors, perhaps two feet wide and three feet long. There was a marble slab in this space, with the name of the church in large letters and the date it was built. I saw all of this with my eyes closed, while I lay some fourteen miles from the place. There is where the trail led me.

I was suddenly hungry for the first time during the nine days and nights. I was very weak and quite exhausted and had to rub circulation into my limbs in a sitting posture before I could stand on my feet or get the use of my faculties. But I finally succeeded in getting down to the house where I had been staying. They did not know where I had been.

I gave the lady a full description of the building I had seen while praying and then asked "Sister, is there such a church?"

"Why, yes, that is our charge here—a nice large church with a strong congregation. Have you been over there?"

"Well, I have seen it."

"Oh," she replied, "I was wondering where you were since you had left your grip here. Yes, we often go over there as it is only about fourteen miles over good roads. There are some fine people over there, but..." and then she stopped, bit her lip and changed the conversation. I knew what was on her mind, she wanted to ask when I had been there.

So I answered, "I just came from there."

That puzzled her as it was very early in the morning. I told her what the elder and the official board said and that I had trailed the thing to that church. I saw at once that this word was a blow to her idea of me. If she had ever had any spark of confidence in me, it was all knocked out then and there. What I had told her was the height of folly.

Now I want to go back to that hollow log where I saw, in addition to the church, a path from the back of the church going down a slope to a fence. Beyond the fence was a grove with a large spring in the midst of it. I told her what else I had seen while in that log and she replied, "Yes," she said, "that is all there." Remember I had never been nearer than fourteen miles of the church. Then I told her of that wonderful sermon the elder preached against the saloon and how it ought to be exposed, as all degeneracy started in the saloon. She looked at me sternly, "Brother Bevington, do you really believe that all this disgrace was wrought through that church? No one had ever been able to glean any information relative to where or by whom it was done."

"Yes, ma'am. It was through a box social, as the Lord has shown me."

"Oh, I can't believe it."

"Well, I can't help that," I said truthfully.

"What is to be done about it? They will never give consent to such a report as that going out against that grand old church. You will have to let it drop and say no more about it. In fact, you had better get out of here before it gets noised around."

I said, "No, I can't let it drop as the four cautioned me to stick to the trail."

"The pastor from that church is down here visiting a member who recently moved. Do you think it best to see him before you go away? If so, I will have the boy go after him in our buggy."

"Yes, I wish you would."

179

When the pastor arrived, he threw his hands up in horror at my report. He shook his head defiantly as he said, "I will not accept that at all."

"Well, sir, you have to accept it whether you want to or not," I told him.

He rose and said, "Mister (he said this sarcastically, rather than addressing me as a brother), you have seen this church or gotten all this from someone. Now you want to bring this awful calamity down upon its pure, unstained portals. Sir, you shall not do any such thing. More than that, I want you to get out of here. If you haven't any money, I will take you to the train and loan you money until you see fit to repay it. If you don't, that will be all right, too."

I decided it was time to recall a few things for him. "Do you remember what you and the other three said—that you all would stand by me and that I should stick to the trail? Do you remember that?"

He didn't reply to my question, but stormed off to drive forty-four miles for the elder, muttering, "Going to have that crank put where he won't be bringing such disgraces in the churches!" I was branded as a genuine church splitter.

The next day they all came—the pastor, elder and official board. Except for the elder, they were all denouncing me. He didn't seem to have much to say and I felt he was thinking it possible, though hardly probable.

They gave me twenty-four hours to get out of that country. Well, I was accustomed to threats—threats of rotten eggs, clubs, tar and feathers and rail, dungeons, insane asylums, pits, jails and even the whipping post. So I was not badly frightened and made no move toward packing up and getting out as they ordered.

"Aren't you going to get ready to leave?" they asked.

180

"I will not be too hasty about this," I said. "I will have to wait on the Lord to get orders."

The pastor rose and said, "We have just given you your orders."

"I will have to wait on the Lord," I insisted. "When He says, 'Go', I will go and not before."

The three said, "It will never do to have such reports go out relative to this grand old landmark."

For the first time, the elder spoke up, "Brother Bevington, it may be possible this is all true. Suppose we admit it is true—would it not be better to drop it? We will pay your way to your next place."

"You told me to stick to the trail. If I should do as you say, then there will always be questions, with me at least. 'What did you do? Did you stick to the trail?' It would necessitate my lying to say I lost the trail. The evil deed was done in that grove at one of your box socials."

Then I turned directly to the elder and said, "Do you remember the sermon you preached against saloons?"

"Yes."

I said very carefully, "You said that every crime that was started in the saloon ought to be published and the saloon keepers made to face it—exposing them as the cause. Now, when a girl loses her virtue in and through a church, is the crime or disgrace lessened any because it was done through the church?"

He admitted the crime stood as horrible in one case as in the other, but insisted, "It must not be exposed here." The other men stood silent.

"Oh, Consistency, thou art a jewel!" I quoted. Then I said firmly, "I cannot keep still on this matter. It is now reported that I lay up in the woods nine days relative to this."

181

"Well, you can't prove it as she will not allow anyone to see her," the three said.

At that I left them, went to the woods and got into my previous quarters to talk with my Master. "Lord, You have permitted me to go this far. Here I am to get permission to see that girl and get the whole truth from her." I realized that was quite a proposition, for she had not allowed anyone to see her.

It took me seventy-two hours to get the buzzards off and then get them entirely out of the way so I could get still. Troublesome buzzards were not only confined to the prophetic days, but seem to be quite numerous these days as well, swooping down upon us to devour the offerings of revelations.

After fighting those long hours and keeping all hell off, I got still and saw myself approaching a house from the back—going down a hill, crossing a creek and going up a bank to a garden fence. Then I climbed over the fence, went through the garden gate and up on the back porch. I knocked at the door and when it opened, there was the mother of the babe. She invited me inside. This was all seen as I lay on my face in the woods.

I got up and ran right into the path that led through all that I just described. I came to the brow of the hill, saw the house, the path to the creek and the garden. I just stopped, got behind a tree and poured out my heart in gratitude to my blessed Leader. I praised Him that He had granted me the privilege of outwitting all men's efforts. I then counted it all done and went just as stated.

The mother of the babe opened the door, invited me in and gave me a chair there in the kitchen. As I was a stranger, she was embarrassed and called her mother. The mother came in and was very surprised to see me there with her daughter, but she gave me a hearty hand shake.

Then they both broke out in tears and wept perhaps thirty minutes. Nothing but deep sobs could be heard—not a word was uttered. I wept too, as I could read between the sobs what it all meant to their precious hearts.

While we were there wrapped in silence, getting down to where the real life was, the father came in. He took in the whole situation at once and threw his arms around his daughter. There was another pathetic scene. Soon he released his hold and clasped my hand. His tears were flowing and his frame trembling until my whole body was influenced. We wept as if our hearts would break.

I felt I had never been under such a holy, pure influence as that which pervaded that kitchen! It seemed the great weight which had been crushing them was being applied to me. I don't remember ever having such intense heartthrobs of sorrow as then.

I wanted to go to the barn, but seemed to be held by an unseen power. Oh, reader, the blessed Holy Ghost was there in the midst of that shame. It was so beautiful! I felt that underneath were His everlasting arms—so real were those arms beneath all four of us that I just burst out between the sobs, "Oh, dear beloved, God is here. His arms are beneath us!"

At that the father released his hold of my hand, reeled back and fell into his dear wife's arms. They both fell on the sofa and gave vent to heart bursts which I will never forget. Oh, reader I can scarcely type these lines as tears flow freely while I go back over that scene.

I cried out, "Dear beloved, His arms are beneath us now, yes now. We are emerging from the awful darkness that has hung like a death pall these seventeen months."

I began to praise God and the mother of the girl rose and clasped my hand, weeping for joy, as she waved her right hand above her gray hairs. I never saw gray hairs

183

look so beautiful as she stood before me, her face radiant with the glow of heaven. She said, "I know that you are a man of God. You are the only one who has been in this home for seventeen months."

Then the father said, "All sit down, please," and we did. The beautiful mother of the babe rose, not beautiful in outward appearance as she was not possessed with what the world calls a beautiful face, but I was getting glimpses of her inner being. And there, so meek and lovely, she told the whole thing from beginning to end.

At the time of this box social, the father was very busy in the wheat field and could not go. Neither could the mother, but seven nice girls came and importuned the parents to let the girl go. They said, "We all will go together, remain together and come home together. We have money to treat ourselves."

So the father and mother consented and the girls went. But as soft drinks and the cakes with a wing in them began to be auctioned off, excitement rose pretty high. Girls were put up for auction at twenty cents a vote for the prettiest girl. Soon everyone was coupled off and parting from the crowd, this girl going along with the proceedings.

After they had eaten, her companion suggested they take a stroll down to the spring and get a drink. She did not like that very well, but finally consented as he said they would return in a few minutes. When they came to the spring, the young man said, "There hasn't been any school here for some time and the water may not be just right. I pass here daily and I like to get a drink, but the doctor told me I should use a preventative. He gave me a powder to purify the water, so I'll put it in now."

He gave her the first drink and she said that was the last that she knew until the next morning when she woke up in her own bed. She had thought it very kind of him to be prepared against impure water. All the time she was telling this, she was in tears and had her head bowed. Finally she looked up and said, "I don't know how this all came about! I have not been able to allow myself to see even my dearest friend. Oooh, " she moaned, placing her hands over her ears, "is this a dream—what have I done?"

She continued, "I have told you all—all that I have ever told even to my dear parents who stood so nobly by me in this fall." At that she fell into her mother's arms. Oh, reader, such a scene. I wish I were able to picture it! She said, "I just don't understand!"

The father rose and clasped her in his arms, "Daughter, this is no mystery. God has answered your mother's and my prayers by sending this man of God here to get at this." Then they asked me how it was that I had come. I related all that had been told me and how I had been in the woods nine days, then again for more than seventy hours. I told them how I had seen the path and followed it to the kitchen. They all marveled at the greatness and accuracy of God.

How long do you think all this took? It took over eleven hours before we were through in that kitchen and then it was nearly midnight. I was shown a good bed and I tell you I appreciated it, for I had spent more than some three hundred hours without a bed or anything to eat. The next morning I enjoyed some good country ham for breakfast.

The family soon sold out and went to northern Michigan to the pine lumber belt. I saw the girl once more at the Cincinnati Camp and she still had a good experience.

Ever since that time, I have fought box socials. I have suffered many times for such stands, but have lived through all. I am as bold against them now as ever. One time I had to walk more than sixty miles, carrying a heavy grip, because of the stand I took against box socials. I will say to our holiness preachers: Take your stand emphatically against the box socials. Cry aloud, spare not, lift up your voice against them; thunder it wherever you go. Let us rise up as one, pierce the serpent to its very center, until we have driven it from our midst.

I was once holding a meeting in Kentucky and was invited to a home for the night. About two in the morning I heard a terrible racket downstairs. I arose and went to the head of the stairs to inquire about what was happening. I heard the answer, "Lucy is dying with terrible cramps." Although it was my first night there and I was a stranger to all of them, I went downstairs. Grandma was rushing in and out to the smoke house and everyone in the house was up doing all they could to save the child's life.

The little girl was writhing in pain. Three were trying to hold her while two were trying to keep the hot cloths and contents of Grandma's smoke house drug store on her. The mother stopped long enough to wring her hands in agony, saying, "Brother Bevington, what more can be done than is being done? My husband is out in the woods after the horses to go for the doctor."

"Sister, if you all let her go and take all of those remedies off her, it may be that Jesus will heal her."

"Oh, no," replied the distraught mother, "she could not live five minutes without these applications!"

As they kept trying to do the best they knew, Grandma suddenly stopped and said, "Mister, did you ever see anyone healed?"

I said, "Plenty of them."

"Well," she said, "I have heard of such likes, but never saw one. No one never round here has done that."

She looked earnestly at me, having done all she knew to help her granddaughter. The child was suffering unbearable pains.

"Well," I assured them, "if you will strip her of those remedies and let go of her, you will all see the power of God."

They were afraid to act on my suggestion. In fact, they wanted me to help hold her down, which I declined to do. The mother said, "Brother Bevington, if we take our hands off her, she will plunge out of bed and kill herself. We will be charged with murder."

"Well," I said, "do as you see fit."

I left the room, but Grandma followed me up the stairs saying, "Don't leave. Oh, I would love to see Jesus heal her. Are you sure He will if we let her go?"

I saw they were so blind to the power of Jesus that I ventured further than I generally do. "Yes, Grandma, He will, but He can't get at her now as there isn't space for Him in that room."

So Grandma led me back into the room and said, "This man says Jesus will heal her if we all get out the way and take the cloths and poultices off."

At that the mother let go of the child and wrung her hands as she wailed, "I can't assume all this responsibility. It is too much for me." The other four were still trying to hold the child down. I raised my hand and the girl dropped down with eyes closed. The mother said, "She is dead."

I said, "She is not dead, but she is quiet. Now remove all those remedies."

Grandma went at it and had a pile on the floor as large as a half bushel. Then I asked all doubters to leave the room. None left. I said, "Do you all believe that Jesus will heal this child?"

187

One spoke up and said, "Well, none of us can say we do, but we will not get in your way in the least. We all would love to see Jesus manifest His healing power on this suffering child."

So I took the oil, anointed her, prayed the prayer of faith and in twenty minutes she was asleep. I went back to bed and when the doctor reached there, he found her asleep. He examined her and pronounced there was nothing the matter with her. He did not leave any medicines as he had been in the habit of doing.

When the father came in, he rushed up to her and laid his hand on her before crying out, "She is dead, Doctor." The doctor just laughed, probably both from nervousness as well as delight. He had never seen anyone healed and it was quite new to him. The father had quite a time believing the child was healed. He probably would have received it more readily if it had been a gradual process.

The doctor went home and all went to bed, exhausted, except the father. He had not struggled as the others had, so he remained up. He expected to have to call them all back at any moment, for he was convinced his daughter could not be healed. I went upstairs and walked the floor, bathed in tears of joy and in praise for what Jesus had done.

Finally I slept, awaking when I was called down to breakfast. Before retiring I had pleaded that the child would get up of her own accord and go to breakfast and eat a hearty meal. When I entered the kitchen, the child was sitting at the table as well as ever. She jumped up, threw her arms around me, hugged me good and laughed. I told her she ought to hug Jesus as He was the One who had healed her. "I know He did," she said, "but you are the only one who has ever been around here with faith for healing."

After breakfast, Grandma said, "Brother Bevington, come out here." She took me to the smokehouse and what a sight it was with the rafters loaded down with all sorts of remedies! Poor Grandma had toiled days and weeks in the fall getting that great display of roots, herbs, leaves and barks—all for the keeping up of disabled and worn-out bodies.

She looked upward and said, "Now, Jesus, if you can heal Lucy, you can and will heal all the rest of us." Turning back to me, she said, "Brother Bevington, I want you to get them all down and I will make a bonfire of them."

"Grandma, are you sure you trust Jesus?" I reminded her I was leaving shortly and she needed to make up her mind for sure before I helped her burn her remedies.

"Yes, sir, I have seen what I never seen before. I will believe and trust Jesus."

"Then you really want to get them down?"

"Yes, sir."

"Hadn't we better see Lucy's father first?"

"You can if you want to, but I assure you he will not object," Grandma said emphatically.

So I went out to the barn and found Lucy's father. "Your mother wants me to haul down that drug store in the smokehouse and make a bonfire of everything hanging there. What do you think about it?"

He went up to the house to see if Lucy were still up and found her out in the swing, laughing happily. She assured him, "Papa, I never felt as I now feel. I know Jesus healed me." That was enough for him.

We went back to the barn and he told me to do as Grandma said. So we stripped those rafters and boxes and hooks of that great store right down to nothing. Lucy, with a radiant face, lit the fire. We all had a great time at that bonfire.

I have seen them several times since and they say Grandma never gathered up any more remedies. Lucy was sound and well and attending school which she had never been able to do before. Oh, hallelujah, to our great Physician! Amen!

I was holding a meeting back at Willard, Kentucky—the former home of the famous Fleming boys. Their mother is still living there. I was invited home by the Ison family who were strangers to me. We were in a jolt wagon and the wife held aloft a large lamp to help find the best route as the roads were quite bad.

When we reached their home, the wife climbed out of the wagon with the baby. Then she turned and the lamp was handed down to her. Somehow that little baby got its tiny hand against the hot chimney and burned it badly. The husband and I put the mules away and hurried into the house. The little one was screaming terribly and the mother was walking the floor in great agony for her child. The girls were trying to do something, but all to no avail.

I said, "Sister," and then paused as I did not know how they would take it, "have you people ever taken cases like this to Jesus?"

The mother was crying like her heart would break with every scream of her child, but she said between sobs, "Do you believe that Jesus can heal my baby?"

"Yes, I do," I assured her.

She handed me the baby in faith and then sat down as calm as though nothing was wrong. I laid my hand on the burned hand and began to pray. In no more than six minutes, the child was asleep. To Jesus be all the glory.

I well remember how near I came to getting tripped up by Satan's schemes when I first thought of mentioning healing to the mother. He immediately warned I had better go a little slow as these were strangers to me and they would not take kindly to my suggestions.

I did hesitate for a moment, but soon rallied from that position. Satan took great pains to tell me none of them were converted at that time and if I wanted to get hold of them, I had better go slow since they would not take any stock in holiness and all that stuff. But I placed my faith in God and ran the chances. In a few moments, I found out that they were both quite saved and were hungering for sanctification. So know that Satan's strategy is filled with lies to bring fear and doubt.

The baby slept well all night. The next morning all the skin was peeled off the back of its hand, but the baby never cried anymore. Praise God for such victories! The parents both got sanctified before I left and two of their daughters got saved.

Now we all know that cause and effect are inseparable—where there is an effect, we know that the cause is around somewhere. One of the main causes for not allowing Jesus to heal us is the lack of entire sanctification. When we fully die out and are dead to this old world and all its environments, we can trust God to do most anything.

For instance, I held one meeting in Ohio where I just trudged along in a slow, hard fight. So far as I could see, just one family was brought in—but the heads of that family were regenerated and sanctified. I was somewhat discouraged at the results of the meeting as it closed. This was helped by the fact that several had deemed it about as near a failure as any meeting ever held there.

Nonetheless, I went from there some twenty-two miles for another meeting. The second night several fell at the altar. Right from the start it looked as though a great revival was just ahead of us. After the first Sunday we began looking for seekers for the Holy Ghost. I preached this second work strongly and incessantly, but no one came although the seekers for regeneration were plenty.

I began weeping over their state, pleading with them, but there was not one seeker for the second work. The meeting closed in what seemed to the people to be a blaze of glory. Some fifty had claimed to have prayed through.

I considered this meeting to be more of a failure than the previous one. In spite of all my preaching on the necessity of sanctification and my fasting for them, not one sought it. I felt pretty bad.

Saturday night I put forth an extra effort and gave one of my best Bible readings on the second work of grace, but still no one made any move. I pleaded with them, "Brethren, regeneration is a most blessed and glorious work, but it does not complete God's ideal for a child of His. If you fail to go on into the second work, you will never stand."

My closing sermon was a strong Bible reading on the second work. No one came. This meeting had been quite far reaching in its sphere. So many came for miles around, it was considered a great meeting. Several asked the reason of the failure of the previous meeting over on the creek. I said nothing, for I felt this was by far the greater failure of the two. I just packed up my tent, went forty-five miles from there, and kept going on. I have been going on ever since, Hallelujah!

But now, back to the "failure." I went to the Cincinnati Camp about nine months after this first meeting and a brother said, "Brother Bevington, I have a call to hold a meeting back on Noose Creek. I was told that you held a meeting there and it was a failure. How about it?"

"Well," I said, "I do not call it a failure by any means, as the heads of a family got saved and sanctified."

"Was that all?"

"Yes, as far as I could see."

"We heard you held a rousing meeting over at the bend."

"That is what they called it," was all I said.

He packed up his tent, turned down the "failure" invitation and went over on the bend where the rousing meeting had been. There he pitched his tent and cut loose, expecting another rousing meeting. He preached eight days with not a soul at the altar. He was somewhat discouraged, but stuck to it until Sunday night—still no one came.

On Sunday, his last day, the sanctified man and wife from over at the pronounced failure asked him to bring his tent over to their neighborhood. The evangelist, not knowing that this was the place where I had the so-called failure, gladly accepted the call. He was pleased to get most anywhere that was away from that place.

The brother came after him Monday with a team. He began his meeting Tuesday night, cutting loose on the second work which they would not stand for over on the bend. He felt impressed to open the altar and eight fell at the altar for sanctification. This brother and wife had been holding cottage meetings during the lapse of time and eleven had been regenerated, with three of them sanctified. The evangelist had not had enough faith to go to the scene of the supposed failed meeting, so God worked around it anyway.

We need power and faith is power. It is hard to exercise faith with the "old man" still active in us.

I was holding a meeting in Indiana where two sisters

193

attended. They were unmarried, lovely girls, both of them being good singers, good leaders and workers with beautiful character. They exerted a fine influence over whoever they met.

The first service was Sunday morning. They were there, at their posts, and I immediately saw they were going to be a great help. But on Sunday night and Monday night, they were missing. So I went over to see about it. They said, "Brother Bevington, we are here with our mother and we make our living on milk and butter. Our cows do not get up here in time for us to get to the night meetings. We don't have enough time to hunt them up any sooner as they have such a large range to run in."

I said, "Well, what time would it be necessary for the cows to be here in order for you to get to church?"

"They would have to be here much, much earlier than they will come. There isn't anything we can do about it, so we just can't come."

"That is not what I asked you. Please answer my question."

"We know that is not an answer—but the cows just won't come any earlier."

"There it is again. Will you please answer my question? What time would they have to be here?"

"There is no use talking about that as they never come earlier."

I could see this was going to take persistence. "There it is again. Now please answer my question. What time would they have to be here?"

The sisters each gave deep sighs and said, "They would have to be here by 5:00 p.m."

"All right, that is what I wanted to know. Do they have a bell?"

"Yes, a large one."

"Well, I want you to listen for that bell at 4:45 p.m.," I announced as they stood looking at me with the strangest expressions.

Then I went to my room, got down on my face and said, "Lord, You know we need these girls there as they will save my voice and add much to the good results of the meeting. So please have that bell in hearing distance at 4:45." It was nearly 2:00 when I went down on my face and I just kept digging in and holding on.

At 4:30, one of the girls laughed and said, "Well, our time is nearly up."

The other one said, "Do you really think those cows will be here at 4:45?"

"Well, he told us to listen and there won't be any harm in listening. In fact, I am going out and open the gate." As soon as she had opened the gate, to her surprise the bell was heard. Quite excited, she called to the sister to come quickly.

The sister came at once and exclaimed, "Well, well, there they come." It was 4:45 exactly. The sisters both came to church early that night, told this experience and it proved to be a great boon to the meeting. At 4:45 every night of the meeting, those cows came up preaching about the power of God with more persuasion than Bevington ever had. It was noised all over and many came to see that fellow who could bring those cows up at that unreasonable hour. I never had tried that before, and never have since—but if God should tell me as He did then, I would do so.

I have more marvels of God's dealings—some I have never told from the pulpit, although I have told them privately or to groups. I suppose those who have heard of my straw stack experience would consider the book incomplete without it. This one will complete the major experiences.

I was holding a meeting in Indiana and the weather was very cold with plenty of snow. People came for miles in old-fashioned, two-horse sleds and their sleigh bells could be heard for great distances. Some even came as far as thirty-five miles as such sleighing did no harm to their horses which were not worked much at that time of the year. Many came to see the sights at the meetings and many of those tumbled into the whirlpool as they took to calling it. Several had gotten down and been actually saved, while four of those who came from a distance got sanctified.

As the meeting progressed, these four said several times that I must come over into their neighborhood. I paid no attention to this as my hands were full there. But they kept urging me until finally I said, "Well, where do you live? How far from here?"

"About twenty-five miles. We have an M.E. church over there and you must come."

As the time came to close the meeting, I asked, "Do you have the permission of your pastor for me to hold a meeting in your church?"

"Oh, that is all right as the church is on father's place. He built it."

"Well," I said, "it belongs to the M.E. Conference and you have to get permission." Then I went up to my room and got on my face. I lay there for twenty-six hours until I felt led to go. The next morning three of their leaders came to see me, but there was no call from their pastor. I sent them back.

The pastor came over the next day and said, "I hear some of our people have been attending your meeting over here and they want you to come over there with us.

I understand that you preach holiness."

"Yes, as hot as I can."

He said, "We are all John Wesley Methodists."

"Well," I said, "I haven't been running into them of late. In fact, I don't find many John Wesley Methodists."

"Do you preach holiness to sinners?"

"I preach just as God gives me the message. Some places it is on holiness as a second work of grace and then at others, holiness is seldom mentioned."

"Well, we would be very glad to have you come over, as it would please some of our people. But I want you to know we consider it very unwise to preach holiness to sinners. We would suggest you preach regeneration to the sinners as that is what they need. Then if you want, we could have some afternoon for holiness."

I said, "Is this merely a suggestion or does it take the form of a command?"

"I think it is the only way we could permit you to come over."

"Well, I can't come on those terms at all," I told the pastor.

He said, "Then how would it do to have one night in the week for holiness?"

"I could not agree to that, either, as it might be all holiness as a second work. I could not come over unless I were to have complete charge and control to preach as long as God said so and just as He prescribes. I could not have any restrictions whatever. I might be led to call on you to pray and I might not."

"Isn't that bordering on fanaticism?" he said accusingly.

Looking him square in the eye, I said, "You can term it whatever you wish. That is where I have to stand if I come over."

197

So he went back and told the people who had sent him, "Brethren, we can't have that fellow over here. He is a genuine crank. He said he wouldn't let me have anything to do with the meeting, not even to pray—he probably wouldn't allow me to be on my own platform. We will not have him here!"

To this outburst, the people replied, "If we can't have him in the church, we will fix up a tobacco stripping house, seat it and put stoves in it. That will hold about as many as the church. We feel that man ought to come here. Souls prayed through every night over there—you have been here three years and not a soul has been regenerated." The pastor saw that this would never do, so he gave in and sent for me. I went over and opened fire on his three hundred members.

The pastor had said that I ought not to preach holiness to sinners, but I said this doctrine of freedom from sin seems to please the sinner pretty well. He said they had three hundred and fifty members and all were saved, of course. Well, I felt the four who had been over to my other meeting and gotten salvation and were then sanctified were probably a pretty safe sample of the whole three hundred and fifty.

After the third sermon, the pastor drew me aside and gave me a surprise announcement. He said the Ladies' Aid had planned quite an extensive program for Christmas and they could not locate any place for their work except the church. He said they were quite sorry as they would dearly love to have the meeting go on, but to please the Ladies' Aid, he had to close the meeting down.

I had papers signed by him that permitted me to remain in the church, yet I would not use them to enforce the meetings. Being permitted to preach the fourth night, however, I announced the action of the pastor and the "Aids."

One man jumped up and said, "We will go over to the schoolhouse." The situation was put to a vote as to whether to go into the schoolhouse and it was said that every hand went up except that of the pastor and his wife. Even his son and daughter raised their hands. So we went over to the schoolhouse the next night.

The following day the pastor hired five boys to cut up the seats so as to stop the meeting. He gave them two dollars apiece and they went at it in good shape. The board met and said, "The boys are cutting up the seats badly and we do not want you to meet in our school-house." So the people went and found another place for the meetings to go on.

That night as I went to my lodging place, I found the house darkened and my grips sitting out by the gate. I took that for a pretty good hint, picked up my grips and started out like Abraham, not knowing where to go. I could have gone, I suppose, to any of those four families. But I did not know where they lived. God did not want me to go there, anyway, as He had a better place for me. By my staying where I ended up, He got far more glory than if I had found any of the people's homes.

I kept trudging on in the snow and it was very cold—so cold that men had been cutting solid ice, twenty-two inches thick, out of a pond. It didn't take long for me to tire, set the grips down and ask, "Lord, where am I going?"

"What is that to thee, follow thou Me," was all I got in answer.

"Right." I sighed, picked up the grips and started on. I found myself in a sort of lane where great furrows had been cut in the road from drawing corn out in the

199

fall. I could not see these deep ruts as they were filled with snow and I fell many times, cutting myself so that my face was bleeding in several places. My hands were so icy cold, I could barely stand it. I said again, "Oh, God, where am I going?"

Again came the same answer, "What is that to thee?" So on I trudged until I saw what appeared to be a great mound in the road. As I was looking down to try to avoid those ruts, I forgot the mound and ran right into it. It proved to be a straw stack. A voice said, "This is the place."

I said, "All right!" threw off my coat and went to pulling straw which helped me get nicely warmed up. I pulled straw until I was back inside the stack some twelve feet, about three feet above the ground so as to be warm. I packed the straw down, took in my grips, put on my coat, dropped down on my back and lay my head on one of the grips for a pillow. Very pleased, I said, "Well, praise God, I don't reckon Jesus ever had much better than this—and probably most of the time not nearly so good."

At that the straw stack was lighted up and I beheld the most beautiful sight I ever saw. It looked just like crystalized straws nearly as large as my little finger, lying in all positions, crossing each other to form a beautiful network. I was frightened and feared I had gotten a match lighted while pulling straw. My fears were soon banished, however, for I threw up my hands and there was nothing except cold straws. Beloved, I will never be able, this side of Heaven, to explain or draw a worthy picture of that scene and the dazzlings going on down in my soul! I have often thought it was a foretaste of what Heaven is going to be like.

We are taught down here to view things according to certain laws. The appearance of those straws did not allow the working of natural laws, as each was apart from the others, yet they did not appear to touch one another. I have thought many times that herein is our trouble—we see things down here under the lights of natural laws. God often breaks through the natural order of things—completely setting the natural aside—so we often fail to get the real import of His designs.

That experience in that cold stack of straw has been a great help to me many a time, enabling me to accept things that I would have formerly rejected on philosophical grounds. While God works through natural laws very much, I have found He has special lessons for us which often go far beyond the natural laws. I have also learned that ruts are dangerous channels to travel.

God wants us pliable so He can twist us up and toss us here or yonder. He wants us to be able to recognize His hand though it appears to be cloaked in other garb or moving apart from those ways in which similar incidents have appeared. There is no doubt that God would give us wonderful revelations if He could get us in condition to receive them.

I am assured the deeper lessons God wants us to have are all in the line of the apparently ridiculous. They are not on the public highway and the casual traveler never sees them, for they are not on his route. These lessons are learned on the unreasonable, out-of-the-ordinary routes, generally routes similar to my getting into this straw stack. I learned invaluable lessons from that.

When I told this to dear Reverend John Fleming, he burst out crying as he said, "Brother Bevington, I would have given a hundred dollars to see that straw stack when it was so luminously lit up."

Had I appealed to reason as I came up against that stack when the thermometer was registering below twenty degrees, everything would have stood against such proceeding. My natural thoughts would have produced this kind of argument: "God has set forth His laws which require obedience relative to taking care of our bodies. I do not accept this stack of straw as the place He wants me to be. He has called me to preach and said the laborer is worthy of his hire. I am His child, Mr. Devil, and I am not going to allow you to run me into such a place as this to bring on a tremendous cold or pneumonia which would more than likely cause my premature death."

Thus I could quite logically have reasoned this all out; though had I have done so, I would have lost one of the grandest lessons of my life. We need to get where we will be willing to ignore all laws of logic in order to get some of the private lessons the Lord has for us. Just those few words of acquiescence to His will when I said, "I suppose Jesus never had a better bed than this," gave me one of the grandest visions I have ever beheld. Those few words spoke volumes which have enabled me to store up great quantities of knowledge of His will relative to me.

I will now proceed with the other marvels of God that were going on at that time. He will open up great and unheard of things if we allow Him to get us where these great and unheard of things are in operation or where He can consistently operate them without knocking others of His lambs flat. While this great manifestation of glory lasted only a short time, raptures of exceeding great joy continued to come in waves one after another. I lay there wrapped in great splendor until I struck a match and looked at my watch to see that it was 4:30 a.m. I turned over and went to sleep and when I woke up and struck a match again, I found it was 5:30 p.m.

I crawled out, shook off the chaff, used my handkerchief for a towel after washing well in the snow and started back to the house that had been offered to continue the meeting. I found twenty-five people there with saws and horses. They had been drawing logs and sawing them into blocks for seats. Both rooms were nearly seated.

I said to the man of the house, "Are these two rooms all you have?"

Surprised at my question, he replied, "But these will hold more than the schoolhouse."

"Is there another room upstairs?" I persisted.

"Yes, sort of an unfinished attic. What do you want to go up there for?"

"I want a place to pray." Then I spied a door on the ceiling and asked, "Can I get up through there?"

He said, "There isn't any floor and it will be cold."

"Just let me get up there." So he got a ladder and up I went. I got close to the large chimney, lying across the joist, and burst into great sobs. I just lay there and wept. I ignored the increasing noise downstairs, supposing they were finishing up seating. Finally I struck a match and saw it was 9:30 p.m., so I got up and went downstairs. I found over a hundred people waiting for me. I had no message, I only had a great burden that souls be brought under such conviction they would see their real condition and fly to the Son of God for refuge.

There was some unoccupied space where I landed from the attic, so I dropped down on my face again. In about thirty minutes the preacher's son came to me and whispered, "Aren't you going to preach? There are over a hundred people here waiting."

I exhorted him and the rest to pray, but he said, "There is no one here who can do any good at prayer. You have spoiled all of us. The only prayer that any of us ought to pray is the prayer of repentance."

I thought he was about right, so I got up and said, "Brethren, this great battle must be fought out on our faces. I have no message to preach. You have had too much preaching. I have only a burden of prayer that each of you may be brought face to face with your real condition as God sees you. I beg you to fly for your lives to the Son of God who has made provision for your complete deliverance from sin."

At that I crawled out of the window nearest me and made a bee line for my straw house. I lay on my face to plead, weep, moan, groan and wrestle all night. When I finally struck a match, I found that it was 5:30 a.m. I fell asleep until late that afternoon. Then I crawled out, took another wash in the snow (it was still freezing) and went back to the house where I found seventy-five people.

More than twenty were down praying as if they really meant business; some on their faces sobbing, others kneeling and praying, others with heads up pleading and weeping, others walking where they could find room. All that crowd pleading for mercy, mind you, were those "saved" people from the church and among them were the son and daughter of the pastor.

I raised the window and crawled back in as there was no room to get in the door. I again climbed up the ladder into the attic. I got on my face across those sleepers close to the warm chimney as a rousing fire was now burning below. After a while the man of the house crawled up the ladder and said, "It is after eight. They all want you to come down and preach."

"Tell them all to go to praying," I said.

"I am afraid they will get tired of this, leave and not return. Then all this work here will be lost."

Here was more logic to contend with, but I remained where I was. I could hear them praying and singing. At about 10:00 p.m., I went down and found about forty in real soul agony. These included the pastor's son and daughter, both of whom had been testifying to being saved for several years. I could see God was working and I knew how foolish it would be for me to try to take the work out of His hands.

I raised the window and slipped back out to my private quarters to plead with God for them. I got back on my face and struggled, agonized, wrestled, wept and held on—expecting God to work wonders. I struck a match and found it was 6:00 a.m., so I rolled over and slept the whole day again.

I had another good wash in the snow, shook myself and started for the meeting. I found about two hundred people there, most of them in great misery. One man and his wife met me outside and began to tell me about the trouble they were having with their bad neighbor. I said, "Go inside, get down on your faces and plead for mercy, throw open your hearts to God, get honest before Him and let Him examine you." They did so.

Another came to me, saying "What shall I do?"

I said, "Get right with God."

"Why, I am a good member here in the church."

I repeated it again, "Get right with God. Repent. Get yourself properly fixed up—then matters can more easily be adjusted."

Two sisters were the next to unload the terrible meanness of their neighbors, saying, "We want you to pray for them as they are a terror to the whole neighborhood."

"You two are the ones who need praying for—never mind those neighbors. Get right yourselves. Go through with God."

Shocked, they informed me, "Why, Mr. Bevington, we

are members in good standing in this church here."

"Well, you are all the worse for that."

"We want to get our children saved—my son and daughter-in-law and daughter and son-in-law."

"Then get in there and get down on your faces and deal with God directly, not with Bevington."

"There is no room inside."

I could hardly believe their excuses. "Make room, then. Go into the kitchen, if you have to," I told them.

"The kitchen is crammed full."

I said loudly, "Go in, go in, go in!"

I left those self-righteous complainers, went to my window, crawled in and slipped up the ladder. Only a few saw me, but soon the man of the house came and said about three hundred people were there. I finally went down and found many on their knees pleading. The man's son was crying as he said, "Oh, won't you preach? I am so miserable and need help. Please tell me what to do. My sister is weeping, too, as if her heart were broken."

There was only room to stand right at the ladder, so there I began my text, "Prepare to meet thy God." I believe that never before nor since have I delivered such a message as was given during that forty minutes. Everyone was writhing in great agony, some walking and screaming. Only about sixty could kneel, but they were doing good work. Oh, how God did send out the lightning bolts in great torrents!

Feeling I had done all God wanted me to do there, I hoisted the window and made for my accommodations. I crawled into the familiar straw cave, got on my face and could do nothing but cry and groan and plead all night long. Then I slept until that evening again. After taking another cool bath, I started back to the house and found about sixty there.

I stopped and stood at the ladder. As I waited there, the pastor came in. He began to lash me with his tongue, calling me about all the names in the catalogue. I was somewhat accustomed to such vocal expressions, so they did not disturb my equilibrium and I just remained speechless through it all. He finally wound up by ordering every one of his members out of there, with the command never to return.

All arose and followed him out except his son, the man and family of the house and one other man and his family. I think there were about sixteen left. Suddenly I felt like preaching and so I did—on the judgment and wrath of God. The son, the man of the house and his wife and the other man prayed through by early morning. We had a blessed time and that son did some wonderful preaching. The night before, the pastor had taken his daughter by the dress collar and dragged her out of the meeting, threatening to punish her severely if she ever returned. The son was too big for that kind of treatment, so the pastor had to go off without him.

I slipped out, went to my straw hotel where I wept until noon and then went to sleep. I awakened that evening and went out for another snow bath in my large toilet room. I went back down to the house and found that only twenty-two were there. But all twenty-two were down pleading for mercy, except those who had gotten through and were now seeking sanctification. The pastor's daughter was there again.

I felt led to remain all night with them, so I stayed until 3:00 a.m. and then went upstairs. Soon the woman of the house came up and said, "I think I am going to throw all those blocks out and clean the whole thing up. I am convinced I am all right. The pastor says I am because I have been a member here for years. You are just making fools out of all of us—my husband and son and daughter."

I said, "Woman, get down those steps as quickly as you can and start screaming for mercy or you may be in hell within twenty minutes."

With a look of real shock on her face, back down she went with me right behind her. I tell you she changed her tune and in forty minutes she struck fire. She did some fine preaching there, too, clear until after daylight. Then I slipped off back to my headquarters.

Now this brings me up to the eighth day. Very early that morning the pastor's daughter got through and in the evening she said, "Brother Bevington, I have disobeyed my father for the first time in my life. I had to come here, as I feared I would lose my soul. Please pray I may be willing and able to endure my punishment." She well knew the temper of her father.

I said, "All right, I will go up into the attic and plead your case. You be loyal to what you have received." So up I went.

She and her brother had about a mile to walk home. He was seeking sanctification, but as he had a whole lot to undo, it was a somewhat tedious matter. I was pleading that the experiences of the two would so melt the father, he would be compelled to surrender. Finally I felt the burden gone. Light was breaking in as I raised up off the sleepers, praising God for the daughter's victory.

I went back to my straw stack, this being the ninth morning. I had not yet had a mouthful to eat or lain on anything except straw and sleepers. When I returned that night, the man of the house met me outside and asked, "Brother Bevington, where are you stopping?"

I said, "None of your business."

"Now see here, it is my business and I am going to make

it so. I went today to the Reynolds where I supposed you were stopping and they said you were not there. I went to all the places there would be any likelihood of your being and none of them knew where you are stopping. Now, tell me."

I repeated, "None of your business. Go on in there and pray through and get the Holy Ghost."

"No, sir, I'm not going in until you tell me."

So I just pointed in the direction of the straw stack.

"Wife, this man has been sleeping and staying in that straw stack," and he capered around about all he dared as a seeker of the Holy Ghost. "Where have you been getting your meals?" he asked next. I just pointed to the skies. So he yelled to his wife, "This man hasn't had a mouthful to eat these two weeks." He was exaggerating by three days. "Come in and get something to eat," he said. But I declined.

As I was listening to his quizzing, here came the pastor, wild eyed and bareheaded, speeding through the snow in his cutter. His son and daughter were with him and the sleigh bells were ringing like crazy. He was being sifted.

The son and daughter had arrived home and gone into the room where he was sleeping, believing his daughter to be upstairs in her bed. She called out to him and said, "Father, I disobeyed you last night. I just had to go back up there or go to hell. Now, father, I am ready and prepared for my punishment."

The son was standing at her side with his head bowed, pleading for the salvation of his father and that this situation would be the means to that end.

"Go on to bed and let me alone," the father said.

"No, father, I want my punishment. I disobeyed you and I am ready."

At that he gave a yell, bounded out of bed, fell on his

knees and went to crying for mercy. The son and daughter dropped on their faces and in ten minutes their mother climbed out beside them. She cried, "Oh, children, pray for me, too. I need what I believe you both have."

So they wrestled in prayer until the following afternoon when the mother prayed through. The father did not get through. He asked us back to the church that night, but as both rooms were full (for many had heard of the pastor's actions and come back) where we were, we held the meeting in our usual place that night. I preached on the text, "If any man be in Christ Jesus, he is a new creature," and God gave me a blessed message.

The mother prayed through for sanctification early the next morning, but the father still did not get through. As soon as it was daylight, he hitched up and went to every one of those men and women whom he had called out of there and asked forgiveness. It took him three days to make the circuit, but he did it.

He said that at the first house he went to, he asked forgiveness and invited the people out to the meetings. They closed the door and he started to leave when a voice said, "And is that all?" He looked all around and saw no one anywhere near him. Not being used to the voice of God, he was quite puzzled. By the time he reached the gate, he heard the same voice again with the same words. He said that he had to go back, fall on his knees before those people and really ask their forgiveness. He gladly knelt and asked forgiveness of all of the three hundred.

We moved the meetings back up to the church and we spent three weeks there. As my straw stack experience had prepared me for a good meal, I had it at the parsonage. I continued to eat only one meal a day during those three weeks.

If I felt clear to tell you, it would no doubt be refreshing to relate many of the incidents which occurred during those three weeks. But I will cut the account short by saying I preached only two sermons and those on the last day of the meeting. The rest of the time I lay on my face on the platform day and night. The pastor's wife, son and daughter prayed through and got sanctified.

There were several incidents in the pastor's seeking that were of interest as it took five days and nights to kill him out. He rolled on the floor, perspired profusely, made restitutions and put up quite a struggle. But he finally got through and was a good witness for several years. I saw him at the Cincinnati Camp three successive years and on the platform he delivered good messages to full salvation.

Yes, if all that was said and done were recorded, it would make an interesting volume to read. They said that over three hundred people fell at the altar and someone was getting through most all the time, day and night. The many who prayed through did some wonderful preaching. Restitutions were made in many instances.

I have left out a lot of this five weeks' campaign, but I guess this will suffice. But I do want you to remember that all the time that I was in the straw stack, it was below freezing. Also, when I trudged up there the first night, I cut my face and hands severely by falling in the frozen ruts. But neither the cuts, the sleeping in the stack nor the struggling for souls caused me any sickness or hardship.

When I was holding a meeting up the river from Cincinnati, I was out on Brother Ben Otten's place making a sled for him. It required a lot of boring with a brace and bit in hard, seasoned oak and as I threw my weight on the brace while boring, a sudden, severe pain took me just above the heart. It rendered me helpless for about an

211

hour. I finally got some strength and went to the house still suffering. Later I went back to boring.

After dinner, however, I could scarcely breathe because of severe pains. I prayed over it some, but kept on working until I finished the sled. That night I slept but little.

Since on a farm there is always so much to do, I was busy puttering round during the morning. After dinner, when I could not straighten up, I told the folks what I had done and explained my present condition. They were a little alarmed, realizing the trouble was quite close to my heart.

I intended to go out behind a shock of fodder and pray, but failed to get there. About an hour later, as the pain was increasing, I realized I had to do something. I finally made it back of the shock where I said, "Now, Mr. Devil, this has gone just about far enough." I fell on my face and began to plead the promises in earnest, holding up the Bible as I claimed the blessed promise in I John 5:14. I held onto that for awhile, but the pain kept increasing. I could hardly even breathe without intense suffering.

Then I got desperate and cried out, "Lord, I am not going to leave this spot until I am delivered." So I began to reckon it so and counted it done. I saw that my faith was getting clearer, hence stronger. I began to praise God and saw I was getting deliverance. I raised my hand, saying, "Oh, hallelujah, it is done, it is done, it is done!" As I said the last word the third time, it was done.

I jumped up running and shouting. Brother Ben and his wife just stood and wept for joy because Jesus had so delivered me. Oh, praise the Lord! Let all the people praise him!

I was holding a meeting in Ohio in a prominent church.

I had preached four nights and on the fifth night, I ate no supper and went somewhat early. I found the door locked, so I sat down on the steps and began reading the precious Word. I got so interested, I did not notice the time until a man stepped up and said, "Isn't the door locked?"

I said, "Yes."

He looked at me rather seriously for about five minutes and then said, "Did you not know that they locked you out?"

I said, "No, have they?"

"Yes, they have."

"Do you live near here?" I asked him.

"Yes, you were at my house last Friday, but I was not at home. You prayed for my wife and she has been well ever since."

I said, "Are you a saved man?"

"No, sir," and with that, off he went.

I said, "Well, Lord, so we are locked out, huh? Now how about that message You gave me this morning? Where am I going to deliver it?"

Satan whispered to me, "You can deliver that tomorrow night, as they will let you back into the church then."

Now note the danger here. This sounded right good and reasonable and would have been accepted by many. It was then well after dark, but I had felt so deeply impressed with this certain message that I could not let go. So I said, "Lord, it seems I must deliver that message somewhere."

There was no one in sight to preach to, but that message kept revolving and enlarging. It continued to gather material at each revolution in spite of the absence of visible prospects. As I sat there, I saw a large oak tree that threw its branches out over the road. While I was admiring its beauty, a voice said, "That is the place."

213

I looked around, but there was no one in sight. So I strolled up to the tree and got down on my face. Soon I heard something. Thinking it was only hogs eating acorns, I stayed on my face. I seemed to be held to the spot, unable to move and that message was still developing. I knew I could not preach to hogs eating acorns.

I began weeping and struggling as I saw the terrible condition of the people. I prayed, cried and wrestled until I heard moaning and groaning and crying and praying. I looked up and there were more than seventy people under that tree with me. About a third of them were praying quite earnestly and they were praying the very message that had been burning on my heart. They all had the same message—I never had to deliver it.

I just remained on my face, pleading with God to burn the message in on them all. The pastor's daughter was among them, desperately in earnest as she kept on weeping and praying. At 1:30 a.m., I got up and closed the message—the part they had not reached as yet. After the firing had ceased and the smoke cleared away, there were thirteen who had been wounded in the spiritual skirmish—so much so that they seemed unable to get up and leave.

Just before dawn, though none had gotten through, nearly fifty men, women, boys and girls lay there. Finally the pastor's daughter got gloriously through. She ran all over the space occupied by those people, shouting and laughing and crying. Within a short while, over a hundred people were under that tree. I was still on my face, weeping and groaning. Many were knocked over by the power of God and someone said that over sixty were praying at once.

While his daughter was preaching, the pastor unfortunately missed this good feast. I was told his wife came down and I remember how I dreaded her appearance, but she had no spirit of interference. She just began helping the rest as did the daughter. The benediction was pronounced late that afternoon. The pastor himself showed up and announced there would be a meeting at the church that night, though he had ordered the church locked against me.

Whether it makes any sense or not, it always pays to obey God.

7
Children's Chapter

To the dear children, Greeting:

This book would be incomplete if there were no children's chapter, so here it is. I will just have a good time with my little friends who have always been such a comfort to me when I needed comfort. I feel Jesus would be pleased to have me tell of several incidents in which He has blessed the children.

Many of these incidents have been told in children's meetings, Sunday schools and by home firesides. I have spent many, long winter evenings amusing children with such stories when I was not otherwise employed.

I feel impressed to first tell of little Katie and Edward. I knew them when I was in the mission work in Cincinnati. Katie lived in a wretched home where both the father and mother drank hard, using up all the money they could get for alcohol. The whole family lived in utter filth when I first found them and Katie was then seven years old. We got clothes for her and put her into Sunday school and in the day school and I looked after them closely.

As little Katie had never been in school, we started her in the kindergarten. This was such a sweet, tiny crowd to look upon. I would slip in many times just to see them in their small red chairs. Katie would take home the little things they were taught to make and she would repeat the songs and blessings at the dinner table which her parents found very amusing.

Her father has told what a time Katie would have in getting him and her mother and the older sister and a brother all quiet while she would ask the blessing. Often times they would be drunk and she would have difficulty in getting them to fold their hands. They thought it quite cute and would always allow her to ask the blessing.

By and by, it got hold of them and before long, both parents were found crying for mercy at the altar. God had a great time in getting them both saved from their awful habits of such long standing, but He did. I was able to get them a job out at Ivorydale at the Proctor and Gamble Soap Factory where the famous Ivory Soap is made. Then some two years seemed to slip by.

One day as I was visiting the poor, I found a family with four little children who had nothing in the house to eat. I started up to Muth's Bakery where I could get bread (baked the day before) for two loaves for a nickel. I had just twenty cents and planned to get a soup bone and some potatoes to go with the two loaves of bread.

As I was walking up toward the bakery, a voice said, "Go out to Katie's." I well remembered Katie, but I was concentrating then on going after something for those four hungry children. It would take my twenty cents to get out to Ivorydale and back from Katie's, so I felt I couldn't go. I kept on toward Muth's Bakery.

But that voice kept ringing in my ears, "Go out to Katie's, go out to Katie's." I stopped and went through my

218

pockets to see if I could find any more money. I had not another cent. So I kept going on after the food.

Then the voice said, "Will you, or will you not, go out to Katie's?" I stopped as if paralyzed and began trembling (something I seldom did).

I said, "Lord, I will go." I looked up and saw an Ivorydale car coming, so I got on and went out to their house. When I arrived, I stepped onto the porch and knocked on the door. I heard a sob and a faint voice said, "Come in."

When I stepped inside, I saw Katie back in the corner caring for the baby. She smiled with trembling lips and said, "Oh, Mamma, here is Brother Bevington."

I saw at once that Katie had been crying as her eyes were all red. I stepped up to her, laid my hand on her head, and asked, "What is the trouble with my Katie?" She had grown so much in two years.

The mother came in, gave me a hearty hand shake and said, "I am so glad you minded God and came. I have been praying for twenty-four hours for Him to send you. Sit down here and I will tell you why Katie has been crying so much. See that house over there?" she asked, pointing out the window.

"Yes."

"And that path going from our house to the fence?" I nodded. "Those people are quite well off and have lots of money. They have a boy about Katie's age, a nice boy named Edward. He has plenty of money to spend, so he bought a croquet set and set it up in the orchard under the trees in the shade. When she is not in school, Katie takes the baby over there and she and Edward play croquet.

"Night before last, they were playing when Edward's mamma called him to go to the grocery. Katie waited for him and when he returned, they resumed their play. Then

219

his mother called again, 'I am sorry, but I forgot something. I guess you will have to go again.'

"So off he went (as every boy should when his mamma calls). He was gone longer than usual, so Katie came back to assist me in getting supper. Edward finally came back and gathered up the set. When he counted the balls, he found one missing. He counted them over again to be sure and one was definitely gone."

Now, children, listen how Satan will always be right on hand to get little ones into trouble. He said to Edward, "Katie stole your ball. She was the only one who was out there."

"Yes," said Edward to himself, "she surely must have taken it and I am going to tell on her." So he ran into his house and called out, "I ain't going to have Katie Brown come over here any more!"

"Why, Edward, what is wrong with Katie?" asked his mother.

"She stole one of my croquet balls."

"You know better than that."

"No, I know she did." Then he ran over to the Brown's house and said, "I ain't going to have Katie come over anymore."

"Why?"

"She stole one of my balls."

"Oh, no!" said Katie's mother.

"Yes, she did. No one else was there and now one of them is gone."

Katie was in the dining room caring for the baby. Hearing this, she came quickly to the doorway and said, "I never did such a thing."

"Yes, you did," Edward shouted. Then he left the house and promptly began nailing up the hole in the fence.

That was a hard blow on dear Katie. Although her

220

parents had been drunkards, now that they had not drunk any for over two years, she was being looked upon as a nice girl. To have this said of her was just about all she could stand. Poor Katie cried and sobbed all night. When the mother told her father how Katie had been accused, he said, "We know she didn't do it."

The next day Katie did not want to go to school, but her parents coaxed her into going. At recess none of the children would play with her or allow her to play with them. Edward was the leader in the school as he would often buy things for the other children, so they all looked up to him. He had told them Katie had stolen his ball and she was a thief. He insisted they must not play with her.

Well, poor Katie was crying hard when she came home at noon. She told how the children had treated her and pleaded, "Oh, Mamma, don't make me go back to school!"

Her mother was hurting for her daughter, but said firmly, "Katie, I think you ought to go to school. I don't want you to miss even a day. I will pray for God to send Brother Bevington out here and he will help us get the matter straight."

Back Katie went and they treated her even worse. They all called her a thief and then walked on the opposite side of the street from her as they came home that night. Even worse, they were saying her father was nothing but an old drunkard and wasn't fit to live with decent folks.

She could not stand that and hurried home crying as if her heart would break. "Oh, Mamma, please don't make me go to school tomorrow. I just can't endure it. Let me stay at home."

When the father came in and heard what had happened, he said, "Let her stay at home and we will pray for

221

God to send out Brother Bevington." And so they prayed. The mother prayed all night.

Now, children, I want you to see how God will answer such prayer. After this mother's all-night prayer, God began asking me to go out to Katie's. Such a trip seemed foolish to me since I was going for food for that poor family, but God wanted to use me to answer that mother's prayer. So He went to work on me that morning.

All the time her mother was relating this to me, Katie sat in the corner crying. I finally went over and laid my hand on her head. She wiped her tears away and then cleaned her face with a damp rag. I assured her, "Now, Katie, I am sure you never took the ball."

"No, I never took it, but we can't prove it. It will kill me unless we move away from here." She began crying again as if all hope was gone.

"Katie, you belong to Jesus, don't you?"

Between sobs, she said, "Yes."

"Oh, yes," said her mother, "Katie is a real Christian girl. Everyone in the school says she is and she reads the Bible and prays every night and morning. Yes, I am sure Katie is a little Christian and she surely does love Jesus. Why, she has gotten over twenty-five scholars in the Sunday school. She is a faithful little soldier for Jesus."

I said, "Katie, don't you remember the time that Jesus healed you downtown?"

"Yes, I do."

"Well, don't you believe that He will still answer prayer today?"

"Yes, I know He will," Katie sighed. "But how could He show Edward where that ball is?"

"Let's get down on our knees and let Jesus talk and work for us," I said as I knelt.

I called on the mother to pray. She prayed, "Yes, dear

Jesus, I know You can do things. I know You healed Katie and have done other things. I know You have and can do these things." She kept praying just that way for some time.

Finally I said, "Sister Brown, you are not hitting the mark at all!"

Children, I want you to know and always remember that we must pray definitely. To know and say that Jesus has done such and such isn't enough. We have to go further than that.

So I called on Katie. She was still sobbing and had quite a time getting out a few words, but she did better than the mother. Finally she got to the place where she said, "I believe you will show him where it is."

Well, that was getting pretty close to the mark, but not close enough. You see, children, if I want to drive a nail into a board, I cannot affect the driving of that nail unless I hit it right on the head. I might just graze it, but that won't do. I can hit close up to it, even all around it and still not get it in. If I don't hit the nail square on the head, I won't get it in the board!

So it is in our praying. We have to hit the matter square on the head by saying, "I know Thou art doing it right now." That is real faith and will bring the answer.

Now I want to show you how Satan will work. It was about 3:00 p.m. when I went to praying, the same time they were having recess at the school. As Edward was there at school, how could we expect him to be finding that ball when he was some five blocks away from where it was missing? So when I began praying, Satan said, "It is foolish for you to say that God is showing Edward that ball now, for he is at school five blocks from here."

Here comes the test. I knew I would have to claim that Jesus was showing him right then where the ball was, so I kept praying up to that point. The Holy Spirit kept leading me on and in two or three minutes I had reached the point where I knew I could say, "Yes, dear Jesus, yes. Thou art showing him right now."

"Hold on," said Satan, "He can't be going that."

So I shouted it out as loud as I could, "He is doing it right now!"

I shouted it three times and at the third time, the glory fell. Katie jumped up and threw her arms around me, laughing and crying at the same time, "Brother Bevington, I believe it. I do believe it! Oh, I am so happy."

I raised my head and looked in her face. All the tears, all the furrows were gone—she looked bright and beautiful as she smiled. I began to praise and thank Jesus. While I was still on my knees, I heard a "rattle-te-bang" outside. It was the newly-nailed board being knocked right off that fence and Edward came running in their door. His hands were all covered with blood and his face scratched, but he was carrying that missing ball. He knelt down in front of Katie and tears began to slide down his cheeks. He said afterward that it was the first time he was ever on his knees.

He just wept there like a good fellow. Then he asked Katie to forgive him for he had found the missing ball. Well, we had a great time rejoicing over it. Finally I said, "Now, Edward, we want you to tell us how you found the ball and why you are not at school."

Now, children, here is something I want you to remember. God knew that morning I would go out to Katie's and I would be claiming Edward's finding the ball about 3:00 p.m. As this was the time Edward was usually in school, his finding the ball at such a time would certainly seem unlikely.

So that morning Jesus made Edward unusually studious. He studied hard and all his lessons seemed to come so easily that, by recess in the afternoon, he had finished all of them. He went to the teacher and said, "I have all my lessons, would you like to hear them?"

"Why, yes, I would." So she heard them and said, "Edward, since you have them all, you may go home now if you want."

So he started running down the street, just so glad to get out of school. I wish I could draw you a diagram of where the schoolhouse was from his home, but I guess I will have to try to explain with words. The schoolhouse was on a street running east and west. His house was on a street running north and south. His was the third house south of the corner where these streets crossed and the school-house was five blocks west.

Edward's father had six acres there which also held a large orchard. His lot ran back to the street west of the one they lived on and part of it extended out to the street the schoolhouse was on. This was the street Edward had been coming down from the school. When the father had been at home more, they used a path running from their house across the back to the street west of theirs and up to the corner of the street the schoolhouse was on. So Edward would go through a gate at the corner and go across to his house to save going down to the east street and then turning south to his house.

His father had gotten into politics and began neglecting this lot. The berries had grown up all over and so covered the path that Edward had not gone through there for several years.

Now I wonder how many, from this explanation, could draw a diagram of how to get from Edward's house to the schoolhouse by the streets? I told this once in a schoolhouse where I was holding a meeting and a boy ten

225

years old gave me a correct diagram of it on paper the next day. So, if you can, make a diagram out and send it to me and I will be thankful. If the Lord has not yet seen fit to take me home and I have any money, I will buy you a present of some kind. That will enable me to get acquainted with you boys and girls. Direct it to Ashland, Kentucky, or Kingswood, Kentucky, and I will get it if I am still this side of Heaven.

Now I will tell how Edward found his croquet ball. He was running down this street east and west on his way home from school. When he got about halfway down from the corner of his father's lot west of him, a voice said to him, "Go back and go through the orchard."

He stopped and looked around, but there was no person in sight. "What could that mean?" he wondered. He started on towards the corner where he would turn south for his home and this same voice said, "Go back and go through the orchard." Edward stopped and looked around again.

"I don't understand what this means," he said, "but I can't go through the orchard now. All those briars in there are covering the path." So he began moving again.

Within seconds he was stopped still and could not move a muscle. The same voice said, "Will you, or will you not, go through the orchard?" Then he could move again.

Now he felt he had better turn back. So he went up to the corner, got down and looked at that path. "I can't go through there and I don't know what this means. Am I going crazy?"

He headed back down the street for home and again was stopped still. He could not move so much as his foot until he tried to turned back. When he found he could move in that direction, back he went. He got down on his hands and knees and began to crawl through those briars,

226

scolding himself almost all the way. When he was about two-thirds of the way through, his hand struck something that moved. He brushed the leaves away and guess what he found? The ball.

Now I want you to see how God answered our prayers and also see the miracles He worked to do so. First think about what a time He had with me to get me to come out there in the first place. Then think about how God made Edward study and helped him in his lessons—for that was the first time he had ever done his schoolwork that fast. Then see what a time God had in getting Edward to crawl through those briars, scratching his hands and face.

God answered my prayer by making that boy do the ridiculous. So now remember this—God will answer prayer in spite of how the circumstances seem! Sometimes we have to shut our eyes to what we might see and just blindly trust Him. Had I failed to mind Him, that opportunity would have been lost and poor Katie would have been wrecked. I had to come to the place where I counted it done, even though Edward was in school.

You see, God had it all planned out all the time. God often wants to perform miracles, children, but we may have to do what seems ridiculous in order that He may.

After this all took place, the mother asked me to stay until after supper. I was glad to do that as it would give me a chance to visit with them a little. I also wanted to find out how that ball got up there in the orchard. That interested me quite a bit.

I felt the best way to get close to that answer was to go out with the children and have a game of croquet. I was praying that God would reveal just how the ball got out in the orchard. And He did, for as we were playing, a half-grown pup ran up and grabbed a ball. Then this pup turned and ran up the path right into the briars. I said, "Look at that, Edward. That is how the ball got up there."

So you see, all things are possible to them who believe and obey God. Amen and amen! If I had not had faith, I might have consulted my watch when we were praying and said, "Edward is in school now, so we will postpone this until later." God's plan would have been frustrated and we never would have found out what really happened. I pray you can readily see how God will work through us if we are fully His and fully yielded up to Him.

I really like to preach to children as they are such good listeners, so I will tell you of another dear youngster. I was holding a meeting one spring not far from Lexington, Kentucky, while I was in the mission work in Cincinnati. A nine-year-old boy got blessedly saved at this meeting. He would gladly testify and pray in public and he was a sweet singer. His name was Harry, if I remember rightly.

In the fall Harry sent me some money, asking me to come back and hold another meeting. He said he wanted to get sanctified. He had gathered walnuts and hulled them all that fall, staining his hands quite dark. He sold the walnuts and sent the money to me so I could come. Well, I tell you, I certainly went.

He was present in the meetings with his singing and prayers until the fourth night when I missed him. I went home and found him in the dining room. He had the table covered with papers he had been figuring all over. I said, "Harry, I know you must get your lessons done, but I really missed you tonight." I went on upstairs where we roomed together and that dear boy never did come up to bed. He figured all night on that sum.

His teacher had said to him, "Harry, I can show you

where the trouble is, but I would like for you to discover it yourself. That will be a great help to you." So, Harry was trying to discover the solution.

The next night he was again missing from the church. When I came back from the meeting, I found him sitting at the same table with eyes all red from studying and figuring. I tried again, "Harry, I don't like to have you miss the meetings. I need you."

Then I went upstairs. Shortly thereafter the father came up and said, "Brother Bevington, what are we going to do with Harry? He has an arithmetic problem there that he may injure himself with."

I said, "Let's go back down." Standing at the table, I spoke to Harry, "You belong to Jesus, don't you?"

He looked up with watery eyes and said, "Yes, I do."

"Do you pray?"

"Yes."

"And don't you believe that Jesus answers prayers?"

"I know he does," Harry said as he rubbed his eyes.

"Can't you believe He will show you where the mistake is?" Well, that puzzled him. He knew God had healed his little sister in the spring and other evidences stood out before him. But to think that God would come down and show him how to do an arithmetic problem was just too much for him.

So I said, "Let's pray." I called on the father to pray aloud. Well, he was about like Katie's mamma. He prayed all around the nail, but never hit it. So I stopped him and called on Harry. Harry came closer, but was not hitting it either, so I had to stop him.

I took it up and in ten minutes was hitting the nail square on the head and driving it through. I brought my hand down on the table emphatically as I said, "Thou art showing him where the mistake has been right now!"

229

I said it three times and as I said it the third time, Harry jumped up and yelled, "Brother Bevington, I've got it." He rushed back to the table, sat down and worked it out on a piece of paper the size of my hand. Up to that point, he had already used up three ten-cent tablets.

The Holy Spirit, in answer to prayer, showed him where the problem was. So, children, Jesus will help you if you will trust Him.

While I was in mission work in Cincinnati, there was a kindergarten there under the charge of Reverend Gilson. A man who had a veneering plant just below us passed by quite often. He often stopped to look at the little jewels there, taking quite a liking to them. Soon he began inquiring as to exactly what we were doing, so I invited him in to see them in their classroom. He had a little curly-headed tot of three years, a sweet little one, who often accompanied him.

One day I was walking up Sixth Street and saw some small, red, white and blue splint baskets in a shop window. I stopped and looked at them, thinking, "How nice those would be for our kindergarten children."

I went in and asked their price if purchased by the dozen and the clerk looked it up for me. Then I went and saw Mr. Gamble, the soap man, and told him about these baskets. I wanted to use them to draw in children, as I knew any child would want one.

Mr. Gamble gave me the money to get five dozen such baskets with the understanding that they were not to be sold and they were to be given only to those attending the kindergarten. So I took the baskets back and gave one to each child. Soon the man with his curly-headed little girl came along just as the tots were walking about with their new baskets. "Oh, Papa," said the little girl,

"I want one of those pretty baskets."

He saw me the next day and told me what the child wanted. He said, "I presume you have seen my little girl."

"Yes," I said, "I have noticed her frequently. She looks like a very bright, sweet little child."

"Well, now she says she just will have to have one of those baskets."

I told him, "Mr. Gamble gave us the money to buy them with the understanding they were only for the kindergarten tots."

"I will give you a dollar for one."

"Oh, no, I dare not sell them," I answered. I said no more, but earnestly prayed that God would bring his child in with us. We had learned that they were Catholics and a very fine family.

So, children, I just kept praying. The next morning, here the little girl came with her big sister looking for one of those pretty baskets. They both coaxed me very hard for one. It seemed that the little tot got about everything she asked for, but I told them I could only give a basket to children in the kindergarten. The man had told his wife about the situation and the tot began to cajole her mamma to let her come to the kindergarten so she could get a basket.

I was praying the Lord would not let him see where I got them. They were wealthy people and could have bought her as many baskets as she wanted if he had ever gone up that street and found the store. The papa was willing that the tot should come to the kindergarten, but the mamma said, "Oh, no, not by any means shall my child go to such a filthy place as that. None but the off-scourings go there."

"Now, now," he said, "I never saw much dirt there. It always looks clean and nice."

231

"Well, I have heard about the place. I have heard that it is a disgrace to Cincinnati as all the bums and drunkards and bad women go there."

At that, the man decided he would investigate the mission for himself. The next night in he walked to sit about midway down in the hall. When I saw him, I went and gave him a hearty handshake. He remained all through the meeting and heard some brilliant testimonies, something they certainly didn't have in his church. I saw he was well pleased with it all, so I invited him back.

He went home and the next morning at the breakfast table, he announced, "Wife, I would like for you to go down to that mission. It is not as we have heard. They are well, if plainly, dressed and they are surely a happy people."

"What! Me go down there?" she said in shock. "Never!" That was the end of that as far as she was concerned.

Their older daughter of nearly fourteen summers had become quite aware of the children going in and out of the mission, too. So one day she stopped and inquired as to what they were doing and she was invited inside. The daughter remained all through the session and then went home to tell her mamma where she had been. "It is a fine place, Mama. Oh, how well they work with the little tots and they are so nice and clean."

The mother was not favorably impressed with the idea of their daughter being mixed up with that crowd, but it was vacation time and the girl became a frequent caller to the school. She learned the children's songs and would play for them. Often she would bring her lunch and eat with the little ones.

I saw that God was answering prayer and we were destined to have that little child. I even saw the whole family in there by faith. The older daughter finally

232

got the mother to come down as the little child was still coaxing and crying for one of those baskets. Once the mother had investigated us, she gave her consent to let the little girl come.

She was a bright child, well brought up. Her sweet and refined ways were a great blessing to those who were not so well brought up. She quickly learned the songs and the blessings asked at the table. I would compose a new blessing each month for the children.

Like all of the other little girls, she wanted to have the blessing asked at her family's table. Well, it amused the parents and the older brother and sister as the tot would go around the table, saying to each one, "Now, Papa, now Mamma, you must fold your hands." Each one would have to fold their hands before the blessing was asked.

Often the brother would unfold his hands and down she would get from the high chair to scold him, "Now you fold your hands, because I'm going to ask the blessing."

This was kept up and how we were praying for God to use those songs and blessings. In less than a year, the older daughter was down at the altar and prayed through. She went wild over her new-found joy. Her brother was also there and he just wept all the time she was rejoicing. Then she went back and led him down to the altar.

Well, we were there so late that night, the father came looking for his children. As he entered, the daughter ran to meet him. She threw her arms around him, saying, "Oh, Papa! Oh, I have something I never heard of before." She was such a sweet child anyway, she just looked like an angel—so innocent and pure. The father was completely melted up when he saw her and then saw his only son there, too.

So, children, see how God can work through a little child. He has said in His Word, "A little child shall lead them." Lots of us big folks can't do that, for it is given for the child.

The father went back home, leaving the son at the altar and the daughter there with him. He wanted to satisfy the mother that the children were safe. Well, the mother was thunderstruck and she raged quite a bit until the son and daughter came home about two hours later. The son, about sixteen, just fell weeping on his mamma's lap with his arms around her.

There was indeed something about the two that their mother had never seen nor felt before. The next thing you knew the mother was weeping and both the son and the daughter were on her lap, hugging her and showering her with kisses. It just broke her all up.

So the next night the whole family came and all were at the altar. They did not get through that night, but the following week they did. They all got sanctified. Then they went to their church and each gave their testimony at prayer meeting which was much against the custom of that church. They were given their letters.

Now, think about this, my little friends. Moses had a rod in his hands, just a piece of wood—but, oh, what he did with that rod. He covered all Egypt with swarms of flies and vermin, turned the waters into blood, walled up the Red Sea so that the people could walk through and so much more. Read it in the Scriptures.

Miracles came about, too, because of that little basket in the hands of a tot. Remember, children, you can do much for Jesus if you have faith.

On another occasion I went into a home in Cincinnati for dinner. The mother kept anxiously going to the window, so I said, "Sister, is there something you want?"

"Yes," she answered, "I am looking for Bessie to come.

I want her to run to the grocery, but she is late today from school."

I said, "Let me do the errand for you."

"I need some bread."

"All right. Where do you get it?"

"Round the corner, first grocery. Here is a nickel."

I took the coin for the bread and went to the store. When I made my purchase and turned to go, the clerk said, "Wait, here is a penny change." I took the penny and the bread back to the house and laid both on the sister's plate.

When she lifted up the bread and saw the penny, she said, "Brother Bevington, do you know how that penny got there?"

I said, "I dropped it there."

"What for?"

"Why, the clerk gave it to me. The bread was only four cents." Well, children, I wish I could draw a picture of that mother's face when I told her this. I could see there was something going on down in her heart and soul as it clearly showed on her face. I said nothing, but wondered what made all those rapid changes in her countenance.

Then Bessie came in and we had our dinner. After Bessie had gone back to school, the sister said, "Brother Bevington, I am in great sorrow."

I said, "I see that something crossed your path from the time you found out where that penny came from. What is it?"

"Well," she said, "Bessie gets two loaves of bread daily and she never has given me any change, as you have. I will go down now and see the grocer."

Soon she returned crying bitterly, saying, "Oh, Brother Bevington, what am I to do? Bessie has been keeping these pennies now for the three months since they cut bread down to four cents. Oh, what does it mean?" She just sat down and cried and cried. I did up the dishes for her and tried to make excuses for Bessie. I suggested maybe Bessie was saving them up to surprise her with a present later on.

"Oh, I wish it were so, but oh, my heart is about broken. I am fearful, I am fearful!" she wailed. How she did cry! I had to leave then and she said nothing further until her husband came home from his work and she revealed the case to him. "What shall we do?" she asked him.

I was gone about two months before I came back to their city. I was anxious to know about that penny affair, so I went to their house and inquired. The mother told me she and the father had waited until after supper and then asked Bessie about the pennies. Well, Bessie just broke down and cried. She got up from the table, went to her Mamma and threw her arms around her. Weeping, she kept saying over and over, "Oh, I am so sorry, I am so sorry." She finally told them how it all came about.

Now children, remember Satan is watching all the time to trip you up and get you to do something wrong. So, you must be very careful to always do right.

Bessie told her parents that when she started out of the store with the first bread after the cut in price, the grocer called her back and gave her the penny. She intended to give the penny to her Mamma, but as she was going out of the door, a school mate met her. The friend asked, "Bessie, did you get a penny?"

"Yes."

"What are you going to do with it?"

"Well..." Bessie knew what she should say, but it just didn't come out.

Her friend had a suggestion, "You know you lost your slate pencil and your mamma will think you very careless in so doing. If I were you, I would get another pencil and then your Mamma won't know you lost one. You can start giving her the penny tomorrow."

Well, that looked all right to Bessie for the moment. So off they went to the store and got the pencil. On the way home, Bessie began feeling quite bad about what she had done. Before she reached home, she had decided what she should do. "I don't feel just right about this. I will go back and get my penny by returning the pencil and then tell Mamma all about it."

But another voice said, "Oh, no, just go on. You can begin tomorrow as the price cut was just made today. One day won't matter."

So this naughty voice prevailed. Bessie went in the house, fully determined to give her mother the next penny. But, as Satan had gotten her to do wrong once, he was right there to see that she kept it up. He had no intention of letting her go once he had gotten her started. So the next day she went again to the store, bought the bread and got another penny.

When she started home, the good voice said, "Give Mamma this penny."

But the bad voice was there, saying, "You know they have taffy on the stick at the candy store for a penny right now. You have always been such a good girl and Papa never gives you pennies. You haven't had any candy for three weeks, so just go over and get one. Tomorrow you can begin giving Mamma the penny and she will never know when the cut began."

So Bessie stopped, looked in the candy-filled window, and said, "Oh, that taffy on the stick is so nice. I want one so bad." She bit her lip as she struggled.

The good voice said, "No, you give Mamma the penny."

Bessie said, "I will," and started for home.

But the bad voice stopped her and Satan made her mouth so hungry for that candy! She turned around, promising herself, "I will begin tomorrow." She again yielded to Satan's bad voice. That night at prayer she had quite a time in stammering any words out, but Satan was there and made her bold. So she got through after a struggle.

Well, the next day it was not much trouble for Satan to get her to get more candy. And each day thereafter, he had some new thing for her to get. Each night at prayer he made her bolder and bolder until she could say, "Now I lay me down to sleep," with no trouble at all.

You see children, Satan was hardening her conscience. He was silencing that alarm bell in her heart so she could steal her mamma's pennies and still say her prayers without any trouble.

But God knew the mother must know what was going on, so He sent me around there to have the thing exposed. He managed to keep Bessie late at school so I would go after the bread. Remember the Bible clearly says, "Be sure your sin will find you out." Bessie thought she had all this covered up and was planning what to do with her pennies from buying the bread each day for her mother.

Well, Bessie came to the altar, confessed it all out and got forgiveness from God. Her parents never whipped her for it, they just let God punish her after He let it all come out. Bessie never did anything like that afterward.

Children, Satan was making great headway with Bessie. He planned to first have her steal pennies, then nickels, then dimes, and on and on. If she had continued, she would someday have been willing to kill a man for his money or sell her virtue to get it. So be sure you avoid bad beginnings. Satan has many a snare to trap dear children.

If he can just get them started to speak or act wrongly, he has many ways of leading them to worse deeds.

Oh, how that mother did weep and pray that God would take care of Bessie and keep her pure and honest. God had to answer that precious mother's prayer by sending Bevington around. God used me in uncovering Bessie's sin. So children, mind your parents.

The next time I saw Bessie, ten months later, she came running and hugged me. She said, "God sent you here to get me out of that tangle which would have made a very bad girl out of me. You came just in time to save me." She was glad that I had uncovered Satan's well-covered plan to ruin her. Bessie grew up to be a fine mother and is carefully watching her own precious jewels that God has given her to be a blessing in this dark world.

When I was in mission work in Cleveland, Ohio, one day I was going down a filthy street among the very poorest of people. I heard a sweet, melodious voice and stopped to listen. I was charmed by that marvelous voice coming from such a quarter. Everyone on that street was very wicked, so I dreaded to inquire as to the voice. I prayed, "God, send someone out so I can find that voice." It seemed to be way back, well out of reach.

As I was standing there, a door opened and a poor, dirty woman said, "Come in."

"Oh, no, I don't wish to come in. But I would like to know where that sweet voice is that I heard a moment ago."

She said, "I reckon it was old Pete."

"No," I said, "it was a young voice."

"That's what everybody calls her—old Pete."

"Where is she?"

"Back there in the dirt," the woman jerked her head over her shoulder.

"Could I see her?"

"I reckon."

Preparing myself to take the plunge, I asked, "Well, how do I get to her?"

"Over that fence," the woman said and then disappeared.

I climbed the high fence and back there in the dirt sat this young girl, jibbering to herself. I said, "Good morning, Sis."

She looked up, and said, "Say, mister, give me a chaw of tobacco."

"I don't use it," I said.

"Well, gimme a nickel and I will get old Sal to buy me some."

I said, "What is your real name, old Pete? Where do you live?"

"There with old Sal," she said, pointing to a shack.

"Is she your mother?"

"Nope."

"Where is your mother?"

"Ain't got any."

"Where is your father?"

"Ain't got any. Never had any father nor mother—just old Sal."

"Could I see her?" I asked.

"I reckon so." The young girl drug the back of her filthy hand across her nose and then yelled, "Hey, old Sal! Come 'ere. Man wants you."

Out came a dirty, raggedy woman. She looked me over and said, "Come on in if you want."

"No, I don't want to come in. I just want to know if this is your child."

240

"No, not mine. I'm just raising her."

What a raising, I thought! I asked, "How long have you had her?"

"Two years."

"How old is she?"

"Don't know."

"Would you like to give her to me?"

"Yes, but she's a no account girl—can't walk nor stand on her feet."

I bent down close to the ground and said to the girl, "Are you the one who was singing Annie Laurie awhile ago?"

"Yep."

"Sing it again."

"I will if you give me a nickel to get tobacco with."

"No, I won't give you a nickel. But please sing again for me."

Finally she did and of all the beautiful, clear, sweet voices I have ever heard, I believe hers was the sweetest. I said to the woman, "If you will give me her clothes, I will take her with me now."

"Laws' sake, man, she ain't got any, only what's on her back!"

So I picked that child up and, oh, what an odor came from her poor, filthy body! I asked, "When did you last have a bath?"

"A what?"

"A bath."

"What's that?"

This poor child, about eleven years old, had never had a bath and had only lived in filth. I carried her across the creek to a home that once had been about like the one I found her in. The good woman took her in and set to cleaning her up while I went for some clothes. I went back the next day and hardly recognized her, except for her beautiful eyes. Those eyes were about all I could see of her face the day before.

I began to teach her our songs. It was wonderful how she would learn and sing them. I would carry her up to the mission and out to the street meetings and she would sing so beautifully. We kept her well dressed and she really enjoyed those nice clothes. She was a marvelous child with wonderful talent.

To cut it short, I kept her for two years. All this time she was learning songs and singing them on the streets, drawing great crowds by her sweet, child-like voice. One evening a man stopped to listen to her. He waited till the service was over and then came up and asked, "Is that your child?"

"No, but she stays with us," I replied.

"She has the sweetest voice I ever heard. Are you giving her music lessons?"

"No, I wish I could. But I am in the mission work here and haven't had the money to do it."

He walked with me as I carried the child back to the mission. I saw he was very interested in her welfare. The next morning he came back and said, "I am a traveling man and I make very good money. If I will give you the money, will you give her music lessons—the best you can get?"

I said, "I surely will." He gave me forty dollars and said he would be back in two months. I secured the best musical talent I could find, taking the child to lessons twice a week. She learned to practice on the mission organ. I made her a high chair with a back to it, so that she could sit and play.

The man came back in two months and was delighted in the progress she was making. He bought her a fine

242

high chair, much better than the one I had made. He left fifty dollars for some clothing and her music lessons, saying he would return. We got her three nice suits and shoes. She had tiny feet about the size of an eight-month-old baby's and had never been able to stand. She was now developing rapidly into a beautiful girl and was such a sweet, cheerful singer.

The traveling man returned in two months and was well pleased with her progress. He went out and came back with a fine, four-wheeled carriage with levers so she could guide it. It had a very nice cover and was quite wonderful. The man paid eighty-eight dollars cash for it.

Well, now she could go anywhere! She nearly went wild with excitement when the man placed her in the carriage. He said, "Now this is yours." She looked so incredulous, he repeated, "Yes, yours!"

"Is it really mine! Mine to keep always?" she asked.

"Yes, it is." At that, she asked me to take her back out and put her in his arms, which I did. She hugged him and showered kisses upon him. Promising to return, the man went on his way.

As usual, I was giving out tracts daily and one day the girl said, "Papa (I had taught her to call me Papa), can't I give out those tracts from my buggy?"

"You certainly can," I said. "Would you really like to?"

"Yes, I can go on the streets and give them out for you." So she did and God would bless her in doing it. For some time I had been trying to tell her what salvation was, what Jesus died for and how she ought to give Him her heart. But it seemed she was so carried away with the great change that had taken place in her life, I just could not get her to see that she ought to be regenerated.

I would pray, "God, what am I going to do? How can I impress her of the importance of this?" I would talk to her, read the Scriptures to her and tell her that if she should die, she would go to an awful hell. That all seemed idle to her, like a dream. I could not get her interested. She seemed to think the transformation that had already taken place was sufficient. So I kept praying.

Now children, listen to how God answered my prayer. As she was giving out tracts, she would find time to study them. I had been teaching her to read all these weeks and months and she could spell out any word.

She had been giving out one particular tract entitled, "Anna's and Nannie's First Prayer," and she really worked on reading that one in her leisure moments on the street. She would also get me to read it to her. So that tract, as well as others, brought her face to face with the question of salvation. She saw where she was and what she must be.

One night as I gave the altar call, she said, "Papa, I want Jesus, too." She was in her buggy, so she just wheeled herself up to the altar. She gave her heart to Jesus and was blessedly saved right there in that buggy. Oh, how she would sing and clap her hands after that!

Her benefactor came back every two months and bought her clothes and paid for her music lessons for four years. She was then about seventeen, as nearly as we could determine her age. She was an accomplished musician.

One day the man came and said, "Mr. Bevington, if you will give me that girl, I will take her to Indianapolis where they make artificial limbs. They would nearly make her perfectly whole."

I said, "Would you want her for all time as your daughter?" The question brought tears to my eyes and he saw it.

"Well," he said thoughtfully, "you really do love her. I will take her there and then bring her back to you—a perfect, walking lady."

I very much disliked the thought of giving her up even for a while, but knew it was best for her. I was then in Louisville in the mission work, having left Cleveland for some time. He took her off to Indianapolis and kept her there over two years. When he brought her to me at Cincinnati, she was a lovely, young lady who could walk as well as I could. She had her artificial limbs and could use them quite proficiently. She had also been studying all this time.

I took her to Mr. Gamble and he sent her to school for another two years. Then she went to the Fiji Islands as a missionary under the M.E. Board. She was there several years and established a great faith home and school. She went from there to Heaven.

See what God can and will do if we will trust Him. I might have said, "That poor, miserable, dirty, ignorant, uncouth girl can never do anything for Jesus." Instead, I saw a glimpse of what God saw in her. He opened the way for her to become a brilliant and accomplished young lady and then sent her to the mission field where hundreds were brought to Jesus. Praise the Lord for her life and that God could use such as I in bringing her out of darkness.

Dear children, if God could take such as she was when I found her and bring her to where He did, just think what He might do with you if you would let Him. You must realize that God can help you and will help you, but He wants you to trust Him. He wants you to give your heart to Him. He says in His Word, "Give me thine heart."

You must be born again, regenerated, made a new creature in Christ Jesus. So see that you do not put it off too long. Jesus said, "Suffer the little children to come unto me...for of such is the kingdom of heaven."

I want to meet every boy and girl who reads these pages up in Heaven. I am going there and surely do thank God for my praying mother. I well remember when I was about seven, after prayer my mother said, "This boy (laying her hand on my head) is going to preach the Gospel."

As a young man I never entered into deep sin, but I was very reckless. I loved the world, dancing, theaters and so many other things. Most anyone seeing me in those days would have said, "Well, that fellow's mother missed it when she said he was going to be a preacher." I forgot my mother's benediction until after I had been preaching some time and then a cousin reminded me of it. God had that prayer of Mother's to answer and praise His dear name, He did. He will make preachers out of you boys and girls, too, if you will just let Him.

When I was in the mission work in Cleveland, I met a crippled girl about fourteen years of age. She was quite small and had never walked. She had a sixteen-year-old brother who had his back broken when he was twelve. He could sit up, but not walk. They were very poor. I got them clothes and wheeled them to and from the mission in a wheelbarrow. They were bright, ambitious children who could read and write. Once after I had given a missionary talk, the girl said, "Oh! I wish I could make some money for those dear children over there." She had never heard of them before and she became greatly worked up about them.

I got to thinking. I went home and made a few lighters out of papers and took them down to a factory to see if I could sell them. I told the foreman about those two children and how they needed help. While I was talking, the manager came in and overheard what I said. He asked the foreman, "Would these be cheaper than matches?"

"Yes, they would," replied the foreman.

"Well, how much could we afford to pay for them?"

The foreman said, "Not over thirty cents a hundred."

Well, that seemed pretty small, but it was a beginning. I went back and got a lot of paper, took it to these children and showed them how to make the lighters. They soon became experts at it and soon could make a hundred a day. This brought them thirty cents, a big pile of money to them. As poor as the parents were, they said the children could give half of everything to the heathen children. So they did.

I took the finished lighters to the factory and got the cash for the children. The factory manager had a cousin in another part of the city who also used gas stoves and he got this cousin to order several thousand lighters. Those children soon got so they could each make two hundred lighters a day or four hundred in all. Well, at thirty cents per hundred, how fast can you figure what they would earn in a day?

Those children bought their own clothes and went to night school. I would wheel them there and their father would come after them. They got saved and we discovered they both loved to sing. The girl even took music lessons and learned to play. This was all from the money earned by making those paper lighters. So, children, where there is a will—there is a way!

They kept giving half of all their money to the foreign field and two years after I left there, they both were engaged in the office of this factory. Both of them had learned stenography. They continued to live good, Christian lives. Four years after that I was at the Cincinnati camp when a young man and a young lady, both on

247

crutches, came up to me. They were fine-looking people. They smiled and said, "I guess you don't know us now."

Well, I admit I didn't. So they told me who they were and, oh, how proud I was of them. They had been faithful to their God and He prospered them. They were living in their own home and paying for it out of the wages they made in this factory and their father and mother still kept them in paper lighters.

Now, one more short story. I was holding a meeting down below Rising Sun, Indiana, and was in a home where there was a little tot. She couldn't talk plain, but would say her, "Now I lay me," every night and morning.

One night she failed to say it. So Mamma said, "Gracie, aren't you going to say your prayer?"

"Nope."

"Well, why not?"

"Because I'm backslid," she replied seriously.

I had never heard anything like that from such a little tot and I was so amused, I had to go outdoors. Mamma just shook her head at me as she went over to the child. She said, "Well, Gracie, how did you come to backslide?"

"I got mad at Jim and said a bad word."

"I see. Well," Mamma said, "you must get back to Jesus again."

So the dear little thing just began to pray and cry. Then she rose and said, "It's all right. I'm all right now."

I tell you that was a good lesson to me. You couldn't get her to say she was saved, sanctified up-to-date, while she was doing wrong. If all children were that honest, it would be a rebuke to many an older person.

Well, dear children, we have had quite a time. I have enjoyed this chat with you all. So in closing this chapter,

I want to invite you all to Jesus, Whom I have been well acquainted with now these more than thirty years since I was sanctified. In Him I have all confidence. I feel sure that if you will give Him your hearts, He will care for you as He has for me. I want to meet every one of you up in Heaven where Jesus and the angels are, where we can forever be with the Lord. God bless you, one and all, and the papas and mammas of all. With love and best wishes, I close.

Your friend and well wisher,

G.C. Bevington
Ashland or Kingswood, Kentucky

8
Instances of Healing

Unanswered prayers avail us nothing. It is the prayers that get through that will count for us and those for whom they are offered. So, do not be careless or indifferent in your praying. God wants real, earnest, effectual, prevailing prayers.

Those prayers are heard and answered. I believe He says to His recording angel, "Get your file and record that prayer. It has a good sound, clear ring to it. We will have to put it on file, ready for adjustment."

God does the giving and we do the taking. What we do not take, we do not get. God cannot give us what we will not take.

> God has His choice things for the few
> Who dare to stand the test;
> God has His second choice for those
> Who will not have His best.

In which crowd are you?

> Faith drops out where our doubts step in,
> And Faith stops just where doubts begin.

> Faith, mighty Faith, the promise sees,
> And looks to that alone;
> Laughs at impossibilities
> And cries, 'It shall be done!'

Yes, it shall be done! Amen!

If you are now ailing and suffering, look up. Count the healing done and it shall be done. Hallelujah! It shall be done "according to your faith." It is not according to how long you have had the trouble or how it has baffled all efforts to solve it. It is "according to your faith." So look up in faith and count it done now.

If healing depended on us to perform it, things would be quite different. But Divine healing is the "shall" as uttered by our omnipotent, omniscient, omnipresent God. Hallelujah! We have a right to trust Him to the limit and count it done.

God wants men and women with iron in their blood and fire in their bones and a pick and a shovel and a subsoil plow to turn something up when real need arises. Amen and amen!

We sometimes get to the place where we can't pray the prayer of faith as we may be too weak or suffering too intensely. This can lessen our faculties and render us incapacitated for such prevailing prayer. This is when we need to hear from God and pray one for another.

I was one of the first students in God's Bible School in Cincinnati. About a month before the first term closed, I was taken down with acute neuralgia. It was very painful and kept getting worse. I was getting to bed quite late in the evenings as I was working downtown for my board and going up to the school in the afternoons for recitations, Bible review and other lessons. That was before I had stepped out entirely on healing, but I was not taking any remedies.

After about a week of suffering, I woke up one night at midnight in terrible misery. I tried to pray, but I was just in too much agony. So I began to cry out to God to make someone else pray for me. I was pleading for about ten minutes, "Oh, God, wake someone up who will pray for me." I began to get better and in thirty minutes the suffering was all gone. I was soon sound asleep, knowing God had answered.

In about ten days I received a letter from California. It stated that on such a date, shortly after midnight, the writer was awakened and a voice said, "Get up and pray for Bevington." She did not know where I was, only that my last address had been Cincinnati, Ohio.

She said, "I am too sleepy and I don't even know where he is," and tried to go back to sleep. But that voice kept calling her.

She finally woke her husband who said, "You are just dreaming. Bevington can do his own praying. I think you ate too much supper last night. Now go to sleep and don't bother about him—he will pull through all right." Well, she tried to go to sleep, but could not for that voice kept ringing in her ears.

Her husband said, "I guess you had better do it. It doesn't matter where he is, go ahead and get up and pray." She did so and the moment her knees struck the floor, she was engulfed with great misery in her head. She called her husband to get up and go to praying with her. He, being a blessedly saved man, got up and it was the same with him—he was taken with severe shooting pains in his head.

So they clasped hands across the bed, he on one side—she on the other, and began to pray for me. In about seven minutes their pains stopped and so did mine. They knew that they had reached the throne in my behalf.

So you see, God had to wake someone up way out in California. That was the first time I ever did that and have never done it since. I don't know when I may, but I will if I have need. The lesson is that we must mind God regardless of how things seem. When God told Samuel to anoint David, a stripling sheep herder, to be a king, Samuel knew that Saul had not yet been dethroned. He was still their actual king and to anoint another would be equal to treason. Samuel had said, "Why, Lord, if I go down there and anoint David as king, Saul will kill me. He is the lawful, legal king and is now on the throne." Yet in face of all this and the danger of being killed, Samuel minded God. God has to appeal to our natural being at times in order to create or stimulate our faith—often to overthrow our own plans.

While at Ashland Heights, I was called one evening to come over to Fairview to preach. As I went by Brother and Sister Wamsley's in Pollard, I stopped to get them to go along. I found Brother Wamsley on his porch and I called to him, "Are you and your wife going over?"

"I guess not. Wife has been suffering for three days with neuralgia and we dare not go out. I don't want to leave her as she is suffering now really beyond her strength."

I said, "Tell her to come out."

"Why, Brother Bevington, she dare not expose herself to the air. She would not live ten minutes."

"Tell her to come out," I insisted. He just stood there and gaped at me, completely astonished at my ridiculous request. I repeated, "Tell her to come out."

"She would not dare to venture out a moment," he said.

"Tell her to come out." I just stood there praying and

repeating this wild request until they got tired of hearing it. Finally, out she came with her head all tied up. I bowed my head and pleaded the promises while standing there on the street. Several others who were unsaved were now standing around looking on. I raised my hand, claimed her healing, then stood still and counted the work done. In fifteen minutes I heard a whoop and off came the bandages. Sister Wamsley had herself a shouting spell right there.

I started on to Fairview with some others, praying the Lord would send them over. About half way there, I said, "Boys, she is coming. She will come soon after we get there."

My companions said, "Oh, I reckon not. She has been in a critical condition and it would be too dangerous for her to attempt it."

I said, "She is coming."

We had just begun singing when in she came, shouting and swinging her sunbonnet until she set the whole house on fire. At the altar service she was all aglow with the power of God on her and prayed a poor, discouraged backslider through. To Jesus be all the glory!

A sister in South Ashland was, according to the doctor, on her death bed with consumption. I was invited over to pray for her and went, taking along another sister with me. I read a chapter and got on my knees, pleading earnestly. I got the victory, claimed her healing, jumped up, grabbed my hat and rushed out as I said, "She will be out of there in ten minutes."

I had not gotten out of their yard before she was out of that bed, praising God for complete healing. She went to the Pilgrim Holiness Church where Reverend John Fleming was pastor and there she testified to her healing.

Brother John witnessed her healing and he will testify to being healed more than once, himself, as will his dear, faithful wife. The first year after he moved to Ashland from Willard, his saintly wife was on her bed very sick. He sent me word and I prayed for her that night. I got blessed during prayer and claimed her healing.

But the next afternoon he drove up the hill after me, saying she was much worse. I jumped into his buggy and went with him to her room. She lay speechless on her bed, very much resembling a lifeless form.

I fell on my face in the corner to ascertain whether God wanted to heal her or not. I lay there over an hour. Finally being satisfied that He wanted to heal her, I rose on my knees and laid my hand on her cold brow. Soon she opened her eyes and smiled and the glory fell! Brother John shouted, "Brother Bevington, she is healed."

I jumped up, walked the floor about five minutes, and then went out and got into the buggy. I drove downtown rejoicing over her healing, though all the visible evidence she had given was the opening of her eyes and smiling. But the glory flooded me all the way. I accomplished an errand and came back under the power of God to find her up and praising Jesus. So, Satan was certainly foiled there. Hallelujah to Jesus' dear name!

I had a number of cases of healing at South Ashland, but cannot remember the details. I do remember while at Willard, in 1917, a case was reported of a very sick woman who was a backslider. She had been in bed six weeks and looked quite helpless. The children needed care and the house was pretty well littered up.

As I approached this case, I felt intense darkness. But I thought, "Can I afford to let this woman die unsaved?" I went to prayer and had a real struggle as everything seemed so black. I kept praying and dynamiting and blasting until, after two hours in tunnels and caves, I began to see streaks of light. I will never forget how that encouraged me.

I don't remember when I have ever been so grateful as when I saw that light beginning there in that dark home. Everything seemed against me except, I think, the five children who appealed to me. I took them as my reasons for pleading for her healing.

As I went to praising God softly, the clouds began to lift. My faith seemed to be climbing rugged peaks, leaping from one to another. Though rather quietly, I claimed her healing and stood to my feet. As I left her room, I met the brother who had sent me there and he asked me, "Well, what did you do?"

"I believe she will be out of that bed soon," was all I could tell him.

I left and went up to the home of Frank Fleming, a brother to the Fleming preachers, John and Bona. This was nearly a mile from where the sick woman lived and I heard nothing from her during the night or early in the morning. So I refused breakfast and held on with good encouragement. I kept pushing right up that dark hill for two hours after I got up. Then I said, "Lord, it is done! It is done! It is done!"

At the third utterance, Sister Fleming came to the door and said, "Oh, Brother Bevington, just listen. That woman is out yelling like a wild person."

I had claimed her victory and now I was rejoicing, sweeping through the clouds and mounting evermore delectable heights, praising God for her healing. The sister was out leaping fences, running from one house to another, shouting and praising God for healing and reclaiming her.

I want to include a letter here which has been addressed to all who would be blessed by reading it.

To the brothers and sisters in the Lord, scattered abroad:

I want to take advantage of this opportunity to testify to all to the glory of Him who said, "I am the Lord that healeth thee."

I am praising the Lord today for healing me of a severe case of gallstones. I feel like saying, sometimes, "This one thing I know, that whereas I was sick, I am now well." Praise the Lord!

Since the flu swept the country, I had been a victim of gallstones which developed after I had the flu. I had always been a believer in Divine healing, but I never could get faith strong enough for the healing of my own body. I remembered that the Bible says: "If two of you shall agree on earth as touching anything that they shall ask, it shall be done," so I wrote Brother G.C. Bevington, who was at Kingswood, Kentucky, at that time.

He joined with me in prayer in behalf of my body and on January 2, 1921, the Lord wonderfully and instantly healed me. Ever since, I have been trusting Him for constant good health and He gives it, praise His name! Of course the devil tries to tell me that I am not healed and that I still have the gallstones, but I know I was healed. So I get the victory over the old devil and go on praising the Lord. Amen!

Knowing there are so many people destitute of faith for the healing of their own bodies, I want to say that it is not an easy thing to give up all remedies and trust the Lord. The devil would like to keep us sick and would even like to kill us. So it takes a lot of encouragement and trusting and prayer and light on how to trust the Lord for complete victory over the devil.

I have often wondered if I would have been healed, if it had not been for the wonderful letters of encouragement and light I received from Brother Bevington while he was praying for me. He has such a matured experience and such a grip on God. He has undaunted faith, especially for Divine healing.

R.W. Wolfe
Fort Gay, West Virginia

On another occasion I went over to Ironton, Ohio, and taught a class in Sunday school where I met an old acquaintance I had not seen for several years. He had been healed in the country.

I was called to his home to pray for his wife's healing. I soon said, "Sister, are you sure you are a sanctified woman?"

She had claimed that experience, but now she broke out crying and confessed, "No, brother, I am not and never have been. I thought I was once and testified to it here in the church, as I was told to claim it and testify to it."

Now here is danger. I never ask people to testify to their sanctification until they are sure they are sanctified. I only encourage them to take it by faith if they and I am satisfied that their consecration is complete. Then they may say they have taken sanctification by faith, believe that they are sanctified and stand on that. Never say that you are sanctified until you know it.

This sister was doing what holiness preachers told her to do, for they are supposed to know. But when she got down face to face with God in that prayer circle, God revealed to her she was never sanctified.

Well, I just turned my whole outfit in another direction from that which she was aiming at and I poured out my desires that she might have a real revelation, a real heart searching. She suddenly raised up and cried, "Oh, brother, I want the real thing this time!"

So I loaded up heavier and bombarded the citadel of hell pretty strong for about two hours until she was suddenly laid out as white as could be. I just kept up the firing until she made an unconditional surrender, which she did in about an hour. I tell you—she took the house sure. When she finally settled down, she said, "Oh, glory, I know it is done now!"

When the bombarding ceased and the smoke cleared away, I heard someone else groaning. I looked behind me and there lay her son of about sixteen years, crying out for salvation. So I turned my guns on him and in ninety minutes he was shouting victory. He grabbed me and carried me all over the room. We had a great praise service.

Then I said, "Now, sister, how about that sickness you called me here to pray for?"

"Oh," she said, "I had forgotten all about that. I guess that is gone with the 'old man'." And sure enough it was. We need to be ready for most anything these days. I just carry a full kit with me all the time, so as to be ready for any emergency.

Here is an incident which occurred in Ashland Heights.

I was going down the hill from the church and slipped and sprained my ankle. Well, it was quite painful, but I went on to walk downtown and back. My foot pained some on my return, but I did not bother the Lord with it for I considered it too small a matter to bring to Him. However, by the next morning it was quite painful and so swollen I could not get my shoe on. The joint was stiff and I could not move the foot. I had planned to put out tracts that day and saw that something had to be done and that right away.

When I had done my dishes and put them all away, I got the Word and opened it to where the lame man was healed instantly. Well, as I plunged down that trail, I was scooping up power at every word. By the time I reached the place where it says, "Immediately his ankle bone received strength," I dropped the Bible and shouted, "Yes and here is the same!"

I jumped up, leaping and shouting, and was perfectly healed right then and there. I tell you I well remember that morning. How the glory did fall! Ah, yes, God will heal.

I see here a record of getting a letter about Bertha Bolander, a former student of God's Bible School. It was a special letter from the husband, stating that his wife was in the hospital with no hopes of recovery. So I took the letter and the Bible and spent nineteen hours pleading for her.

I saw her rise up and raise her hand as plainly as I ever saw anything, though she was two hundred miles from me. Well, you might again ask, "Why did it take that long, inasmuch as she was suffering so and needed immediate help?"

As usual, it took me some time to get still as many other cases were clamoring for a hearing. Satan is always around to remind us of the many other "important" cases

261

we ought to attend to. He knows that will divert us from the main line, switch us off and blockade the whole thing.

So it did take me hours to find out if the Lord wanted to heal her, but it took only two hours to see her raised up after those seventeen hours were spent in getting the mind of Jesus. Many devices of Satan were used to head me off. I would get drowsy, sleepy and unconcerned, all of which were only to get me discouraged and to drop the case.

But I felt the case was worthy of my best efforts and I well remember while I was pleading, I brought up some pretty good reasons for her speedy recovery. I would quickly be met by just about as reasonable logic as I was presenting—that is from the natural standpoint. A particular stress was put on the point that we must not close our eyes to the natural as God is the founder of natural laws and we must give heed to them.

All of these arguments often present a pretty broad and solid front that can be somewhat difficult to break through if others are clamoring for attention. But I had the assurance God wanted to heal her and I continued the fight for her life.

I saw her lying just like a corpse, but I did not give up at that. Satan said, "She is now dead. There is no use putting in any more time on her case. You have been very faithful and done your best, putting in seventeen hours of your valuable time."

All this was tinged with logic, even if it was somewhat laced with flattery. I fought all this logic and rose from my face, demanding immediate attention. I held up the Bible, saying, "Lord, Thou dost hear and Thou art interested in Thy children. Keep Satan off. Is she dead? I am now listening to Thee." Soon the scene changed, the clouds vanished and no more logical presentations were given. I said, "Lord, I can't believe she is dead."

Now listen to what was given me. "The afflictions of the righteous are many, but the Lord delivereth from them all." I grabbed my Bible and began praising God. I soon had the evidence that she was not only alive, but healed. Oh, hallelujah! How the glory did fall! In a few days I received notice of her sudden recovery.

I have another letter of testimony I would like to include right here from Sister G.L. Medler regarding her healing at Kingswood, Kentucky, in May of 1921:

> I want to tell that God has wonderfully relieved me of my very severe suffering. Divine healing is wonderful and it shows God's love for us. I have been Divinely healed many times, though this time seems more wonderful because the suffering had been of so long duration.
>
> When a girl in my teens, I was taken with a very severe case of rheumatism. I do not know that I was ever free entirely from suffering from that time until now. Praise the Lord, He has removed the suffering! Many physicians did their best to relieve me, though the disease only tightened its already fastened fangs. As time went on, I think there was none of my flesh or sinew that had not experienced this sawing, cutting, gnawing pain through and through.
>
> No joint or nerve escaped the continual suffering. When I slept, my hands swelled, the joints becoming stiff and useless. When the worst suffering settled in my hands, they would be so out of shape, they hardly looked like human hands. Then the suffering would move to some other part of the body and the joints

would loosen. My hands would return to a semblance of hands, though not normal as the joints would be enlarged and knots formed.

I do not claim to be healed from the effects of rheumatism, though I am relieved from the awful suffering. I do thank the Lord for it. It was His love and His power that relieved me. I cannot describe what a sufferer I was for forty years.

One doctor refused to do anything for me as he said it was an incurable case. He said I was past help and never would use either of my hands again. From about twenty-three years since I was taken ill, I suffered every winter with rheumatism in my head and many other times, also. One doctor said, "I will send you another medicine. If it does not help you, there is not anything that will." I took that medicine exactly as directed, regarding my diet and everything, but grew worse every day.

Over a year ago the rheumatism settled in my head and my brain. I cannot explain the suffering. My neighbors offered to come and pray for me, but I said, "I have no faith for my healing; I have suffered so long and so severely. This is a hopeless case." This Spring a sanctified physician, Dr. Shoemaker, advised me to ask Brother Bevington to pray for my healing.

At first I was not much interested. There had been so many other attempts, I had given up all hope. But after some time of continual suffering, the Lord began to talk to me about asking Brother Bevington. I began to take heed and hearing of others who were being healed through his prayers, I began to get interested. The third week in April I decided I would ask Brother Bevington to pray for my healing, though I had not decided just when and how I would put this decision into action. However, the Lord knew it was time for action, so it was settled on Sunday, April 24th.

When I attempted to get up that morning, I just fell back on the bed. I did not give up and lie back down, I fell. When I decided to wake Mr. Medler and tell him he would have to get up and get his own breakfast, the Lord said, "You get up."

I replied, "I did not suppose I could get up." The Lord never tells anyone to do anything impossible, so I saw that I could in His name.

When it was time to get ready for Sunday school, the Lord said, "You get ready and go." I was more surprised at that command than the other, though again I believed that the Lord knew and I obeyed.

About two-thirds of the way there, I felt I could go no farther though I kept saying, "Well, the Lord told me to go, so He will help me the rest of the way." When I arrived, I was very, very sick.

Then the Lord said, "Get Brother Bevington to pray for you." I was so blinded that I could not see to write a note to him, so Mr. Medler wrote Mr. Bevington that I was at the college and very sick. He asked him to pray for my relief. That was all I would have asked, as it was as far as I could see—just relief. I had no faith in healing.

265

After I went in and took my seat, there seemed to be a black, weighty something about ten feet square with the center of it pressing on the top of my head. Our pastor told me that was the devil trying to keep Brother Bevington from getting a prayer through for me. After a while, that was removed and the blind, dizzy, deathly sick feeling left me, though the severe pain did not cease until the next afternoon. When we got home, the pastor told us how Brother Bevington got down and talked to the Lord about my case and how he felt the mighty presence of God. He said that Brother Bevington prayed, "Now, Lord, I believe she is Your child and if she is, we have a right to claim healing for her—yes, complete healing."

It was right then that my faith took hold for the first time and I said, "Yes, Lord, I am Thy child. I shall be healed on the ground that I am Thy child."

That noon I went to bed, as I thought, for the rest of the day. But after I took a nap, the Lord said, "Get up and go to the class meeting."

I did so and gave my testimony. I said, "I have suffered very much the last few days, and especially today, though the Lord is healing me. Brother Bevington is praying for me and he said if I am the Lord's, I can be healed. I know I am God's child and I am going to be healed. Praise His name!"

It was nearly five weeks before I reported to Brother Bevington that I had complete relief from rheumatism. I had suffered much during that time and even had tonsillitis. Our pastor,

Sister Brown, came and prayed with me and I was instantly healed of that and a severe cold. The devil tried hard to keep me from getting the victory.

The Lord did not remove the rheumatism suffering all at once, but the Lord's way is the right way always and the best for us. Praise His Holy Name forever and forever! I praise Him for victory for the soul and body. Through the precious blood I am saved, sanctified and completely healed. Hallelujah.

Mrs. G.L. Medler
Kingswood, Kentucky

While I was at my home at Ashland Heights, Brother White came over for water and brought his boy of four summers with him. The boy's head was covered with eczema. I inquired about the case and was informed of the details. Then I said, "Well, I guess our Doctor can cure that. Brother White, don't you know that Jesus can heal that head?"

"Well, I reckon He can, as He can do all things."

I said, "Come in, let's anoint him for healing."

"But I am afraid I haven't the faith," he said in an apologetic way.

"Well, come in anyway." So in they came and I anointed the boy and prayed the prayer of faith. They came back the next evening and the little fellow was healed. Oh, how blessed to be yoked up with such a power to relieve the suffering and that without money and without price. Hallelujah!

That particular water well was the only one right near

there and many numbers of people came to get water. I would give them tracts and talk salvation with them. A neighbor once told me, "Brother Bevington, there is a spring on down the hill a ways. You had better send these people down there or your well will soon go dry. Too many are drawing from it and it always goes dry in the summer."

Well, the water soon got roily, but still the people came. It was suggested that I put a sign out asking them not to get any more water until it rained. I thought that was all right and even went so far as to write it up. I got the tacks and the hammer and started out to put the sign up, but when I got part way out to the gate, a voice said, "Where are you going?"

Well, I was startled and looked around, really expecting to see someone behind me. But there was not a person in sight. I just stood there and again the voice said, "Yes, where are you going?" I tell you that settled it. I tore up the sign, dropped on my knees and asked God to forgive me for venturing that far into the realms of the doubting castle. I began praising Him for rebuking me.

Just as I got off my knees, here came three women with large buckets. I promptly got a small bucket and gave it to them to draw with, as their large buckets would get but little. I availed myself of the opportunity of going in to get some more tracts and then began talking salvation to them. One of them had never been there and I felt that God really sent the message home to her, as she had four precious children to train for the kingdom. Left alone, those children would not need any training for hell as they had the thing in them that would land them there without any human help.

Well, they had a time getting their three buckets full, but I just kept sweet. I said, "Lord, You keep sending them here. I would rather pack water from the spring ninety rods away than to miss an opportunity of warning those lost mothers."

The day passed. I went out in the evening with a two-quart bucket, let it down and got it half full of roily water. I just said, "Well, amen, I can go the spring." So I started off with two buckets. But because I had two hills to climb, I soon was impressed to leave one bucket and did so.

I set the bucket down and started on to the spring and, lo, the voice said, "Bevington, where are you going?" Well, I knew the voice—hence I never even looked around, but instantly turned and went back into the house.

I had somewhat of a struggle in getting where I could easily praise the Lord for rebuking me, as I had to have water and I was thirsty. I prayed my way through the darkness, though, and got up. Just then my neighbor came in with a quart of nice, cool water she had gotten some distance from home.

Well, I began to see that God wanted to send water into my well though there was no signs of rain and the well had always gone dry at that season. It often remained dry for three, four or even five months or so they said. I got down and began praising God for stopping me and for sending in the sister with the water.

I was in the habit of taking a good drink just before retiring and this is where Satan had confused me. He kept saying, "What are you going to do for that cool drink that always helps you so?" I had to tell him it was none of his business what I was going to do about it. I had a struggle for three hours over it, but got the victory. I claimed two feet of water in the morning, which had not been such since I lived there.

I told the neighbor that we would have at least two feet of water in the morning. She was a dear woman, a member of a church, but knew nothing about God answering prayer. She looked at me, quite puzzled, and then said, "Brother Bevington what makes you think that? I have never known of there being two feet of water in that well. When there comes a freshet, it just leaks out." The well was seventy-two feet deep.

"Well," I assured her, "we will have it."

She peered up at the sky, "I cannot see any signs of rain."

I said, "I do."

Well, that puzzled her more than ever as the firmament was decked with brilliant stars. I went to bed, praising God for two feet of water in the morning, so I could have plenty for the neighbors.

I had a two-quart bucket that I usually drew out with the windlass and, without thinking, in the morning I started out with this two-quart bucket. I had to be rebuked again. It seemed that the bucket spoke up as did Baalam's ass and I dropped it as if it were a hot poker. I stopped and cried out, "Oh, God, forgive me! Oh, forgive me!" I felt His touch.

I went to the well and let down the large bucket. I gave it the usual time to sink and then started to draw it up. I could tell by the pull that it was full. I shouted, "Oh, glory!"

Out came my neighbor. I called to her, "We have our two feet in this morning." She came right over and by the time I had the bucket up and out, there it was full and as clear as a crystal. I just stood there weeping for joy.

She ran into the house, got a cup and took a drink before she could believe it. Then she said in amazement, "Well, this is a marvel. Your God surely has answered your prayer." She broke down and we both stood there by that well, weeping. Finally she spoke again, "Brother

Bevington, this is something quite new to me. Do you really think there is two feet of water in there?"

"Yes, I do."

"Well, please measure it."

"No, I would not do that, as it would be displeasing to God."

"Well, may I measure it?"

I saw no problem with that. "Certainly," I responded.

So she measured it and found there were two feet and nine inches of water. That amount was kept up all summer and fall.

Now I have left out what, to my thinking, was the cream of it. Satan bothered me and tormented me all he could all that night long after I had prayed. He woke me up to notify me that it had not rained during the night. "Well," I said, "I am not looking for rain. I am after water, rain or no rain." While I was dressing, he just poured out his logic and came near downing me in it. But I rallied, got dressed and dropped on my knees, as prayer is generally the best weapon I can use. Pray as I might, I seemed to make slow progress for the heights.

So I jumped up and said, "Mr. Devil, I have two feet of water out there!" That seemed to have no effect on him whatever. So I said, "I will see what my calendar says." I struck a light and referred to the daily Scripture on the calendar. Now listen what was there: Isaiah 33:16, "Bread shall be given him; his water shall be sure."

Oh, how I did rejoice. Think of it, that after all that struggling, God had that very passage there on the canvas for me—just for my special use. I tell you I have never been without a Scripture calendar since. Oh, God answers!

I see here, recorded in 1920, several cases of the flu. I

271

remember one family that had two doctors all night. Nothing seemed to help and as they were sinking fast, they sent for me. I went and anointed them and began to pray. Soon they showed signs of life, so I held on. Then the woman opened her eyes, smiled and said, "I am healed." In a few hours she was out of bed and gaining strength. The next morning she got breakfast for the family and there was no more flu in that home.

I was called to another sister who was very low. Her husband had just gotten out of bed after a long siege of it and she was well worn out from caring for him. He was still very weak and two children were in another bed with the same disease. When I arrived, I felt awful darkness—it was, oh, so dark. I sat there wondering what could be done and was almost persuaded to leave.

Oh, such a pressure! There was nothing congenial, no encouragement whatever. The sister was unconscious. She had not lived any too close to the Lord as she had many hindrances in the home with unsaved girls and an unsaved husband. Well, as I sat there, I said, "Oh, God, what can be done?" I seemed to get no answer, no light, but there I was. I had been sent for by one of the daughters. There was a possibility and should I ignore that?

I had not been where there was such a heavy pressure in a long time, but I was held there by the power of God. I looked at the sister where she lay with no sign of life. The medicine was sending out its fumes which had a stupefying effect on me. But I rallied and said, "God is able." At that, the man raised his head from an apparent stupor and nodded assent.

Satan was there and warned me about remaining in that atmosphere. There had been several severe cases over four weeks and the rooms had not been fumigated. Well, all this was logic and rather hard to meet and I was having such a hard time in breathing that I could scarcely get my breath. But could I leave one of my sisters, who was so needed in that home and who was evidently at the point of death? Could I leave her? Would God get any glory out of my leaving?

Then came more logic. "But you surely can't stand it long in here with this flu odor so thick and you were up all night last night. If you undertake to pray through, you will smother in here and hence fail. It would be better never to have come. You must remember that it was the unsaved girl who sent for you. She did it through simply human desires to have her mamma get well—God has nothing to do with your coming here!"

Well, I tell you, all these arguments were staggering and it was getting very difficult for me to breathe. Then I compared the sister's usefulness to mine. "Ah, Lord, mine is of little importance, but there are three babies and two in their teens here, all needing her."

I stepped out onto the porch, got a whiff of fresh air and called for a drink. But I had to get it myself, as there was no one to wait on me nor any of the others. I fell on my knees, but I could scarcely get a word out. I pushed on through, crying to God mightily from my heart, if not with my voice. "Oh, God, Thou wilt hear! Oh, God, Thou wilt hear!"

I got this out audibly and that encouraged me. So I proceeded up the hill of faith, grabbing a root here and there, and soon saw that I was coming to the top. That gave me courage and I tell you, I did some earnest scrambling. As the footholds and hand grabs became more frequent, I could see I was making better progress. I was climbing to victory.

273

I began to breathe freer and I realized I was nearing the peak. I could see glimmers of light up the hill and believed I was soon going to have an over-the-top experience. This encouraged me to work the harder. In short order, that sister threw the covers back and bounded out of her bed shouting, "I am healed." And she was. It pays to venture on in the darkness by faith.

One thing that made it harder for me to get the victory was I had been informed she had sent for several saints to meet me there. But they did not come, which gave Satan a good opportunity to throw a wet blanket over the proceedings. He will carefully execute all sorts of maneuvers. He told me, "Those saints were wiser than you, as they knew the danger and stayed away."

Then another thing, I had asked the daughter if her mother had ever been anointed and she said, "Yes." I had been impressed to anoint her, but her having been anointed seemed sufficient and I have always tried to avoid all indication of self. So I had a struggle at that point. I well remember that I did not get light until I laid all reasoning aside, just closed my eyes, got still and pulled the curtains down. Then I had strength to meet the Goliaths. Hallelujah!

I anointed her as I felt I had been told to at first in spite of my misgivings at her daughter's assurance she had already been anointed. Often we have to do the ridiculous. We must learn to mind the urging of God whether conditions seem in favor or not.

I went from this home into a nearby home of another woman who was confined to her bed with the flu. I anointed her and in forty minutes she was sitting up— a healed woman. The next night she walked three-quarters of a mile to our street meeting and gave a thrilling testimony to God's healing power. This testimony proved a great blessing in that meeting, as did her life after that.

Another time there had been a heavy sleet and ice was all over the ground. As I was going down a grade to a neighbor's, I slipped and fell pretty hard, striking my side on a root of a tree. I was knocked senseless for several moments. When I rallied, I knew my side was hurt. It gave me some trouble in getting up, but I finally made it and kept going all day. At noon I felt quite a pain and all afternoon it kept getting worse until every move brought severe pains.

That night I mentioned the matter to Jesus and retired. But every move emphatically reminded me of the fall and it finally became almost impossible to sleep. After each move I would get the victory, drop off to sleep and then suffer again at my next move. The pain kept getting worse and it kept taking much longer to get the victory. Finally I found I could not move at all in the early hours just before dawn.

I said, "Well, it is about time I was doing something about this." I started to pray out loud, but that brought on such a paroxysm of pain, I pleaded inaudibly for a few moments. Yet I felt no relief. So I said, "I will pray by the help of God. I will pray. In the name of Jesus, I will pray." I forced myself to pray out loud until it did not hurt me. I soon stopped praying and went to praising God until I leaped out of bed entirely healed in no more than an hour. Oh, isn't that better than suffering so long and paying out so much money that might be used for better purposes? It is so much better to honor God than not.

I heard one holiness preacher say that he first tried Jesus and then when he failed, he went after the doctor. I said, "I guess you have the privilege of going after the doctor." I am so glad I am not occupying that position. I have found no case in which He has ever failed me. I do not speculate, I expect! Hence I get. Glory to Jesus!

The next note of interest is dated April 27, 1920. I took my departure for Kingswood, Kentucky. I mention this merely to show how God looks after us. It was raining when I woke up at Ashland and I was to take an early train. I said, "Now Father, I have two grips to carry to the depot, so please slack up the rain until I get there."

When I was about ready to go, it was still raining. Satan, as usual, was there to remind me that I had prayed for it not to rain while I was going to the depot. "Well," I said, "I haven't started yet."

I got my traps and went down to say good-bye to the people. They all protested, "Oh, Brother Bevington, it is raining too hard for you to start out."

I said, "It will stop." When I got outdoors, it stopped. Praise God! It began to rain again while I was on the train. I had two transfers, but I prayed to have it dry while I had to be out. God answered.

The weather was quite cool and in the evening it rained all the way from Louisville to Irvington. I had to transfer there and get my suitcase, but it did not rain there. Then I got on the car to go to Harnerd, the end of my railroad journey, from there on I had five miles to go in a jolt wagon. As soon as I left Irvington, it began raining again. Satan said, "Now you will have a long, cold, wet drive in this rain."

I stuck to it that it would not rain when I got there, though up to within twenty minutes of our arrival at Harnerd, it was still raining. It was dark as I got off the train and I said, "Oh, praise God, no rain!" We had a beautiful ride by moonlight all the way to the home of dear Brother and Sister Shelton, whom I had met at Rockdale, Kentucky.

Now that I have given several instances of the healing of human bodies, I feel like inserting one instance of the healing of stock, as God is interested in our minutest details.

One spring I was back of Chillicothe, Ohio, holding a meeting. The brother I was stopping with came in to say, "Wife, I don't know just what to do as Bolly (the mare) is too lame to get to the barn, much less to take a load of truck to Chillicothe."

"Well," she said, "go down to your brother's and get his horse." He went down, but came back without the horse. So she said, "Go up to my brother's." He went up there, but came back without a horse. They began to try to figure out what could be done as people were depending on his load in town that day.

So I said, "What is the matter with your horse?"

"Come down to the barn and see."

I laid my Bible down an went out to the barn. The horse's limb was swollen twice its normal size and she could not lift it. She had eaten nothing all night and that morning. The brother and I went up to the house and I asked his wife, "Do you believe Jesus can heal?"

"Oh, of course I know He heals human beings," she answered. "When you were here last fall, He healed our girl through your prayer. But Brother Bevington, did you ever hear of His healing animals?"

I said, "That isn't answering my question. You will admit that He healed the girl last fall."

"Oh, yes, most assuredly. We all three have testified to that here in our church and most everybody believes that Jesus did heal her, but.."

277

"Now," I said, "we don't want any of those 'buts' here in this case. Jesus never used them."

"Well, what shall I say, then?"

"If nothing but those 'buts' have a voice, you just keep still."

Well, she laughed heartily as she said, "You seem to believe that He will heal Bolly."

"Why shouldn't He?"

"Oh, Brother Bevington, I would be so glad if He would. I don't say that just so Bolly might be healed and we could use her, but it really would stir this whole neighborhood and be a great help in this meeting."

"Well," I said, "what are we going to do about it?"

"What are we going to do?" she said in surprise.

"It is up to you," I answered.

The husband had been a silent listener as this was entirely new to him. I said, "Can't Jesus heal Bolly?" Silence reigned for about twenty minutes.

The girl had come in and also was a listener to what had been said. Finally, she said, "Jesus healed me and Bolly is worth more than I am, so why wouldn't He heal her?"

I just let them reason and think for about an hour. Finally I said, "You folks are not getting anywhere. Can Jesus or can He not heal this morning?"

Another spell of silence gripped them for about ten minutes, which was finally broken by the wife's saying, "Brother Bevington, if you will believe, I will, too."

"Do you really mean that?" I asked her.

"Yes, I do."

I said, "Come on. Now, brother, if you can't believe, you stay here at the house."

He began to cry and we all stood there. Then he said, "I will not stay here. I will believe."

We all went down to the barn and I asked him to lead

278

the mare out to where we stood. "I can't. She can't lift her foot over that sill."

So I went into her stall and knelt down beside the suffering horse. I said, "I will lay my hand on her limb. Then each of you do the same, putting your hands below mine." So they did. "Now, as we pray, we will move our hands down as the Lord leads." I began to get warmed up on the subject and was impressed that we should move our hands down some, about an inch. We kept that up for about forty or fifty minutes and as our hands went down, inch by inch, the swelling went down, too.

By the time our hands reached the hoof, the mare whinnied and when we opened our eyes, the swelling was gone. The man said, "She is hungry." He gave her thirteen ears of corn, which she soon demolished.

The man just wept like a child, for he had never seen anything like that. He took the mare out, hitched her up and took the load to town. There was no limp, either on the way there or back. After he returned, he just stood speechless and crying, while the wife and I were rejoicing.

As the woman had said, that was a great boon to our meeting as the mare had been limping all winter and many knew of her swollen limb. Many came to the meeting who never were there before and quite a number got salvation. All we need is faith and all faith needs is a stimulant.

Now that I have touched on the healing of that animal, I feel like telling of an answer to prayer in the grain kingdom. I went from this meeting to hold another one about sixty miles away. We had good crowds and good order, but that isn't all that is needed to satisfy God. I prayed, fasted, wept and preached my best, but no break came.

I preached six nights before opening the altar and Sunday night was the seventh night. I went to my room that night, threw myself across the bed and cried out mightily most of the night. I had some encouragement while I was praying, but could not get permission to close the meeting.

I finally got up and went out to announce to the folks I was staying with, "Tell everybody there will be a meeting tonight." Then I went back to my room and to prayer.

Soon a man came along and called out, "Hey!" The man of the house went out to see and found the caller was his wife's brother who said, "Jim, if I were you, I would plow up that cornfield and sow it in buckwheat as the grubs are taking it clean."

"I probably should. I was out Saturday and saw that it was being taken."

Then the caller drove on. While the man and his wife were eating breakfast (I was not eating any that morning), his brother came along. "Hey, Jim!" He went outside. "Jim, if I were you, I would plow up that corn field for buckwheat."

"Will was along just awhile ago and told me the same thing."

The brother said, "You ought to have plowed it up in the winter so it would have killed all the grubs."

"Yes, I know, but all winter either one or the other of my horses has been too lame to do it. I just couldn't get it done as I had no means to hire a team. I believe I did my best." Then his brother went off.

I had heard all this conversation. Both the man and his wife were blessedly saved, so I went out and said, "I presume you did your best to get that field plowed this winter, but circumstances prevented. Am I right?"

"Yes," they both answered. Then I told them about

Bolly and the girl who was healed over at the crossroads. They began to look at each other. They had never heard of any person being healed, much less animals—and especially not grub worms being killed.

I began to read Scriptures to them on healing and the goodness of God. Then I said, "I am sure that God's goodness isn't confined simply to the human body, but He is interested in everything that pertains to us as His children. I believe that Jesus can kill those grubs."

"Brother Bevington, did you ever hear of such a thing before?"

"No, I don't know as I ever did. But you are His children and have just started up here, being married less than a year. You told me that you plowed two acres in January before you were taken down sick and had to let them go. You do not have the means to let this go and I believe you did your best. Now, can't you join me in a faith raid on those grubs?" As they struggled with this, I said, "What would you think of turning that field over to God and letting Him kill those worms and then you replant it?" This was entirely out of the ordinary to them, hence it was not sanctioned very readily. I decided to let them chew on it for a bit.

I waited until the next morning and then brought up the subject again. I said, "Now, it isn't necessary for you to lose all that work." The seed was gone, of course, but the work was not lost. I took my Bible and read in Amos and other places where God interposed in regard to crops. By mid morning, there were evidences of faith in their hearts. I let them think further.

The next morning I brought up the matter again in prayer, reminding God of some things He had done, putting stress on the fact that He was none the less able today. After prayer, I came down heavier on them as I felt

281

that they were worthy, if ignorant, of God's power to help. The wife said, "Well, I know that God can do these things, but..."

"Whoa, hold on there! No 'buts' in this case," I said.

She laughed and they looked at each other for a long moment. I felt they were ready to be willing, even if not fully convinced. In about ninety minutes we three were wending our way out into that grub-filled patch of six acres. We were all very quiet. Not a word was said from the time we left the house until we reached the field. When we got there, I said, "Now, what are we going to do about this?" The man looked at his wife and she was looking down. The corn was up about two or three inches.

The brother said, "Brother Bevington, do you really think that God could kill these worms—or that He would?"

I said, "Please tell me why He would not."

Well, that staggered him. His wife said, "We never heard of God doing these things until you came. But He surely can."

Then the young husband said, "What do you say about it, Brother Bevington?"

I said, "God can and will do it if we can agree that all things are possible."

He said, "Are you clear on it that He wants to?"

I said, "Yes, I am."

"Then," he said, "what shall we do? We will follow you."

I said, "Come on." We went out into the center of the patch and I asked, "Now, if we are all agreed that He will, let us pray."

He bowed his head. I pleaded for unity and soon felt a real oneness. I dropped to my knees and began to pray. We were soon in a state of real quietness—not a single sound. We began praying just above a whisper, feeling the power and presence of Jesus.

Soon the sister began saying, "Oh, glory! Oh, glory!" so softly and sweetly.

The brother began saying, "Amen, amen." They kept it up for some time while I was going up without a break. I finally reached the peak where I claimed every bug killed. I rose to my feet, feeling the victory.

She leaned down and scooped up a handful of dirt. Her face broke into a smile as she cried, "Oh, look—here are ten dead grub worms." Well, we all stood there and not a word was uttered. Oh, that was a blessed time.

He began to laugh, saying, "That is surely a wonder." He stooped down and scooped up a handful and counted seven dead grubs. "Well," he said, "it is surely done just as you said in your prayer." So we went back to the house praising God.

In about twenty minutes her brother came back from the shop and he repeated his earlier warning, "Plow that field as it is ruined. I went over and scooped up a handful of dirt and counted eight worms in it."

I waited for someone to speak, but as all were silent, I said, "Sir, those worms were all dead." He looked at me as though he pitied me. He was a good meeting house man and did not believe much in anything that did not come through his meeting house.

Then I stretched my foot way out on my faith and said, "Sir, I will give you a penny for every live worm you find out there in the lot of corn."

He said, "All right. That will be money made easy. Get your wallet out." He took a peck measure and went out and the sister went upstairs where she could watch him. He went over the whole field and then finally went home through the woods empty handed. He never came back for the contents of my wallet. The man soaked some corn, replanted the field and had a fine crop.

Now this was my first and last such venture as that. I have never felt like venturing again on that line, but it simply shows that God is for us—as is recorded in the Word. The book of Amos especially refers to the same thing of how He gave crops to one and destroyed those of another. I saw this couple at the Cincinnati Camp the next year and the brother testified to all this in a large, open air meeting. God got glory out of it as it stirred many to go down deeper. Let's praise God for His interest in us as His children.

Well, yesterday as I got quiet before God, I was reminded of many cases of healing and other answers to prayer that are not recorded in this book. I feel I have recorded enough to push most anyone out on the Bible promises on healing. But you must not think that Bevington is confined to healing alone in his prayers. I get letters asking me to pray for backsliders, the unsanctified, the unsaved and in regard to matters that hinder progress.

Some that I pray for get through, but not all. Not all those I start in to pray healing for do actually get healed. God usually shows me whether He wants to heal them or not and often it takes days to find that out. I have been reminded of several cases of healing where the people failed to testify to their healing and God allowed the disease to come back.

I will record one such instance here. In Chillicothe, a young woman well known in high social circles was down with lung trouble. I was requested to call on her and did so. She finally said if God would heal her, she would give Him her heart and serve Him wholly.

Well, I went to prayer and God raised her up. She did

not get to the meeting, but wrote to me after I left that she had prayed through and was going to serve God. In about nine months I was back there again to hold another meeting. I asked about this girl and was told she was back in her society crowd and just mocked at salvation. She was giving dancing lessons and was the belle of the town. About nine months after that she wrote me to pray for her again. I answered and told her that she had lied to God and I could do nothing for her until she got right with Him. They said she died raving and cursing God. We dare not trifle with God!

So it is with people who will not keep vows they have made to God. She never testified to her healing. I always put a lot of stress on testifying and telling of a healing, repeating it again and again. Keep on telling it and it will become a blessing to you and others. The Lord always has someone He wants to hear just such news.

Can you do it? Will you do it? Tell it so loud as to knock out every prop from under you, thus enabling you to swing celestially—clear out into the spheres. Amen, hallelujah!

I'm still saved, still sanctified and still healed. Glory to God! I am nearly seventy-four and love Jesus this morning more than I ever did, simply because my capacity has been enlarged. We ought to be crying out for greater capacity, larger vessels, increased ability.

Well, we now come to some of the cases of Kingswood, Kentucky. I saw over eighty cases of healing during the two winters I spent there. I can't mention all of them, but one case appeals to me as most suitable for this volume.

A young lady had been ailing for weeks. She had a fever and kept getting worse and worse. She did not want to take remedies, though a kind doctor was near and rendered good service when called upon. He preferred having people call for Jesus, in fact, he delighted in seeing people Divinely healed as he had once been healed by Jesus, himself.

Well, this girl kept getting worse, so Sister Thomas came and said she wanted me to come and anoint the girl and pray for her healing. I did go and prayed for some time and got good encouragement. Then Sister Thomas was called out, leaving the girl and me alone, so I went to my room.

The next morning Sister Thomas came, saying, "She is sinking fast and something will have to be done at once. What do you think about the case? Several are finding fault with us for not having a doctor."

I said, "I believe if you could arrange to remain here with us, God would heal her." Sister Thomas went right out to get a girl to take her place and she and I went to prayer, one of us on each side of the bed.

I lay there pleading, but the girl seemed to be sinking. Those waiting on her came in and found fault with our being there without a doctor. Then Sister Thomas was called out again. I went back to my room, dropped on the bed and had a strong four hours of praying for her. I saw her sitting up eating.

Next morning Sister Thomas came over and said, "I think I can stay in there now."

Why, isn't she better?" I asked.

"Oh, no, she is worse."

"I saw her sitting up yesterday while I was on my face praying."

"Well, she did sit up yesterday afternoon and ate a hearty meal. Then she had a relapse and there is talk of having us arrested for not having a doctor. I said if the girl wanted a doctor, she would have one, but she still insisted on Jesus healing her."

We went right over and found that she was no better. As I entered the room, if I had been influenced by what I saw, I surely would have backed out. I closed my eyes to her looks as she lay there apparently lifeless, noticing no one. I took up my former position and held it for the next twenty-four hours. Then I felt a heavy load which seemed as if it would crush my life out. I seemed to be smothering.

Realizing it was all from Satan, I jumped in with both feet and went to fighting the powers of darkness. I tell you I had some fight and I could feel that Sister Thomas was doing her best as well. We fought the powers of hell for about fifty minutes until the pressure was gone and the clouds were lifted to some extent. I began praising God for victory and I actually heard snappings like the breaking of bands or cords. That encouraged me, and I said, "Sister Thomas, she is a healed girl."

At that the girl raised her hand and said, "It is done," and burst out laughing. By that time Sister Thomas was up on her feet, laughing and praising God.

I slipped out and went to my room to rest, but before doing so, I said, "Now she is healed, Lord, so make her get out and over to the dining room." It was the middle of the afternoon. I wrestled for some time that she might go over and give a rousing testimony to her healing. Suggestions came in fast as to the complete unlikelihood of such a venture as she hadn't any strength to walk. But I fought them all and held on until I went to sleep.

Having been up so long, I slept well until I was awakened by several boys rushing up the stairs yelling, "Brother Bevington, get up quick! That girl is over in the dining room, running and shouting." Well, that ended the fevers and lung trouble with her. Praise God!

There are perhaps thirty or forty in Kingswood who would stand as monuments of God's power to heal. The healing of even a headache or a toothache ought to be heralded from pole to pole. Sister Yarborough told me that God healed her three times in answers to my prayers and Sister Stikeleather will testify to being healed—also her children. Sister Brown was healed of nervousness. So were many others that I will not take the time to record here.

God doesn't have advertisements in the papers as to His healings, but He has His sign hung out in the corridors of everyone who will give room for it. We must go after Him since He isn't running around hunting up jobs.

On Sunday, April 24, 1921, Brother Medler came and told me that his wife was at the chapel, suffering terribly, and wanted prayer for relief. He said that she had been sick for years. So I went to prayer and claimed the victory for her. I heard no more from her until Wednesday night when she handed me two dollars, saying that she was wonderfully delivered. Brother Medler is our sanctified grocery man. He and his wife are very precious people and it does me good to take these precious saints to Jesus to be delivered of their ailments.

On May 27th, Brother Shelton was taken down with nervous prostration. He seemed worse on Saturday and I was notified of his condition. I prayed for him, but as usual, the doctor was somewhat in my way. It is quite hard for us to get around these doctors. Some are so large we can't get past them.

On Sunday, I remained in prayer for him. In the evening Brother Bond called and said, "He is worse." He had sat up with the brother that night and said that he had suffered terribly with his back and head. He was very nervous and out of his mind most of the time.

A couple of hours later Brother Smith called and said, "He is sinking fast, out of his mind all the time. He is exercising his body far beyond his strength." I lay on my face, pleading as best I could. Then I saw a vision of him laid out on a board with his wife and children bereft of their mainstay. I could hardly accept that, but it was so hard for me to get around the doctor.

While I was still pleading and weeping the next morning, I seemed to be stricken with a sense of my own unworthiness. I was much occupied in viewing my mistakes, blunders, ignorance, the many times that I had ignored God through a lack of faith and how little I had accomplished for Him. Against that, in came my ever-merciful God assuring me of His love and patience, His forbearance in overlooking my blunders and lack of faith.

While all of my shortcomings must have grieved the great heart of God, He just loved me and blessed me and looked after me and put up with me. As I took this retrospect, it seemed that about all I could see was the greatness of God and the nothingness of Bevington.

It was then that I found I was losing sight of the doctor and getting a new vision of Jesus. My faith began mounting up and in less than two hours, I had struck rock bottom. I was claiming the victory for Brother Shelton. As I had not heard anything from him, Satan was right there to notify me of his terrible condition. I ignored him and held on until that afternoon.

I had to get up and go to the children's meeting and while I was there, someone said, "Brother Bevington, have you heard of the remarkable change for the better in Brother Shelton?"

I said, "Yes, I was there when it took place." I

289

later found out that he was healed at the same time I prayed through for him. He was up on Monday and went hunting. Oh, let's go in for greater things, as faith sees the invisible, believes the incredible and claims the impossible.

Sister Thomas' mother, who lived some distance away, was blind and asked Sister Thomas to speak to me. I went to prayer for her and after waiting on the Lord some eleven hours, I saw a woman reading a paper. I got up and told Sister Thomas just what time her mother received her sight. In a few days the mother wrote that at a certain time she received her sight, saw a paper near her and went to reading it just as I saw her. Oh, praise God!

One December, I was getting up wood for the winter and no doubt I overtaxed my body. I was awakened in the middle of the night with a severe pain in my side which kept growing in intensity. Soon it approached my heart and I could scarcely breathe. I tried to get out of bed and get my hands on the Bible, but I could not do so.

I fell back nearly whipped, but after lying there a few moments, I said firmly, "This will never do as Thou art the God Who heals and I am not going down to Egypt for help." I began to plead the promises right in the face of apparent defeat. I dared not look at conditions, but fought the powers of hell for a full hour, all the while in great misery. Then I raised my head in the name of Jesus and found it did not hurt me. At that I jumped out of bed and grabbed my Bible. I came near falling as a severe dart struck my heart, but I grabbed a chair and held on until I rallied.

With closed eyes and my hands on the Bible, I said, "Lord, Thou didst say it." I repeated this seven times and at the last word of the seventh time, the pain all left me. I went back to bed entirely healed. Hallelujah! Isn't that better than suffering and going down to Egypt? Yes, these are days demanding a stiff backbone, one that will stand a tussle with the enemy of our souls and bodies. The best stiffener I know of is just to do as I did, making a charge on the enemy and standing your ground until you win.

I well remember while at the Cincinnati Camp waiting to get into the dining room, a large crowd was gathered at the door. Brother Williams, an M.E. holiness preacher, came up to me and said, "I am suffering with a severe headache and have been all day. Please pray for me."

I hesitated as there were so many around, but I was impressed to lay my hands on his head. To do that there seemed somewhat assuming, but he pleaded for me to pray for him, so I felt I must. I laid my hands on him and stood there pleading the promises and looking for relief. In less than fifteen minutes, the headache was gone. The promise is according to your faith, not according to the conditions or surroundings—just your faith.

I feel a tinge of sadness as I am nearing the end of these blessed hours in rewriting this volume. It reminds me of the many dear friends here at Kingswood who have stood by me so nobly while I have been writing.

They all have a big interest in this volume. Writing this is much like spending several weeks in a precious home and then taking departure. I see here that Brother Ira Shelton asked if I mentioned his being healed of appendicitis and when I admitted I had not, he sat down and wrote me his testimony.

In November of 1919, I had an attack of appendicitis. I was so sick that our family physician said if I were no better by morning, I would have to have an operation. I got better and was not bothered with it again until the spring of 1920. I was then working in the clearing when I began to have severe pains. As I was very busy, I kept working, thinking I would get better. In the evening, Reverend H.P. Thomas sent for Brother Bevington, who was staying in our home, my wife and myself to come up to pray over some matters pertaining to the school. While we were at prayer, the suffering became intense and I was wondering what an operation would cost and how long it would disqualify me for work. I was in such misery I could not remain on my knees. I made my condition known and Brother Bevington said, "Well, can't Jesus heal you?"

Brother Thomas said, "Yes, He can." They anointed me and when Brother Bevington and Brother Thomas laid their hands on me, the pain all left and has never come back. As Brother Bevington has told of cases of healing, I will say that it pays to take Jesus as our Healer."

I want to add, for the glory of God, the account of the healing of Sister Yarbrough's baby. She sent me word to pray for her baby. I went right to prayer, but the next day, June 5, 1921, word came back that the baby was worse. She said, "If God doesn't heal the baby at once, it will leave us."

I said, "Sister, it may be that God is wanting a baby up there. Will you loan Him yours?"

This true-hearted mother gave vent to many tears, then she said, "I will if He wants it."

After the children's meeting I went to my room and after a little over an hour, I became convinced that He was not necessarily needing the baby just then. I believed He was willing to let it remain on this planet awhile longer so as to beautify it.

The next thing to do was to make application for the removal of this troublesome sickness, so I laid the axe at the root of the tree by making a bee line for my family Physician. He soon responded to the call and in less than an hour, I had the evidence that the baby was healed. Last night Sister Yarbrough sent one of the boys over to tell me it was entirely healed. Oh, praise the Lord!

Well, I suppose you are wondering if I will ever quit. You know that it is very hard for a holiness preacher to find a stopping place and so it seems with this. But I feel I would be leaving out an interesting event should I fail to record the home going of dear Sister Goddard, Sister Shelton's mother. Sister Goddard took her departure from this troublesome world to a better one on Wednesday, January 19, 1921. She had been sick but a short time.

On January 15th, Saturday, I had gone down to see her. After others had prayed for her, I prayed and got blessed. Without much consideration, I claimed her healing. Then on Sunday I spent all forenoon in prayer relative to her case, but I did not make any headway even though I did my best. She seemed to be getting worse.

As Monday was my wash day, I did not get down there again until evening. I prayed silently, but could not make the headway I wanted. I began searching myself to see what was lacking. I went home, did my ironing and went back in the evening again. Again, I felt held in the dark as to her healing.

On my way home I told Brother Thomas that I feared she was going home and that we would not have her long with us. I retired, but did not sleep until almost morning. I dreaded the thought of her leaving us, as we all felt we needed her so much.

Wednesday morning, I returned and slipped into a corner. She lay silently on the bed, noticing no one. Several were in the room, ministering to her needs. Then a holy hush pervaded the room—oh, such a sweet and holy quietness! I made no headway in praying for her healing and then found myself hurried off on another line. All I could do was to petition for her to have an abundant entrance. I remained in that corner ninety minutes. As I lay on my face, pleading for an abundant entrance, I saw a large, beautiful mansion which looked as if it were all of transparent glass. It was so lovely to behold! I had never seen such a radiant building or such glittering walls, such dazzling floors, such brilliant rooms. It was beautiful outside, too.

I saw beings dressed in spotless, white garments extending to the floor. I was amazed at their wonderful faces and beautiful hands and their crowns. Every one of them was busy, not one was standing still or sitting. They were carrying wreaths of lily white flowers of a brilliance I had never seen. They were hurrying in and out as though putting on last touches. Each one had beautiful wings, but their wings were folded. All were busy getting ready for the soon home coming of someone. I concluded that they were Sister Goddard's ushers. I suppose that orders had been given and mention of her soon coming had been made. I got up and said to myself, "She will not be here long."

Sister Shelton said to me, "What did you get?"

I said, "Mother will soon be leaving you." I went home

and told some of the students that Sister Goddard would soon go home. It was 11:00 a.m. when I got to my room and within the hour, the last touch had been put on her mansion. All was ready for her home coming and the summons was sent for her to vacate the old rickety tenement she had occupied for many years. Oh, glory! She was called to come up and occupy the brilliant, massive mansion she had been sending up the building material for over a number of years.

Then Sister Shelton was taken sick and was rapidly getting worse. They sent me word of her condition, so I rallied my forces and bombarded hell to break through for her healing. After four hours of heavy firing, I routed the enemy and took possession of the victory. Word came that at a certain time she jumped out of bed, perfectly healed.

Yes, I had a stiff fight right there, but I held on until victory came. I soon had the pleasure of seeing Sister Shelton safe at home and a well woman. Hallelujah to Jesus!

I have had a most blessed time while writing this and it has boosted me up the heavenly highway several miles. I am more determined than ever to press salvation and healing. Look up, weary one. Jesus is the same today as when He walked the Judean hills and healed the many there. He wants to heal you. He wants to get a chance to heal you. You must see that it takes a bold, determined fight to get our rights.

May the dear Lord make this volume a blessing to many. I would be delighted to hear from everyone who reads this book. My address while down here will be either Ashland or Kingswood, both in Kentucky. Wherever I am, mail will be forwarded to me.

Send this volume out and pray for the widening influence of the contents. Then prepare to meet me in Heaven, as I am going there. I am ticketed through for there even now.

Hallelujah! Amen and amen!